The Peacemaker's P

Expanding from her path-breaking work in *Unspeakable Truths*, Priscilla Hayner focuses on a new challenge in *The Peacemaker's Paradox*: the age-old problem of negotiating peace after a war of atrocities. Drawing on her first-hand involvement in peace processes and interviews from the frontlines of peace talks, the author recounts many heretofore-untold stories of how justice has been negotiated, with great difficulty, and what this tells us for the future. Those with the most power to stop a war are the least likely to submit to justice for their crimes, but the demand for justice only grows louder. She also asks how the intervention of an international tribunal, such as the International Criminal Court, changes how a war is fought and the possibility of brokering peace. *The Peacemaker's Paradox* looks far and wide, from Gaddafi's Libya to the FARC talks in Colombia, to provide an unparalleled exploration of these thorniest of issues.

A combination of interview-based reporting and political analysis, *The Peacemaker's Paradox* brings clarity to a field fraught with both legal and practical difficulties.

Priscilla Hayner has worked in the field of transitional justice for twenty-five years, the last ten years focused on the challenge of justice in contexts of peace negotiations. She co-founded the International Center for Transitional Justice in 2001, working as program director and head of its Geneva office. Her first book, *Unspeakable Truths: Transitional Justice and the Challenge of Truth Commissions*, helped to define that field. She has served as human rights advisor in a number of peace negotiations, from Kenya in 2008 to the recent talks in Colombia. In 2017 she was appointed to the United Nations Standby Team of Senior Mediation Advisors. She is based in New York City.

The Peacemaker's Paradox

Pursuing Justice in the Shadow
of Conflict

Priscilla Hayner

Routledge
Taylor & Francis Group

NEW YORK AND LONDON

Published 2018
by Routledge
711 Third Avenue, New York, NY 10017

and by Routledge
2 Park Square, Milton Park, Abingdon, Oxon, OX14 4RN

Routledge is an imprint of the Taylor & Francis Group, an informa business

© 2018 Taylor & Francis

Library of Congress Cataloging-in-Publication Data
A catalog record for this book has been requested

ISBN: 978-1-138-30342-3 (hbk)
ISBN: 978-1-138-30343-0 (pbk)
ISBN: 978-0-203-73108-6 (ebk)

Typeset in Galliard
by Apex CoVantage, LLC

Printed and bound in the United States of America by Sheridan

Brief Contents

Detailed Contents

Acknowledgments

Little has been published that records the inside story of peace negotiations, and thus this book depended on interviews with those closest to these processes. I am most grateful to all those who have shared these experiences with me: mediators, former warring parties, and other close participants and observers.

Many local experts were particularly generous in sharing their wisdom, experience, and perspectives. Several helped guide and advise me in my research travels, in some cases accompanying me to regions that were difficult to access. My many thanks to Michael Otim in Uganda; Mohamed Htewish in Tripoli and Mahamud Tawel in Misrata, Libya; Isaac Lappia in Sierra Leone; Aaron Weah in Liberia; and Maria Camila Moreno and the staff at the International Center for Transitional Justice (ICTJ) in Bogota, who kindly assisted during my first research visit to Colombia in 2012.

I undertook my first exploration of this topic, in Liberia and Sierra Leone, while on a short sabbatical from ICTJ in 2006. I collaborated in this early research in Sierra Leone with Kristina Thorne and the Centre for Humanitarian Dialogue (HD), and in the Democratic Republic of Congo with Laura Davis and ICTJ; my thanks to both for this partnership, and to these organizations for their early interest in this subject.

Colleagues in Geneva, where I was based for part of the time that I was doing this work, were immensely helpful. I am very thankful to Robert Archer, an early editor and friend who helped me give shape to a complex array of issues that at times seemed impossible to untangle. Terrific colleagues at HD, where I served as senior advisor, opened up the often-closed world of mediation as we collaborated on a number of tough mediation cases, where questions of justice inevitably arose.

When I turned to the impact of international courts working in contexts of war, I greatly benefited from insiders taking the time to talk through policies and difficult dilemmas, including at the International Criminal Court and the Special Court for Sierra Leone. My specific research on the "interests of justice" and prosecutorial discretion began during a mid-career executive masters on the international law of armed conflict that I undertook at the Geneva Academy of International Humanitarian Law and Human Rights (based at the

University of Geneva and the Graduate Institute of International and Development Studies). My thanks and appreciation to many good colleagues there, including Andrew Clapham and Nicolas Michel.

Policy discussions and debates on these overall peace-justice dilemmas have advanced each year at the regular Amsterdam Dialogue meeting hosted by the Dialogue Advisory Group and at the annual Oslo Forum organized by HD and the Norwegian Foreign Ministry. These meetings bring together some of the best minds on these issues and were always valuable in helping move forward my sometimes-muddled thinking.

My work on this book was in its final stages during the two years that I took part in the periphery of the Colombian peace talks. It was an honor to be part of the extraordinarily complex and difficult brainstorming of the "New York Group" that took place regularly over this period, where we tried to find solutions that might assist the Havana talks. The depth and breadth of the issues that we debated was a constant reminder of how difficult this subject is, and will remain. There is no easy shortcut: that became clear. My thanks and appreciation to the members of this group who brought rich expertise to these meetings, which inevitably fed into my own broader thinking on the subject. In particular, my thanks to Dag Nylander and Idun Tvedt of the Norwegian Foreign Ministry, who first identified the need and opportunity for such a brainstorming group and with whom I worked closely in facilitating these meetings. I would also like to thank the following scholars for their comments on an earlier form of the manuscript: George A. Lopez, Notre Dame; Kenneth A. Rodman, Colby College; Michael Stohl, University of California-Santa Barbara; and Jennifer A. Yoder, Colby College.

My appreciation also goes to each member of my family, who have been supportive throughout, and who have never questioned my sometimes unusual and obsessive path. Likewise, my dear friends in New York have offered much-appreciated support.

This book would not have been possible without two critical grants that allowed me to dedicate time and resources to independent research. I am indebted to Tony Tabatznik and the Bertha Foundation, in London, who provided a generous grant and vote of confidence in my work, all the more appreciated because this is outside their normal area of grantmaking. Much earlier, in 2006, the U.S. Institute of Peace supported my initial research on peace and justice, which formally started me down this road.

Finally, my literary agent, Malaga Baldi, and my editor at Routledge, Jennifer Knerr, have been wonderful partners. The input of Karen Kornblum Berntsen has also been much appreciated in the last stages. My enormous thanks to each, and to others unnamed, for giving shape to this book and helping me put it out into the world, at long last.

Priscilla Hayner

Part I

Peace and Justice in Perspective

1   The Problem

War crimes hamper peace talks. This is no surprise.

No armed rebels have agreed to disarm and demobilize in exchange for a prison cell. Nor has any country's military offered to send its generals to jail, even if their complicity in atrocities is clear. Both sides of a war may have committed horrific crimes. But these can no longer be buried in impunity, as may have been true in another era. What to do about these crimes, while prioritizing the need to stop the violence? Thus emerges the classic peacemaker's paradox: how to obtain sufficient justice without scuttling the possibility of peace.

On the face of it, the problem is perfectly clear: any peace agreement that grants impunity for a war's serious crimes may risk being short-lived, will be legally questionable, and will almost certainly meet loud opposition from both national and international observers and advocates—whose support will be needed to build a durable peace. But if a mediator insists on accountability, the armed groups will likely resist, and a peace deal may become impossible. Both peace with justice and peace without justice are difficult propositions.

Virtually all negotiated peace processes confront this problem, and even more so now, with the greater reach of international courts. How this dilemma is resolved, or sometimes fails to be resolved, can be startlingly different in different contexts and will often fundamentally shape both the success of a deal and the contours of the peace.

This is evident with a glance at a few examples:

Kenya descended into horrific violence in early 2008 after the official results of a presidential election were deemed suspicious, and anger spilled onto the streets. Soon the country was on the precipice of all-out war, as political and ethnic loyalties merged and the violence spiraled out of control. Former United Nations Secretary-General Kofi Annan led a mediation effort to find a political agreement that would end the violence. Several weeks into the talks, Annan's team asked me to come to Kenya to help devise a plan for justice and reconciliation, knowing that these crimes, and the intense anger between communities, would have to be addressed. I arrived in Nairobi just hours before Annan secured a critical power-sharing agreement and ceasefire. Kenya celebrated. The relief was palpable. But this political deal was only the first item on the agenda.

I was briefed: the next issue for the parties to address was to be justice. No one had had a moment to plan for this. In the two months since the contested election, over a thousand people had been brutally killed and many others targeted and chased from their home; the parties sitting at the peace table were directly or indirectly responsible. How could this be addressed? My task: propose a solution, or at least a strategy for broaching the issue, when the parties reconvened three days hence.

The good news: the mediation team was supportive and understood the difficulty at hand. The bad news: we had 72 hours to prepare a plan.

We were lucky. After consultations and brainstorming, especially with Kenyan experts, we felt ready to gently suggest a model specific to Kenya that responded to the demands and dilemmas at hand. The idea was fairly simple: the appointment of an independent commission to investigate the post-election violence, with powers to recommend prosecutions and also to make recommendations to a longer-term truth commission that would follow. Both parties immediately accepted the idea, each insisting that justice was essential for what they and their supporters had suffered, and the next day they signed an agreement setting out this plan.

Most peace negotiations don't resolve their justice quandary so quickly. And of course, many difficult justice issues demand attention as an agreement is implemented. This was certainly true in Kenya, as the possibility of criminal justice was left open and soon emerged as a major political issue, when the legislature balked at taking the necessary steps to allow independent prosecutions. Ultimately, the International Criminal Court (ICC) intervened, which was highly contentious and had significant political ramifications.

While the Kenyan negotiating parties agreed unusually quickly to a means of addressing past crimes, there are a surprising number of similar cases where this issue is addressed very late in a process, or in a very cursory way, and without fully considering the ramifications of decisions reached.

A better-prepared peace negotiation was taking place simultaneously with the Kenyan talks in a directly neighboring country, although ultimately without a successful result. Mediators of the conflict in northern Uganda struggled for two years under the challenge of outstanding indictments from the ICC: they were trying to broker a peace deal with the very people who were subject to ICC arrest warrants. The mediation team tried to construct a justice package that was acceptable to the rebel leadership and complied with the legal demands for accountability, but in the end the rebels balked, refusing to sign. To be clear, their distrust was not limited to this issue, but it played a part. This brutal armed group, the Lord's Resistance Army, continued to wreak havoc in the region for many years more.

Five years later, when Colombia opened peace talks to end its fifty-year war with the FARC (the Revolutionary Armed Forces of Colombia), the contrast with the process in Kenya couldn't have been greater. The four years of talks dedicated the most time to the question of how to deal with past crimes and what exactly would happen to those who were complicit in serious abuses from either side of the conflict.

The parties grappled with huge legal and political difficulties related to the question of justice; many observers predicted that it would be impossible to find a solution that was satisfactory enough to give the guerrillas the confidence to disarm while also meeting Colombia's obligations under both national and international law. The ICC Prosecutor made clear that she was watching closely and was ready to intervene if any agreement didn't pass muster.

This was one of the last issues to be addressed in the talks. After eighteen intensive months on this subject, including detailed technical input from dozens of national and international experts and emotional meetings between the FARC and government negotiating teams and direct victims of the war, the parties concluded an extraordinarily complex 63-page justice agreement. This essentially set out a new truth and justice system to be created within Colombia's national legal framework. This was the major turning point in the peace talks. Colombia celebrated. Now, with this justice agreement, everyone realized that peace might in fact be achievable.

Why This Book

Kenya, Uganda, and Colombia are but a few examples of the tension between the demand for justice for crimes of a war and the real limitations that must be faced when brokering an agreement between warring parties.

For a variety of reasons, this issue has been getting more attention in recent years, but the discussion often takes place with a frustrating lack of familiarity with past experience. A common refrain in meetings and conferences that touch on this subject is that we simply don't know enough to untangle the various policy and legal dilemmas or reach any broad conclusions, despite a considerable number of countries that have confronted these very issues and worked out solutions in different ways.

The intent of this book is to peer behind this quandary and to look at what has actually happened when peacemaking and justice seeking come together, including when they sometimes collide. The book does not delve into great detail on the law and legal parameters; this has been done elsewhere at length. Rather, the intention here is to focus on actual experience and practice in specific cases, and to pull lessons from these. The sometimes overly simplified "peace vs. justice" debate, which has played out among policymakers, rights advocates, and scholars, has relied on selective accounts rather than a comparative or detailed case analysis. The narrow lens of a very few individual countries' experiences has led to overreaching claims and presumptions that do not always hold up against the broader record to date. Some of these claims have led to quite unhelpful policy prescriptions.

As I ventured into this research, I became increasingly uncomfortable with some of the claims that are repeated on both sides of the argument. The realities of countries at war—always struggling with an extraordinarily complex and painful set of choices, pressures, and risks—are simply not well reflected in some of the positions put forward in the international sphere. It is important to consider the views of those who have lived these experiences most closely and can reflect the nuances and difficult choices they have confronted.

This book offers a comparative look at past (and current) experiences in this realm of negotiating justice, unraveling the complications and dilemmas that have emerged in very different kinds of cases. In brief, the book asks the question, What has been the impact when issues of justice for past crimes have come to the peace table, and how have these dynamics played out? If we take an unvarnished view, what do these experiences tell us?

It is easy to see, scanning the cases, that the impact of "justice" on "peace"— that is, the impact of pushing for accountability for crimes of a war while actively negotiating to end the war—has been (perhaps unsurprisingly) sometimes positive, and indeed sometimes negative. While it used to be common to grant amnesties and essentially turn the page on the past, that is no longer considered acceptable. Rather, there are now both legal obligations and strong political expectations, both nationally and internationally, that serious crimes will somehow be accounted for and attention will be given to victims' needs.

For the first time, slowly taking shape over the last fifteen or twenty years, the world is confronting the realities of real legal limits on the level of impunity that can be granted to combatants for war crimes or crimes against humanity. If combatants demand such immunity as a precondition to setting down their weapons, and especially if an international prosecutor has jurisdiction to open a case against such persons, the inescapable difficulties quickly become clear.

This is not only a question of international justice, as the threat of national trials equally presents a challenge. But the possibility of justice clashing with national peace processes has become more likely as the reach of the International Criminal Court has expanded. It is now clear that this Court is investigating crimes primarily in contexts of ongoing armed conflict, rather than after a war has ended. This naturally raises questions. Indeed, as I will show below, the involvement of an international prosecutor has influenced in fundamental ways the course of peace processes or the possibilities of a negotiated peace in a number of different contexts.

Two Core Questions

The first issue that this book will consider is how human rights violations and war crimes have been addressed during peace negotiations. This has been a significant challenge. Nevertheless, there is a growing recognition that, with creativity, conviction, and a nuanced understanding of justice, rights, prevention, victims' interests, and the reality of local constraints, it is possible to address the imperatives of both peace and justice.

A second and distinct issue is how international criminal courts may affect ongoing or planned peace talks, or affect the war itself. Investigations, indictments, or arrest warrants against persons engaged in peace negotiations—by the ICC or another international tribunal—will impact peace talks. The relatively new factor of an independent international prosecutor can be destabilizing to peace efforts.

Both of these issues—how a peace agreement handles accountability and the impact of international prosecutions—may directly affect the stability of peace in the long term. On the one hand, granting impunity for well-known human rights abusers, and failing to compensate victims and investigate the truth, could lay the ground for further abuses and win thin support for the peace by the most-affected population. On the other hand, a move to prosecute those taking part in peace talks or those who signed the peace could bring peace negotiations to an end or put a newfound peace at risk.

These two questions are distinct, but they ultimately point to the same core problem: threatening to bring leaders to justice makes peace negotiations more difficult. Both sides to a conflict might easily agree that the rule of law and functioning judicial systems are critical to a healthy, peaceful society, but they are likely to resist applying these laws and principles to themselves, at least in relation to events of the war.

Structure of the Book

This book considers the experiences of many different countries that have struggled with these questions.

Part I is focused on cross-cutting thematic issues. Chapter 2 explores the overall parameters of the peace-justice debate and the contrasting perspectives of those in the peace mediation and human rights fields. Chapter 3 and Chapter 4 then delve into more detail of how justice has been negotiated in specific cases, and how these issues continue to be effectively "negotiated" long after a peace agreement is signed.

The following four chapters turn to the impact of the ICC and other international courts on peace negotiations and conflict. Chapter 5 explores what this impact has been in specific countries in the midst of (or hoping to begin) peace negotiations; Chapter 6 assesses more specifically whether international courts have helped to deter or prevent war crimes. Chapter 7 argues that there is considerable discretion for international prosecutors to choose how and when they engage in contexts of war, and that they should be strategic in their actions, with an eye not to worsen violence or derail any serious chance of a brokered peace. Chapter 8 shows how the ICC Rome Statute already contains language to allow for such strategic analysis, in its call for the ICC Prosecutor to act in the "interests of justice."

The final chapter of Part I highlights some of the overarching themes and lessons that have emerged from these cross-cutting chapters.

Part II offers a deeper exploration of five specific country cases: Sierra Leone, Liberia, Uganda, Libya, and Colombia (in chronological order of the main events analyzed). Each of these are also briefly addressed in the thematic chapters of Part I, but these five more detailed case studies offer a better picture of the peace negotiations, or in the case of Libya, how the ICC impacted that conflict in 2011 and 2012. We can see the shifting dynamics, and the diverse actors and interests, that influence how the peace-justice equation is decided.

Both the case studies and the thematic chapters are based on extensive interviews with national and international participants in the events under study. I focus on cases that offer the most useful lessons, where international attention (including from international courts) has been significant, and that together offer a diverse range of experience.

2 The Peace and Justice Debate

The tension between peace and justice, or between those who prioritize one over the other, is a bit of a misnomer. The "debate" is not really between peace and justice. Everyone agrees that both are important and valuable. But there is much less agreement on how to achieve both when they are in tension. It is here that the conversation begins, and too often ends, usually without much understanding between the different perspectives. Recognizing these differences is the first step.

This book brings together the interests of two overarching and largely distinct groups of people: those whose principal aim is to protect human rights and ensure justice for rights violations, and those engaged in the work of mediating or facilitating peace negotiations. There are of course differences of views within each of these two general groups, but also significant similarities in focus of work and priorities.

It is notable that the distinction between these two groups is usually more pronounced at the international level than at the national level. In the face of a specific raging conflict, those working in-country for human rights usually put a high priority on preventing new victims, so they value the possibility of stopping the fighting and giving space for a peace agreement to take root. International rights advocates have been more strict in their views, less flexible in relation to national context, and less willing to recognize the human rights interests in ending a war.

Discussions of these peace and justice dilemmas can raise strong passions within both the peace mediation and human rights communities. There are usually many unstated assumptions, including concerns about the other's intentions, that heighten a sense of mutual misunderstanding. Human rights proponents worry that peace mediators will too easily sacrifice justice and that an impunity deal will only lead to more abuses. Their first priority is justice. Peacemakers worry that demands for justice may be a hurdle too high when trying to reach peace. First stop the killing, they say; justice will more easily come later.

These worries are usually most focused on the possibility of criminal prosecutions for atrocities committed in war. Parties to peace negotiations, those who fought the war, will want to know: is there a risk of going to jail? Is a full amnesty possible? If there is no amnesty in the agreement, what does that mean for those who might be accused of crimes? And if an international court holds jurisdiction, should commanders trust that a national agreement (for a conditional amnesty or for reduced or alternative sentences, for example) will be sustained? The concerns and tensions are very real. Other forms of justice, such as establishing a truth commission or providing victims with reparations, are usually less controversial and might be agreed to in general terms fairly readily. But this is not always true: the negotiations over both truth and reparations have been extremely contentious in some contexts. More locally rooted conceptions of justice are given even less attention as a criminal justice focus has gained in prominence.[1]

This is almost never an easy subject at the peace table, neither quickly dispensed with nor forgotten, as may have been possible decades ago. Especially at this moment in history, with international courts gaining in reach and an increasing sense that broad impunity for massive crimes is simply no longer acceptable, questions of accountability are virtually inescapable.[2] The issue is now usually addressed with great seriousness and complexity, with a host of options considered and debated.

The debate that has ensued at the international policy or advocacy level, however, is sometimes frustrating in its simplicity. At its most simple, it is sometimes described as a debate between those who insist on justice first, others on peace first, and a third reasonable group that argues that of course you can have both. A more nuanced exploration of the issues and choices is often lacking. There is rarely a close look at what actually has been discussed on the subject during peace talks. Admittedly, this information is not always readily available, since peace negotiations are often held behind closed doors, and there are few written accounts of these conversations. Intentional or not, the debate and discussions in the policy and advocacy worlds, focused on the principles of peace and justice and especially on the narrow question of amnesty, seem to somehow miss the larger and more important story of these processes, including the missed opportunities and lessons to be learned.

Despite differences in views, it is also true that some principles are now widely accepted, and in the generic not particularly controversial: basic principles of the rule of law for the future, for example. Those involved in war also usually understand, or come to understand, that in today's world it's not likely they can simply "turn the page" without some measure to address past atrocities. While full justice may be impossible, complete impunity is now generally recognized to be unacceptable.

A Change Over Time

The question of war crimes, and more specifically the increasing discomfort with impunity for massive atrocities, has haunted peacemaking for some years. As the human rights field became stronger in the 1980s and into the 1990s, there was increasing criticism of arrangements of impunity that allowed dictators—or other perpetrators of serious crimes—to walk free. In the nego-tiated agreements in El Salvador (1992), South Africa (1993), and Guatemala (1996), the parties agreed to compromises that kept a blanket amnesty out of the negotiated text. These more human rights–friendly arrangements were negotiated in an ad hoc manner, at the insistence of the individual mediator or one of the negotiating parties, and sometimes under pressure from human rights advocates, but with no explicit guidance or clear rules from the interna-tional community per se.

The United Nations formalized a position against amnesty for those crimes known as "international crimes" in 1999, when UN Secretary-General Kofi Annan released a guidance note to UN representatives in peacemaking con-texts.[3] This said that UN representatives could not give their support to amnesties for war crimes, crimes against humanity, genocide, or other viola-tions of human rights that would violate treaty obligations.[4] Meanwhile, in 1998, a treaty was signed in Rome that set out terms for an International Criminal Court. The ICC came into force in 2002 with over sixty state parties, with many more joining later. Regional courts, particularly the Inter-American Court of Human Rights, were also reaching firm decisions that set out an obli-gation to prosecute serious crimes, as well as to establish the truth and provide reparations to victims of a war.

All of these developments made it increasingly clear that the space for impu-nity arrangements was shrinking, quickly. But the demands from those coming to a peace table had not necessarily changed. Many international mediators (in particular those representing the UN) were now required to oppose any proposal that would grant immunity for the most serious crimes of the war. At the same time, it became clear that any national amnesty that might be agreed would have no effect internationally. Senior force commanders increasingly felt the threat of criminal justice as they calculated the possibility of a ceasefire, peace agreement, and ultimately demobilization of opposition troops.

Thus, by the early to mid-2000s, there was a lurking question in discus-sions between justice advocates and peace mediators, and among mediators as they considered the challenges of different contexts. Were the new legal and policy developments, which understandably had the interest of strengthening rights and the rule of law, also inherently making peace negotiations more dif-ficult? In short, were these interests in justice damaging the broader interests in peace? The limited future options for dictators and warlords seemed an obvious constraint on the possibility of reaching a deal: there were few places where someone could flee and effectively escape the reach of international jus-tice. In the context of strengthening human rights standards and an increas-ingly robust ICC, peace negotiations had evidently become more difficult.

A diverse array of conflicts and attempted negotiations were bringing these dynamics to the fore. In Colombia, beginning in 2002, attempts to demo-bilize paramilitary groups became a long and difficult struggle to implement sufficient criminal justice for more than 20,000 armed men, many of them complicit is serious brutalities. In Uganda, from 2006 to 2008, peace talks struggled with accountability for massive rebel crimes, made more difficult by ICC arrest warrants for the rebel leadership. And in Darfur, Sudan, the ICC indictment of the president in 2009 raised questions from some about the balance of priorities between peace and justice and led to significant protest from many African states.[5]

In Libya, where the ICC entered with indictments at the height of war in 2011, the question was a different one: What impact would the ICC have on the ongoing conflict? Did it not force President Muammar Gaddafi into a corner and make it more difficult to end the fighting?

Protests from the African Union (AU) started in response to the Darfur indictments, especially the arrest warrant for the president of Sudan, and increased with the indictment of Gaddafi and the ICC's charges against two who were to become president and vice president of Kenya. In each case, the AU framed its complaint by insisting that peace and stability must take priority. It also called for immunity from prosecution for heads of state and other senior officials, saying that such prosecutions were destabilizing and a violation of sovereignty. Many of the over thirty African state-parties to the ICC threatened to withdraw from the ICC, en masse, and repeatedly pushed for the UN Security Council to halt the ICC's action on Kenya and Sudan.[6] The protestations of an interest in peace were met with skepticism by human rights advocates and by the ICC Prosecutor. But over time the disagreements with the manner, timing, and perceived exclusively African focus of the ICC were conflated; legitimate interests in peace and stability in some contexts were melded with a sense of offense at the way the ICC did its business. It became nearly impossible to separate out genuine concerns of the AU about the ICC damaging peace prospects from what were seen as political and self-interested complaints against the ICC.[7]

In 2015, the European Union adopted a policy that formally backed the UN's position against amnesty for international crimes.[8] For a number of years previously the EU had already held essentially the same position, but it was ad hoc and grounded in upholding ICC obligations, since all EU member states are also members of the ICC. EU representatives had resisted amnesty for Rome Statute crimes even in non-ICC member states, such as Sudan in 2005.

As human rights legal standards strengthened over these years, a new field of "transitional justice" was also developing. This offered a broader array of policy responses to massive human rights abuses and focused on the needs of victims and societal healing, as well as the prosecution and punishment of perpetrators. Truth commissions, victim reparations, and systemic reforms to prevent further abuses were central elements of transitional justice, intended not to displace criminal justice but to work hand in hand with any possible action through the courts. As more and more post-war countries were drawn to these measures, it became evident that a prosecutions focus alone was insufficient.

Meanwhile, ever since the conclusion of the ICC Rome Statute, a quiet discussion was taking place, mostly in academic circles, about a provision in this Statute that allowed the ICC Prosecutor to hold off on an investigation or prosecution if he or she found it to be in the "interest of justice." Most commentators and legal experts read the Statute broadly; the language clearly suggested that the "interest of justice" went beyond very narrow prosecutorial interests. Two groups of people disagreed with this reading: a few international nongovernmental human rights advocacy organizations and, more importantly, the ICC Prosecutor and staff. Thus, the tool that was inserted into the Statute for the purpose of allowing flexibility for national circumstance, potentially including an "interest in peace," was largely off the table. It wasn't helping to solve the dilemmas at hand. As the ICC became increasingly focused on contexts of ongoing conflict, the ICC's second Chief Prosecutor, beginning in 2012, began to explicitly acknowledge these tensions and to emphasize her interest in not only preventing violence but also promoting peace, and not wanting to be a spoiler of any peace process.

Mediation

The relative youth and rapid development of the international human rights movement, and institutions such as the ICC, is matched by recent advances in the mediation field. Both mediation and transitional justice have matured and strengthened over the last two to three decades, largely progressing in parallel and quite separate from each other. With this progression, each of these fields has developed specialized institutions, expertise, generally accepted principles, and some sense of standard practice.

While transitional justice has been seen as a subset of the field of international human rights, traditionally dominated by lawyers, mediation is most closely aligned with diplomacy and often carried out by current or former diplomats. The persons and institutions in these two fields have not naturally overlapped, and the understanding between them (human rights professionals' understanding of mediation practices, or mediators' knowledge of the intricacies of human rights and transitional justice) has remained fairly limited. Certain biases, fears, and false assumptions are still quite evident when these two separate worlds intersect.

While there are centuries of examples of negotiations to end or prevent conflict, the practice picked up considerably after the Cold War, when shifting tides in international relations opened the possibility of negotiating an end to many long-entrenched conflicts. By 2004, more conflicts had been settled by negotiation in the previous fifteen years than in the previous two hundred, according to the United Nations.[9]

The post–Cold War model of peace mediation has included a stronger framework of international norms and recognition of international law, usually starting with a substantive agenda far beyond simply ending fighting and demobilizing and reintegrating troops. International mediators from the UN or other intergovernmental organizations, from individual states, such as Norway, or from specialized nongovernmental organizations have brokered processes that address a wide range of policy and societal issues. These may pertain to constitutional affairs, minority rights, regional autonomy, distribution of land, economic inequality, or illegal drug cultivation, as well as of course political rights and representation, particularly for groups that have been fighting over inequality and access to power. Even against these very demanding issues, reconciliation and justice for past crimes have usually been seen as among the most difficult.

Those working in the peace mediation field are well aware of the limited duration of many signed peace agreements, let alone the long peace processes that never reach fruition with a final accord, despite behemoth efforts to create space for the warring parties to talk, and despite in some cases the successful completion of important interim agreements.[10] Mediators and local peace advocates also understand that reaching a peace agreement, even if a very important turning point, is only one step towards long-term peace.

Even the meaning of peace is controversial. The focus by mediators on ending or preventing violent conflict between armed groups, and defining this as peace, is criticized by those who see this as far too limited. The parties may try to address root causes of conflict, but a peace accord leaves much undone, including building reconciliation between former enemies.[11] But of course a conflict-free society cannot be the aim; rather it is a question of how conflict and differing interests are managed.

Claims and Confusions

One difficulty of the issue of "peace and justice" is that many of those who have ventured into drawing conclusions—and there have been quite a few—have based their conclusions on the experiences of a small number of countries. And within each case, they draw from a narrow part of the story, thus losing the larger context and any measure of nuance in the lessons drawn. Certain anecdotes—and sweeping policy recommendations adduced from them—have been repeated many times. Some of these, regrettably, are not confirmed by a broader review of the facts. A closer analysis, especially relying on inputs from national experts and participants in each process, may lead to a different set of conclusions.

Indeed, the details offered by these closer accounts bring out the complexity of the issue in ways that are not only more accurate, but also much more interesting. The lessons are more nuanced. The oversimplification that has been typical in "peace vs. justice" debates begins to fall away.

So what have been the claims? From human rights advocates, the following: a peace deal without justice is not sustainable. Impunity deals encourage more abuses. Impunity leads to more conflict. The engagement of the ICC (or another international court) in contexts of peacemaking spurs peace and diffuses tensions. It sidelines perpetrators, making peace possible. The ICC's involvement improves the security situation. The ICC prevents and deters crimes. Where it hasn't sidelined perpetrators, ICC indictments have pushed them to the peace table and pushed them to take peace talks seriously.

Most of these arguments sound quite plausible and logical, and thus likely. From a perspective of strengthening human rights protections, they are also usefully coherent and consistent with broader interests. After having looked closely at many peace processes that grappled with questions of justice, I agree with some of the assertions here, but not with others. Some are only sometimes true, in part.

These positions are linked to the core foundation of international human rights work, that of the law, and the legal obligations of states and non-state armed groups to respect certain principles and practices. One core obligation is to prosecute gross violations, as well as to establish the truth and repair harm.

A difficulty arises, however, when the prioritization of accountability leads to positions of advocacy that are almost intentionally blind to the realities of context. In one case, a prominent international advocate told me that he refused to consider what the possible "solutions" might be to the peace-justice dilemmas in the current negotiations. "That is not my problem. That is not my issue. I am not a mediator," he said, emphatically. "My job is simply to let them know that in the 21st century, there are some limits." Unfortunately for those seeking fair and legal solutions, his definition of the limits included a strict requirement to prosecute all serious crimes and significant jail terms for the guilty. At the level of either political or operational reality, this was not feasible.

Human rights advocates may understand that they are taking positions that are impractical and making demands that are unrealizable. They might be hoping to make certain principles clear and to pull the final outcome at least somewhat closer to their position. This is to some degree effective, but such a strategy risks doing damage to peacemaking, and thus damage to broader human rights interests—stopping the atrocities of the war—when it is pushed too hard. Human Rights Watch, for example, was strongly criticized for its vehement opposition to the justice agreement in Colombia, which fed into the defeat of the accord in a national plebiscite, and ironically strengthened the hand of Colombian politicians on the right who are the least interested in accountability.

On the other side, from those engaged in mediating or facilitating peace talks or trying to forestall or lessen violence, there is worry that justice has been unreasonably put before interests in peace. Human rights demands make it more difficult to attract parties to the table and create a stumbling block to reaching an agreement, they say. Taking a quiet approach to the problem of impunity is both smarter and more effective. The most successful examples of justice are those that develop after peace is established, usually after a number of years have passed. Indictments from the ICC when talks are under way have damaged prospects for peace. No combatants have ever agreed to go to jail or on trial in exchange for putting down their arms. Preventing tomorrow's victims must be at least as important as providing justice for the victims of yesterday, they insist.

These views are felt most strongly by those who have worked closely with warring parties in peace processes and who are well aware of the fragility of peace negotiations. Mediators often expect that perpetrators will want amnesty, or at least some form of guarantee for their future; most mediators also understand, however, that this is a difficult proposition under international, and often national, law. They are likely to advise the parties against it, warn that any amnesty deal is unlikely to hold, and work to find an alternative arrangement that the parties might accept. At the same time, they know that whatever arrangement might be found is unlikely to satisfy the strongest demands from rights advocates.

These concerns do not only arise from mediators. Some independent advocates in national contexts have argued that a national amnesty is the best route not only to peace, reconciliation, and rebuilding, but also to a much stronger transitional justice policy overall. In Uganda in 2013, many victim-focused organizations came together to insist that the government reinstitute a lapsed amnesty for rebels. The Refugee Law Project, which works closely with victims in northern Uganda, commended the government when the amnesty was finally reinstated, saying that this would "promote reintegration and reconciliation among the affected communities" and that it demonstrated the government's willingness to pursue a peaceful end to hostilities.[12]

Do the concerns of peace mediators accurately reflect the experiences to date? Again: partly true, part of the time. Some of the assumptions don't fully represent past experiences; others are legitimate and quite logical concerns, although perhaps they assume too quickly that some forms of accountability are impossible.

However, there is no sense in rejecting or dismissing these mediators' concerns or pretending they are not there. It can only be wishful thinking to suggest that a threat of justice—which suspected perpetrators understand to be a prison term—would not give a leader pause, whether a rebel leader or an army commander. We must begin with the recognition that justice is indeed a challenge for peacemaking. This book hopes to increase our understanding of these challenges and to suggest some possible approaches to the dilemmas at hand.

Hints at a Solution: Colombia

The Colombia case has helped focus attention on the complexity of the problem and also suggested ideas for a solution. In part, Colombia has reframed the issue, expanding it out from what has traditionally been a too-narrow focus on prosecutions and punishment. A legal foundation to any peace agreement is essential, but insufficient, and a legal perspective alone misses other interests of victims.

As the recent talks between Colombia and the Revolutionary Armed Forces of Colombia (FARC) unfolded, beginning in 2012, the issue of justice became the most contentious aspect in the view of the Colombian public. Many human rights and peace advocates, as well as protagonists directly engaged in the process, worked to find a reasonable and acceptable solution.

Colombian President Santos insisted repeatedly that preventing further victims in the future was certainly as important as obtaining justice for victims of the past. He pushed back against those with unrealistic demands, including a singular focus on criminal accountability, and those who were unwilling to recognize the importance of stopping the fifty-year war in order to prevent further atrocities.

War opens space for horrific violations. In this sense, wouldn't a ceasefire and ultimately a full peace agreement be in the interest of protecting human rights? This is not as self-evident as it may seem, and many international human rights organizations do not take a position on war or peace or even on whether a peace agreement in any country is a positive development, believing that this extends beyond their human rights mandate.

But in addition to prevention and protection against further war and the war's abuses, a peace agreement may advance human rights in other ways. Typically, there are detailed provisions for reforming state institutions in a way that would protect rights in the future. These provisions should be of direct and immediate interest to those with a rights focus. A singular emphasis on punishment for past crimes has the effect of undervaluing these other goals. These debates have come through clearly in Colombia.

Some lawyers have pointed to the competing obligations of a government to provide security and a peaceful environment for its citizens, which should be recognized as parallel obligations to that of seeking justice for past crimes.[13] As Colombian human rights experts Rodrigo Uprimny and Camilo Sanchez argued, "The duty to prosecute is not an absolute rule, but rather a duty that should be considered in the face of other obligations on the state."[14] From this broader legal understanding, they and other scholars insist, it would be irresponsible to allow justice for past crimes to take absolute precedence over all other goals.[15]

The Colombian context also crystalized the concerns about the impact of international courts, and in particular the ICC. Uprimny and Sanchez argued that if the ICC maintained too rigid of an understanding of the duty to prosecute, this could "threaten the possibility of negotiating an end of the armed conflict. That can't be correct; the purpose the ICC was certainly not to make it impossible for wars to end through negotiated peace processes."[16] It is for these reasons that the possibility of a more nuanced understanding of the interests of justice, and the interests of peace, has attracted attention.

As the Colombian talks progressed, and after many hours of debate, discussion, and legal analysis, there was a sense among Colombian experts that a solution to the justice quandary might be found in an interconnected model that would, in a sense, balance perpetrators' contributions to peace and to victims' rights with some measure of benefits for those perpetrators, including reduced or alternative penal sanctions. The requirements could include providing the truth about past crimes, contributing to peace-building or victim reparations, helping to dismantle criminal networks, locating human remains or buried land mines, or a range of other measures. Surprisingly, the legally required minimal sentence for these crimes was not clear, from an international law perspective: the ICC judges had never addressed the question of minimal sentence requirements at the national level, and there were no good reference points from other courts. These many interrelated ideas were slowly shaped into a final agreement, one of great length and legal complexity.

The Colombian peace process had already gone further in incorporating victims into the process than any previous peace negotiations to date. Delegations of victims had been invited to speak to the negotiating parties in Havana—a total of sixty individual victims, in five high-profile visits. Their stories were heart wrenching, but they also made clear that their demands for justice were not limited to trials and punishment. Rather, these victims emphasized ending the war and the need for truth and reparations, and for dismantling paramilitary and other illegal armed groups. These messages were echoed in national victims' conferences that the United Nations helped to organize, which engaged several thousand victims in consultations.[17] Few victims argued that criminal prosecution was their primary or sole priority. Rather, their desire for accountability was naturally balanced against the need for security and recovery for individual victims, communities, and the country as a whole.

Conclusion

Among its many lessons, Colombia certainly confirms what is clear in so many peace negotiation contexts: that the peace-justice equation is not static. National and international actors, very much including the ICC, affect these dynamics through their decisions and actions. Past experience suggests that the timing and nature of ICC engagement can be improved. The issue is not only the fact of indictments (or threats of indictments) in a conflict situation, but the style, form, and timing of their issue.

In each situation where an international prosecutor has engaged, there have been many choices to be made, and reasonable alternatives existed that could potentially have strengthened or weakened the effectiveness and impact of this engagement. These choices affect the Court's own direct interests, such as the likelihood of an arrest, as well as the interests of those focused on stopping the violence. These issues will be addressed in more depth in the following chapters.

Notes

1 Many writers and rights advocates equate the notion of justice with criminal justice—that of prosecuting and punishing perpetrators—but this has had the effect of sidelining alternative conceptions of justice that might have much more resonance at the local level. See Sarah M. H. Nouwen and Wouter G.

Werner, "Monopolizing Global Justice: International Criminal Law as Challenge to Human Diversity," *Journal of International Criminal Justice* 13 (2015), 157–176. These authors identify, for example, the restoration of relationships, ending ongoing violence, redistribution, alternative forms of punishment, and equality as examples of how justice is defined or understood by interlocutors in Uganda and Sudan.

2 In the past, immunities from prosecution, especially for the highest officials of the state, were not always spelled out explicitly, in part because of the common notion of how far the law could reach. As Ron Slye notes, "Historically, amnesties for war crimes and what we today call crimes against humanity were less common precisely because there was little acceptance of the notion that state officials could be held accountable for such acts." Ronald C. Slye, "The Legitimacy of Amnesties Under International Law and General Principles of Anglo-American Law," *Virginia Journal of International Law* 43 (2002): 175, digitalcommons.law.seattleu.edu/faculty/433.

3 Office of the United Nations Secretary-General, "Guidelines for United Nations Representatives on Certain Aspects of Negotiations for Conflict Resolution," 1999; updated 2006.

4 The Guidelines state, at p. 2:

> Demands for amnesty might be made on behalf of different elements. It may be necessary and proper for immunity from prosecution to be granted to members of the armed opposition seeking reintegration into society as part of a national reconciliation process. Government negotiators might seek endorsement of self-amnesty proposals. The UN, however, cannot condone amnesties regarding war crimes, crimes against humanity, genocide, or gross violations of human rights, or foster those that violate relevant treaty obligations of the parties in this field.

5 This book uses "indictments" and "arrest warrants" interchangeably, in reference to the ICC and other international courts, as is common practice. Technically, the ICC Pre-Trial Chamber first submits an arrest warrant (or a summons for someone to appear voluntarily) and only later, after the person appears, will it confirm the charges (or perhaps not confirm the charges and thus release the person). There is a higher evidentiary threshold required for the confirmation of charges. The Rome Statute does not refer to "indictments," but in most systems this refers to the confirmation of charges. For other tribunals, such as the Special Court for Sierra Leone, the indictment took place together with the confirmation of the arrest warrant.

6 See, for example, African Union, "Decision on the Progress Report of the Commission on the Implementation of Previous Decisions on the International Criminal Court (ICC)," Doc. Assembly/AU/18(XXIV), Dec. 547, 31 Jan 2015. These views were further detailed in interviews by the author with AU officials, Addis Ababa, Ethiopia, 20 Apr 2016.

7 For example, see the opinion piece by Desmond Tutu, "In Africa, Seeking a License to Kill," *NY Times*, 10 Oct 2013, criticizing those who were pushing AU member states to leave the ICC.

8 Council of the European Union, "The EU's Policy Framework on Support to Transitional Justice," 13576/15 Brussels, 16 Nov 2015. On amnesties, this states:

> The EU firmly believes in the principle that there cannot be lasting peace without justice. Therefore the EU supports the established United Nations policy to oppose amnesties for war crimes, crimes against humanity,

genocide or gross violations of human rights, including in the context of peace negotiations.

9   UN Secretary-General's High-level Panel on Threats, Challenges and Change, *A More Secure World: Our Shared Responsibility*, 2004.

10 The record on the durability of peace agreements is difficult to quantify, depending on what factors are measured, and how. For a useful analysis, see Barbara F. Walter, "Conflict Relapse and the Sustainability of Post-Conflict Peace," *World Development Report 2011* (background paper), World Bank, 13 Sept 2010, web.worldbank.org.

11 Academics draw a distinction between "negative peace" (the absence of violence) and "positive peace," which includes the restoration of relationships and social systems that serve all. The Norwegian sociologist Johan Galtung, often referred to as the father of peace studies, coined this terminology in the 1960s. Johan Galtung, *Peace by Peaceful Means: Peace and Conflict, Development and Civilization* (Oslo: International Peace Research Institute, 1996). See also interview of Johan Galtung by Amy Goodman, *Democracy Now*, 9 July 2012, www.democracynow.org.

12 Refugee Law Project, Makerere University, Kampala, "A Renewed Promise for Peace and Justice: The Reinstatement of Uganda's Amnesty Act 2000," press release, 29 May 2013, www.refugeelawproject.org.

13 See, for example, Transitional Justice Institute, *The Belfast Guidelines on Amnesty and Accountability* (Belfast: Transitional Justice Institute, University of Ulster, 2013), 6–7. See also Slye, "The Legitimacy of Amnesties."

14 Rodrigo Uprimny and Nelson Camilo Sanchez, "The ICC and Negotiated Peace: Reflections from Colombia," *OpenGlobalRights* (blog), 11 Feb 2015, www.openglobalrights.org.

15 See Mark Freeman, *Necessary Evils: Amnesties and the Search for Justice*, (Cambridge: Cambridge University Press, 2009).

16 Uprimny and Sanchez, "Negotiated Peace."

17 See *Sistematización* and *Informe y Balance General: Foros Nacional y Regionales Sobre Víctimas* (Bogota: UN Colombia Office and Centro de Pensamiento y Seguimiento al Diálago de Paz, Universidad Nacional de Colombia, 2014).

3 How Justice Is Negotiated at the Peace Table

If rights are guaranteed, they should not be negotiated. But a central agenda item of most peace talks is exactly this: working out a legal framework to respond to egregious crimes of a war. In most cases, the mediator is sitting with those who are in some way responsible for these very acts. The subject matter is sometimes labeled "reconciliation," "victims," or "transitional justice." The first question on the minds of the parties, though, is likely to be that of criminal justice and, most often, how they might avoid any possibility of trials and prison time.

The combination of developments set out in the previous chapter—the UN policy against amnesties in the late 1990s, the start of the ICC in 2002, a number of key decisions by international courts—has led to a general understanding that blanket amnesties are unacceptable. Peace agreements have reflected these changed parameters. Judging only from the specific language of recent peace agreements, the record has not been bad. The great majority of these peace accords do not grant impunity for serious crimes. Most include proactive measures for truth, reparations, or other nonjudicial forms of accountability. Some set out important reforms for justice in the future.

This general record of good intentions, and many reasonably good outcomes (again, based on what is included in the text), only tell part of the story. The often-fraught processes to reach these agreements offer important lessons. Equally, we must recognize the considerable difficulties in actually implementing a justice program after an agreement has been signed and the guns stop firing. The record in this area, set out below and in the next chapter, is sobering.

Much focus has been given to the issue of amnesty, and it is now common to find language in a peace agreement that prevents any amnesty from being applied to serious international crimes. Meanwhile, factors outside the control of those directly involved in the talks may have the greatest sway in shaping the justice agenda: the direct engagement of the ICC, in particular, has had a considerable impact on several peace processes.

A special mix of factors makes this issue in some ways unique, in the landscape of difficult issues confronting mediators: the constraints of international law and advances in the accepted norms against impunity; the likely complicity in serious crimes even of persons sitting at the negotiating table; the intensity of interest by outside observers, including victims and the international community; and the likelihood that the outcome on justice—be it the announcement of a truth commission, some form of amnesty, or a reparations or vetting program—will capture immediate public attention and serve as a lightning rod either for accolades or for condemnation of a peace agreement as a whole.

What's on the Table, and Why?

The issue of justice might encompass a wide range of judicial and nonjudicial subjects. The question of how the subject of justice is defined, and indeed who defines it, is the first matter for consideration by those who intend to see this on the agenda for negotiations. The mediator or facilitator may play an important role, especially in helping to set the initial agenda, but he or she cannot move without the parties' support and consent. Some issues may be uncontroversial, even if they require a detailed and technical working through. Others, of course, are not.

Justice for the Past and the Future

The issue of justice emerges in peace negotiations in two different respects. One is focused on accountability for the events of the past. After atrocities have taken place, it is natural to ask what happened, who did it, and will anyone be held to account? Who were the victims, and what reparations are due? This may include an aspect of "undoing" the past: the return of refugees, the release of political prisoners, the return of land.[1] A second manner of thinking about justice is focused primarily on the future: what needs to change in order to prevent further abuses? What reforms of state institutions, such as the judiciary, military, or police, are needed? Should the state sign onto international human rights treaties or create an independent oversight mechanism to guard against abuses? How might reconciliation be promoted?

Of course, there are important areas of overlap between these past-focused and future-focused approaches to justice. Broad investigations into past abuses almost always aim to affect future policy, by learning lessons and recommending reforms. A reparations program should represent contrition on the part of the state, which can reduce anger and resentment and advance reconciliation. And a critical piece is identifying those with an abusive record and removing them from the security forces so they will abuse no more.

But despite overlaps, it is still useful to recognize these two distinct baskets of work. The second of these—the broad array of future-oriented reforms and initiatives to protect human rights—is important. It is not the subject of this book, however. Other good resources are available in this area.[2] In brief, while these are certainly not simple aspects to work out, they are generally not a major source of controversy and disagreement. As Christine Bell pointed out in an important book on the subject, there is often a positive incentive on both sides to ensure protection of those whose power will be reduced in the new political order.[3] In Northern Ireland, for example, the 1998 Good Friday Agreement included a host of provisions for human rights protections in the future, but said almost nothing about accountability, truth, or reparations for abuses of the past.[4]

Perhaps as a testament to the relative lack of controversy on future human rights protections, much of the literature on these aspects of peace agreements has reasonably been based on a study of the texts—the agreements themselves—as well as the implementation after signing, rather than looking at the process to arrive at the agreed language. In contrast, on the subject of accountability for past crimes, a study of the final text alone misses an important element, which will help explain what the parties intended and why certain sometimes-odd language was used. While the interpretation of the signed agreement shouldn't be determined or influenced by unwritten side deals, in fact it often can be, since the parties at the table usually have an oversized role in implementation as well.

Why Do Warring Parties Sometimes Demand Justice?

One would think that warring parties, well-known for atrocities, would start into peace talks with an explicit demand for full immunity from any prosecution. It's true that some have.

But surprisingly, many leaders have launched into formal peace negotiations with a call for justice. The logic of this isn't obvious: if both parties have a record of serious crimes, which is often true, why would they push for accountability?

This is partly answered by a strange aspect that seems common in the psychology of war: a tendency to misperceive one's own crimes.

When fighting parties come to the table, they are usually quite aware of the kinds of atrocities that have taken place in conflict. It would be surprising if they were not aware of what their own side has done, at least in general terms and probably in specific terms. But they are more focused on the atrocities that they and their supporters have suffered, and thus they see themselves more as victim rather than perpetrator. The notoriously abusive rebels in Sierra Leone and Liberia, for example, both opened their respective peace negotiations by demanding justice for the government's crimes. In the Kenya talks in 2008, both parties pushed to strengthen accountability guarantees in the agreement to investigate post-election violence, each of them profoundly aware of what their supporters suffered.

Meanwhile, each party may see their own acts as justified for the purpose of self-defense and their own motivations as almost pure: fighting for the people, fighting to defend the people, fighting to change a corrupt and abusive system, or defending the country from "terrorists" or "communists." Thus, their own crimes fade, or they may simply not see them as crimes—or, if crimes, they are somehow justifiable for a greater cause.

Whether this is founded on self-delusion or on a lack of information about the atrocities of the war remains an open question. There are surely examples of both of these. A foreign diplomat closely involved in the Sierra Leone peace talks recounted an exchange with Foday Sankoh, the head of the notorious Revolutionary United Front (RUF) rebels that were still wreaking havoc in Sierra Leone even while the talks were under way in Togo. The diplomat visited Sankoh in his hotel room, in Togo, to show him clear satellite pictures of the aftermath of rampages by RUF forces over the previous days. Sankoh was visibly startled: he had been denying outright that these abuses were happening. Sankoh immediately called his commanders in the field, and these actions largely stopped.

Another dynamic at play is a keen interest by many warring parties to guard their own political future, and they know that pronouncing a commitment to human rights will be well received by the international community. Indeed, if they demand an amnesty for atrocious crimes, it would suggest they know they're guilty, and it may only bring more attention to this record. The ICC is also a factor: as explored in a later chapter, rebel groups are usually quite aware of the new international legal context, even if they may misunderstand its reach. Legal advisors are likely to warn them that any blanket amnesty won't stick and may only bring international prosecution.

If these leaders begin by justifying or denying their abuses, this usually changes as they realize that these actions are crimes and they are at risk of prosecution. Thus follows, usually, a difficult discussion on what form of immunity from prosecution might be possible and whether there are other ways to provide legal security to armed groups as they demobilize.

Ultimately, the strength of feeling around these issues, and the level of difficulty that this presents, is determined by the perceived threat of prosecution—especially the personal risk felt by those sitting at the peace table. Mediators in some peace processes say that the parties, and especially the government or army representatives, have shown surprisingly little concern that they might be the target of prosecution. Decades of impunity for these very crimes give them considerable comfort, and a demand for legal guarantees of protection might seem superfluous. In the Aceh talks, the Indonesia military rejected the idea that they might need an amnesty. They simply didn't see themselves as having committed crimes, close experts say—despite reports of serious abuses by the army over many years of the conflict.

In the major peace agreement in the Philippines, signed in 2014 between the government and the Moro Islamic Liberation Front (MILF), there is neither an amnesty nor any specifics spelled out on justice. Instead, the issue was transferred to a follow-up Transitional Justice and Reconciliation Commission that was to be created after the peace agreement was signed. The rebel leadership was not worried about disarming and joining open society without judicial guarantees. Prosecutions were not in the spirit of the accord and were simply not expected, a leading participant told me.[5] Indeed, the transitional justice commission did not have a criminal justice mandate, but rather was tasked to recommend measures "to address the grievances of the Bangsamoro people, correct historical injustices, and address human rights violations," as well as promote healing and reconciliation.[6]

In other instances, parties who felt victimized assumed that justice was impossible and that it was unrealistic to push the issue. Thus, there are cases where, despite great numbers of atrocities in the war, the question of amnesty vs. justice was not identified by the parties as a priority issue. They were more interested in ensuring political benefits in a transitional government, pushing for a clear regional autonomy arrangement, or addressing other broad issues relating to the post-conflict political dispensation.

However, in most cases it is indeed the parties to the conflict who insist on attention to this issue. It is this element of risk (especially to the leadership on either side), and perhaps also desire for justice for what they and their supporters have suffered, that leads naturally to a central plank of the peace negotiations being dedicated to questions of past crimes, individual culpability, and possible benefits for victims.

Where the parties do not prioritize this issue, civil society and victims' groups are likely to push it onto the agenda, or alternatively the mediator may raise it. Some form of accountability for massive atrocities has become a priority for the international community; it would now be seen as odd and impractical to conclude a major peace agreement that lacked at least indicative language on how this subject would be handled after the signing.

Negotiating Amnesty, Accountability, and Truth

Looking at the many peace negotiations over the last decades with the question of justice in mind, a general pattern begins to emerge. First, it has been rare that proactive criminal justice measures are considered, such as a special court or special prosecutor, although there are some important recent examples where new tribunals have been agreed. More often, rather than measures for criminal justice, the question that garners the most attention is: What kind of restrictions on accountability might be possible, through some form of amnesty?

Indeed, an amnesty law is usually necessary after war, and especially a civil war in which citizens have taken up arms against the state. Armed rebels are by definition breaking national law—committing treason, sedition, or the like— and the state has the full legal authority to imprison those it has been able to capture in the course of the conflict. In principle, those prisoners of war who are not accused of war crimes or other serious abuses should be released at the end of a conflict. This is affirmed, for example, in the 1977 Protocol II to the Geneva Conventions, which states that there should be the "broadest possible amnesty to persons who have participated in the armed conflict." This has generally been understood not to apply to grave war crimes, crimes against humanity, or genocide, but this is still under debate. It would be more accurate to say that international law is not perfectly clear that amnesty can never be provided for serious international crimes.[7]

As indicated above, the policy of the UN, and some other states or institutions, is another matter. The UN first set out its own restrictions on amnesty in Latin American peacemaking contexts, in the El Salvador (concluding in 1991) and Guatemala (1996) peace negotiations. The UN mediators in both cases advised against including an amnesty for human rights crimes in the final agreement. But elsewhere, at exactly the same time, another UN representative expressed no objection to a broad amnesty proposal, which resulted in a blanket amnesty included in the Sierra Leone peace agreement of 1996 (an agreement that ultimately did not hold). Indeed, the maturation and clarification of this principle against amnesty for international crimes, at least from the perspective of UN policy, can be seen in Sierra Leone in the space of time between 1996 and 1999, when the UN position on amnesty firmly changed.

It must be recognized, however, that amnesties are not uniform. Their parameters can be very broad or very narrow, or conditioned or limited in a host of different ways, as Mark Freeman makes clear in a book on this subject.[8] Freeman's study of hundreds of amnesty laws offers a range of options for those crafting future amnesties, so that they might exclude, include, or condition very specific kinds of immunities.

My analysis, for our purposes here, is focused on both the process and outcome of the negotiations. If serious crimes were explicitly excluded from an amnesty, what was the nature of the discussion, and what were the specific factors that decided this? How did this issue affect the peace negotiations, and what was the effect—amnesty or not—on whether criminal prosecutions took place in the years following a peace deal?

Interim Immunity Arrangements: Perpetrators at the Peace Table

A wrinkle may come up early in a peace process, for those intending to set out a hard and fast rule against immunities for those accused of serious crimes. Often it is necessary to provide some kind of provisional amnesty or pardon, as the rebel leadership may be either imprisoned or facing arrest warrants, to even begin peace talks. Those living in exile, or still living in the bush, at war, are under the threat of arrest if they present themselves for peace talks—either very simply for the crime of rebellion or for specific war crimes or crimes against humanity. Arrest warrants may have been extended internationally, also complicating the idea of talks outside the country.

In 1999, the leader of the RUF in Sierra Leone, Foday Sankoh, well-known for horrific acts, had been captured and convicted and was on death row in Sierra Leone. He was released from jail to travel to Lomé, Togo, for peace negotiations. His fate was dependent on the outcome of the talks; he even referred to himself, during the months of negotiations, as a "prisoner of peace." Ultimately, in the context of a blanket amnesty awarded to all fighters on both sides, Sankoh emerged from the peace talks with the "status of vice president" and with a full pardon for his outstanding sentence.

In 2012, the Norwegian government hosted the official opening of the peace talks between the Colombian government and the Revolutionary Armed Forces of Colombia (FARC), Colombia's largest rebel group. However, there were outstanding arrest warrants against many of the FARC leaders, including from the U.S., France (for killings of French citizens), and Colombia itself; these had in most cases been transferred to Interpol, so that arrests could be made internationally. However, it became clear that it was impossible to lift or waive these arrest warrants, given their multiple national sources. Rather, there was an informal arrangement for the FARC delegation to travel to Oslo without risk of arrest. During the course of the talks in Havana, Cuba, the Colombian government put all legal action against the FARC delegation members on hold. Meanwhile, however, U.S. authorities denied a request to release a FARC leader from a U.S. prison so that he could join the FARC delegation in Cuba.

When peace talks begin, of course, it's never clear if they will succeed, and thus both the current and future legal risk to the participants may be in question. In South Africa, several African National Congress (ANC) leaders returned to South Africa for the first rounds of confidential talks without legal immunities in place, aware that they were at risk of arrest if the talks were to collapse.[9] This has in fact happened in other cases: for example those representing the armed opposition in Aceh, Indonesia, were arrested by the government when an early attempt at peace talks soured.[10]

These interim measures certainly don't resolve the longer-term questions of what will happen in relation to accused war criminals at the conclusion of a peace agreement—if there is a successful conclusion. In some ways, these temporary immunity measures only highlight the dilemmas further: it is unrealistic to expect to send a Foday Sankoh–type figure back to jail after signing a peace deal. Sankoh's claim of being a "prisoner of peace" is understood in this sense. But this also becomes an incentive for peace. Although the Sierra Leone talks were sometimes at the edge of collapse, the government held extraordinary leverage over Sankoh on this point: in theory, a failure to reach peace would have returned Sankoh to his jail cell, and death sentence, in Freetown.

Outside observers and human rights advocates sometimes protest the very premise of inviting the worst rights abusers to high-level peace talks, where they are wined and dined and live in considerable comfort in a nice hotel for weeks or months on end. The greater the abuses, the greater the chance perpetrators are invited to the table, they say, and the greater the chance they'll emerge with political power and benefits. There is some truth to this, but it may be unavoidable. Those who control the levers of war have to be included, or any peace effort will fail.

In the peace talks between Uganda and the Lord's Resistance Army (LRA) from 2006 to 2008, which took place in Juba, Southern Sudan, the LRA struggled with how it would be represented at the peace table. Because there was an ICC arrest warrant for LRA leader Joseph Kony and others in the leadership, they wouldn't leave the safety of their command base. Kony first sent two low-level LRA members, but soon pulled them back, afraid they might be detained or manipulated. Ultimately, the LRA was represented by a group of Ugandans in exile who apparently had some historical links to the group, but it wasn't always clear, despite their regular consultations with Kony, that their positions truly represented the wishes of the LRA. Already suspicious of the process, Kony soon lost trust in his delegation, foretelling—and in part causing—the eventual collapse of the talks.

There are very few examples of successful peace talks that excluded leaders or specific groups from participation because they are accused of war crimes or other atrocities. On the contrary, in almost every case some of those sitting at the table are under credible and often specific accusations of serious crimes. This is true equally of government and rebel representatives. There are many examples: if one considers those involved in the peace talks of El Salvador, Mozambique, Sierra Leone, Northern Ireland, or the recent examples of Colombia, South Sudan, or Afghanistan, as well as many others, one finds many central participants who were implicated in serious crimes, according to the records of independent groups that tracked these conflicts.

For mediators, this presents in part a location dilemma: finding a place to meet where the parties feel safe from arrest. The recent strengthening of universal jurisdiction laws in a number of countries, especially in Europe, has de facto limited who can be invited. In Switzerland, which has had a long tradition of hosting peace talks, any well-founded accusation of serious war crimes or crimes against humanity would require national authorities to arrest and prosecute the person accused, regardless of their involvement in a Swiss-hosted peace process.

To date, the few persons excluded from talks because of war crimes accusations have generally been under specific legal indictment by an international court. In the case of the LRA, Kony and the others excluded themselves, unsurprisingly, to avoid arrest. Charles Taylor removed himself from the Liberia talks as soon as a warrant for his arrest was released by the Special Court for Sierra Leone. For a mediator, the decision on inclusion and exclusion is more often determined by broader interests and particularly a judgment on what is required for a workable peace process. The U.S. government prohibited Bosnian Serb leaders from attending the Dayton peace talks in 1995, based on their indictment by the International Criminal Tribunal for the former Yugoslavia (ICTY) just weeks earlier. U.S. Ambassador Richard Holbrooke, who arranged this peace conference, threatened to have them arrested if they landed on U.S. soil. But this also served Holbrooke's practical interests: Holbrooke had already concluded that the meeting might only succeed if these two polarizing individuals were excluded. They did not attend, and their interests were represented by Serbian President Slobodan Milosevic.

Debating the Parameters of Amnesty and Truth

There have been few examples of broad, all-inclusive amnesties included in peace agreements over the past twenty years, but there have been many examples of limited or conditional amnesties. Most agreements have language that excludes serious international crimes from any amnesty. Many peace agreements also include a truth commission, but sometimes with few details on its powers and mandate and little evident political commitment to a rigorous investigation. This becomes clear in the difficult years of implementation that follow.

The sections below set out several prominent cases where the issue of amnesty and truth has been particularly contentious, and where the outcome on these issues has helped define the nature of the peace that followed.

El Salvador (1992)

Although the official UN policy on amnesties was not established until 1999, as described above, some UN officials took a clear position against blanket amnesties much earlier. The first place this arose was in El Salvador, where a specific proposal for amnesty arose very late in the talks.

El Salvador was one of the first countries in which the UN held an active peace mediation role, beginning in 1990. This was a new area of work, soon after the Cold War ended, and there was little in the way of UN guidance or policy on many of the specific issues that arose. Given the massacres and targeted killing of thousands of civilians in the twelve-year civil war—and the majority of these crimes committed by the government's forces—it was natural that issues of justice and impunity became central to the talks.

The armed opposition, the Farabundo Marti National Liberation Front (FMLN), insisted on the need for trials and punishment for the war's massive crimes in order to send a clear signal that there would be no more impunity. The government resisted. Government representatives asked, Under what law would such trials take place? And in what courts? It was widely known that the judicial system as a whole at that time was extremely biased and lacked independence, and any trials would not have been credible or successful. It was impossible to deny this reality, which created a real problem around the fact of impunity and the opposition's demand for justice.

UN mediator Alvaro de Soto saw this as a possible opportunity. He studied the experiences of other countries, including Chile and Argentina, where truth commissions had recently concluded. De Soto put the idea of a truth commission to the Salvadoran negotiators. They liked the idea, but they wanted to include a specific list of acts or events to be investigated by such a commission. Agreeing to such a list proved impossible. The mediation team then proposed language that would direct the truth commission to investigate "serious acts of violence that have occurred since 1980 and whose impact on society urgently demands that the public should know the truth." The parties agreed, and one of the first pillars of the peace agreement was in place. The parties also agreed, several months later, that there should be a separate "Ad Hoc Commission," in which senior members of the armed forces would be vetted on human rights grounds and removed from their positions if complicit in serious abuses.

But questions of criminal justice remained outstanding. After concluding agreements on many other issues, towards the end of the negotiations, de Soto learned that the parties had discussed the possibility of a broad amnesty, and one of them sought de Soto's view on the matter. "I made clear that the UN would not go along with this," he said.[11] But de Soto recognized that he was in uncharted waters, as the UN had no established policy on this at that time.

There was no further discussion of the issue. The final agreement, signed in January 1992, included no mention of amnesty. Instead, it stressed the need to put an "end to impunity" and called in general terms for criminal accountability in the courts. The agreement read:

> The Parties recognize the need to clarify and put an end to any indication of impunity on the part of officers of the armed forces, particularly in cases where respect for human rights is jeopardized. To that end, the Parties refer this issue to the Commission on the Truth for consideration and resolution. All of this shall be without prejudice to the principle, which the Parties also recognize, that acts of this nature, regardless of the sector to which their perpetrators belong, must be the object of exemplary action by the law courts so that the punishment prescribed by law is meted out to those found responsible.[12]

Shortly after the peace agreement was signed, the National Assembly of El Salvador passed the Law on National Reconciliation, which provided amnesty for political crimes and offenses during the war, but excluded particularly violent acts and those incidents that would fall under recommendations of the truth commission. This allowed the release of the eighty persons who were in prison on charges of supporting the FMLN. The next day, in a rare example of justice for crimes by the armed forces, two military officers were sentenced to thirty years in prison for the infamous murder of six Jesuit priests in 1989.

When the truth commission concluded its work a year later, its final report named dozens of senior officials, both military and civilian, and both government and FMLN, responsible for specific killings and massacres during the twelve-year civil war. It did not recommend they be tried, given the state of the judiciary, but rather urged that these persons be removed from public or security positions. Five days later, in an uproar over the naming of such high-level persons, the Salvadoran legislature passed a sweeping amnesty covering all acts of the war. Even the two officers convicted in the Jesuits cases were promptly released.

This 1993 amnesty law was challenged repeatedly in national courts and at the Inter-American Commission and Inter-American Court of Human Rights. In 2000, the Salvadoran Supreme Court ruled that the amnesty was constitutional but generally inapplicable. The Inter-American Commission and Court then ruled that the amnesty was illegal and illegitimate. Despite these rulings, national prosecutors and judges resisted opening cases from the war, and amnesty remained de facto in place.[13] In 2013, human rights organizations again brought a constitutional challenge before the Supreme Court, and in 2016 the Court finally declared the amnesty unconstitutional. A judge soon opened investigations into several prominent cases from the war, but it was not clear if these would move forward given political resistance and prosecutorial reluctance. Meanwhile, Spain brought indictments against twenty retired Salvadoran officers for the Jesuits murders, based on the fact that several of the victims were Spanish citizens.[14]

The resistance to criminal accountability in El Salvador reached across many sectors. When the Supreme Court said in 2013 that it would again review the amnesty law, the Catholic Archbishop abruptly sealed its human rights archive, Tutela Legal, which was the most important repository of case files in the country.[15] Twenty-five years after the peace agreement, criminal justice for the crimes of the war remained contentious and unresolved.

Guatemala (1996)

The UN mediator in Guatemala, Jean Arnault, also resisted a broad amnesty for serious crimes, supported by a vocal human rights community that organized in advance to prevent an impunity deal. Human rights and accountability emerged at several points in the five years of talks. Early, perhaps too early, a truth commission was agreed, but the final language on a limited amnesty was not concluded until the end.

One of the first items addressed by the parties was a general accord for monitoring ongoing human rights violations, which established a UN human rights monitoring mission. This successful agreement led to an expectation for the parties to next address past crimes, and specifically a proposal for a truth commission. Some worried that broaching the contentious subject of truth about past crimes, so early in the process and before there was sufficient trust between the parties, might be unwise; unfortunately, this turned out to be correct.

The sessions were very difficult. The military representatives at the talks had no interest in a commission like that of neighboring El Salvador, which had just submitted its report and was perceived as going further than the parties had intended.[16] The armed opposition, the Unidad Revolucionaria Nacional Guatemalteca (URNG), faced with unyielding demands from the government, came close to backing out. They ultimately signed the truth commission agreement under pressure, without the time to consult, and worried that it might be badly received by their supporters.[17] Indeed, the text was seen as far too weak. Human rights advocates and others were sharply critical of the terms of commission, which included explicit limitations to narrow the commission's reach and impact. For example, the commission could not "attribute responsibility to any individual" and its work could have no "judicial aim or effect."[18] Even the name that it was given—the "Historical Clarification Commission"—suggested that the parties were not comfortable with the truth.

A *New York Times* op-ed lambasted the agreement as opting for ignorance and surrender.[19] The avalanche of criticism, and the protests from within the URNG itself, resulted in a suspension of the talks that lasted for a full five months, as the URNG tried to regroup.

In retrospect, both Arnault and the parties felt that they would have reached a much better and less timid agreement for a truth commission if they had waited until later in the talks, when there was much greater trust between the parties.

The difficult question of amnesty remained outstanding until the very end, two and a half years later, understood to be one of the most sensitive and critical elements of the final agreement. The government (and especially the military) wanted robust protection from any prosecutions. Guatemalan civil society was pushing hard against further entrenched impunity. Arnault took counsel from the legal office of UN headquarters in New York, which set out the legal arguments against amnesty for serious human rights crimes. After making no progress, the parties finally accepted a proposal from Arnault for an amnesty that excluded "genocide, torture, and forced disappearance." Human rights advocates pushed for extrajudicial killings and illegal detention to also be excluded from the amnesty and to explicitly allow prosecution of those who ordered, and not only committed, any of these acts, but they were not successful in getting these changes.[20] Still, the explicit limitations to the amnesty was seen as a considerable success and one of the first such examples anywhere.

But there were still many years to come of resistance to prosecutions, and obfuscation, by the authorities, and little progress on criminal accountability for the crimes of the war. Only in 2013 did a major high-level case come to court, with former President Efrian Rios Montt convicted of genocide for his actions thirty years earlier. This conviction was overthrown on technical grounds, however, and the prosecutor was removed from her post.

As the case against Rios Montt was under way, Arnault returned to Guatemala to assess the impact of the peace accords almost twenty years later. He urged caution to those who found any model of success in the limited amnesty that they had managed to reach in the Guatemala negotiations. Ultimately, he wrote, it was premised on a false assumption on the part of the military. Regardless of the text, they simply did not believe there was any risk of prosecution:

> (T)he issue of criminal prosecution for past crimes raises the most daunting challenge of all, because no party to a conflict—short of capitulation—will sign a peace agreement if they expect that criminal prosecution and imprisonment will follow. The Guatemalan army would certainly not have signed the peace accords in 1996 had they expected that senior officers would end up being prosecuted on charges of genocide.[21]

Sierra Leone (1999)

The text of the Sierra Leone peace agreement, signed in 1999, included a blanket amnesty for all crimes. The UN's rejection of this amnesty applying to serious crimes was the first clear statement from the UN on the matter of granting immunity for atrocities, and human rights advocates have since pointed to this as a critical moment.

The war in Sierra Leone was marked by massive atrocities targeting civilians, especially by the opposition Revolutionary United Front, known for instilling terror by cutting off the hands or arms of their victims. A previous peace agreement, three years earlier, had failed. A blanket amnesty in that agreement had received no opposition from national or international participants, who generally saw it as a necessity. When the Sierra Leone president was preparing for the new talks in 1999, he accepted that the amnesty in the previous peace agreement would need to be updated, pushing the date forward to cover all years of the conflict.[22] Thus, the decision to include a general amnesty in the 1999 peace accord was essentially concluded before the peace conference even began.

The 1999 talks were held in Lomé, Togo. In the first meeting of the working group tasked to address political issues, a blanket amnesty was quickly agreed. There was little debate on the issues among the Sierra Leone delegates, representing the government and the RUF. Civil society was present as observers and had no voice in the discussion. The UN was not in this working group. Both UN staff and human rights advocates tried to raise the issue of amnesty in side discussions with the parties over the next months, but it was made clear that this was not open for discussion.

It is in this space of time that we see the break between the accepted tradition of simply turning the page on past crimes, with an assumption that a blanket amnesty will have to be granted in the interest of peace, and a new age in which the international community began to redefine such impunity deals as legally or politically untenable. The experiences of El Salvador and Guatemala, described above, were a few years ahead of their time, before a new policy on amnesty began to be formalized.

In Sierra Lone in 1999, the senior UN representative at the talks, Francis Okelo, had seen the amnesty in the final text and intended to sign without objection. He served as deputy chair of the overall peace conference and led the final sessions. The signature of the UN was seen as critical to its success.

But Okelo seemed to be unaware that just weeks earlier, UN Secretary-General Kofi Annan had issued new policy guidance that prohibited UN representatives from endorsing amnesty for international crimes. UN staff in New York received an advanced copy of the Sierra Leone accord by fax, due to be signed the next day, and when they saw the amnesty language, they immediately understood that the UN could not sign on.

It was thus with some surprise that Okelo received a call from New York the day before the scheduled signing of the final accord, with the Secretary-General advising him he couldn't take part in the signing ceremony if such a blanket amnesty was included.

Okelo considered his options. If the UN backed out of signing, the agreement would have been seriously weakened and perhaps doomed; it also would have been difficult for the UN to carry out its planned role in monitoring and implementation. Instead, Okelo decided to sign but to add a disclaimer, written by hand next to his signature, that the UN understood that the amnesty would not apply to serious international crimes. But the parties saw this disclaimer only at the moment of signing, and some—especially the head of the RUF, Foday Sankoh—raised questions as to the UN intentions. But the signing ceremony continued. The legal status of this now-famous UN disclaimer remained quite unclear for some time.

At the national level, however, the amnesty was in force. Known human rights abusers were incorporated into the transitional government. International human rights advocates have often cited the amnesty as the reason for a relapse in violence the following year, which nearly restarted the war. But Sierra Leoneans site many other factors, such as a delayed deployment of peacekeeping troops.

The parties also agreed to a national truth commission, but after a much more vigorous debate and initial disagreement on terms. A first proposal from the government set out a one-sided investigation into RUF crimes only. The RUF strongly objected, refusing to move forward, and there were angry exchanges between them. The civil society observers helped resolve this impasse, engaging the RUF to help propose a more balanced investigation. Once revised to include crimes and abuses on all sides, the RUF became quite supportive of a truth investigation. Indeed, as they made clear over the next months, they had many questions about abuses committed by government forces and were keen to have an investigation into this matter.

The agreement also included the creation of a victims' compensation fund, which was agreed quickly but provided little detail on funding or implementation and remained largely unimplemented in the following years.

Liberia (2003)

A few minutes before the opening ceremony of the 2003 Liberian peace conference, which was held in Accra, the capital of Ghana, Liberian President Charles Taylor was told that the Special Court for Sierra Leone had released a warrant for his arrest. Taylor had sponsored, sheltered, and financed the Sierra Leone RUF in its first years, causing mayhem across the border, and therefore fell under the jurisdiction of this court.

In response to the indictment, Taylor took the stage at the opening ceremony and surprised everyone by offering to resign from the presidency if that would be good for the country. He then left directly for the airport and returned to Liberia, where he could better avoid arrest. A few days later he gave his formal agreement, through his representatives at the talks, that he would indeed step aside from politics and that the final peace agreement should not grant him any continued role. This fundamentally changed the nature and prospects of the peace talks.

But the question of justice remained alive, even more so because of the dozens of victims, mostly women, who encamped on the periphery of the talks and were vocal and organized in their demands: first priority was to stop the war, they said, but this couldn't be done through impunity. Accountability was first broached in a plenary session with a proposal from civil society—who were full-fledged delegates in these talks—for a national war crimes court. This was countered with a proposal from the warring parties for a broad amnesty. But they didn't push this very hard: insisting on an amnesty would have been seen as practically admitting their guilt, participants recount. Meanwhile, quiet assurances, never written into the agreement, persuaded the combatants that prosecutions would not take place, that they would be safe. In a context where no one had been held accountable for anything in fourteen years of war, the possibility of criminal prosecutions was really not seen as much of a threat.

The tension between the two proposals—a war crimes court vs. a general amnesty—was resolved, unsatisfactorily, with an agreement to instead create a Truth and Reconciliation Commission. The parameters of the TRC were set out in a total of five sentences: it would investigate the past in order to "address issues of impunity," "deal with the root causes of the crisis in Liberia," and "recommend measures to be taken for the rehabilitation of victims of human rights violations."[23] With this agreement, the proposal for a war crimes court was put to rest.

The final agreement ultimately stated that the transitional government could "give consideration" to a general amnesty, without promising anything.[24] A government advisor explained later that this vague wording was intentional: they didn't want to grant the rebels amnesty because it might encourage future wars, but it would be difficult to end the current war if they went so far as to threaten prosecutions. The transitional government never returned to the amnesty question, and the mild risk of national prosecutions was largely forgotten by the former warlords.

The Accra talks also addressed the terms for integrating the armed forces, and agreed to screen out human rights abusers: "Incoming service personnel shall be screened with respect to educational, professional, medical and fitness qualifications as well as prior history with regard to human rights abuses," it said.[25] The UN mission in Liberia was ultimately tasked to carry out this screening, responding to specific complaints from the public.

The delegates then turned their attention to the matter that truly focused their minds: the post-agreement political order, and specifically, who would get which position in the transitional government. They spent much of the next months locked in negotiations over this question. In contrast to the screening provided for the armed forces, the agreement for political posts provided no exclusions or limitations on persons who were deeply involved in the war, and in many cases had instigated, commanded, or authorized the horrendous practices of the war. Many prominent participants from all sides of the conflict took up key positions in the two-year transitional government, including in Congress, the Supreme Court, and elsewhere, and many of these extended well beyond the period of the transitional government.

When the truth commission concluded its work three years later, it published a long list of names of persons accused of serious crimes and recommended they be prosecuted; many of these were now high-level officials. The former warlords who had taken part in the peace talks quickly came together for a press conference: if there was legal action against any one of them, they said, they were ready to go back to war. No prosecutions took place.

As of 2016, no one has yet been prosecuted in Liberia for crimes of the war.

Sudan (2005)

The talks between Sudan and the rebels in southern Sudan, which concluded in 2005, aimed to end a horrible, decades-long civil war. There was little discussion of victims or any form of transitional justice. Only in the very last days of the talks did the parties turn to the war's crimes, with an old-fashioned approach of the parties granting themselves a blanket amnesty, quietly inserted in the text by the two parties.

One international participant described his surprise: "They slipped in the amnesty: one morning we woke up and there was an extra article in the text. It might have taken them ten minutes to negotiate." The many observers or advisors to the talks from the international diplomatic and donor community outright rejected the idea of a blanket amnesty. The agreement would lose all legitimacy, especially because the proposed amnesty would directly benefit the two parties, they argued. It would weaken the agreement and have no legal force under international law. The broader international community wouldn't accept it, they said. Some important donor states specifically threatened to hold back all funding for implementation of the agreement if a blanket amnesty was included.

The lead negotiator for southern Sudan, John Garang, was furious at the internationals' response, and stormed out of the room. Several days of tension followed. Some foreign participants, feeling pressure from a self-imposed deadline, began to suggest that they accept the amnesty in order to allow a rapid conclusion of the final agreement. But in the end, the parties were finally persuaded to remove the amnesty clause, thus leaving the agreement silent on the question of justice. Instead, a provision calling for national reconciliation was included; researcher Sarah Nouwen found over the next years that Sudanese officials continued to refer to this as the "amnesty clause," and "considered 'national reconciliation' to be synonymous with forgetting the past."[26]

In the years since the signing in 2005, there has been no criminal or other accountability for the widespread abuses in the war between the north and south of Sudan. This was always seen as unlikely in a context of so many other major conflicts brewing in both Sudan and South Sudan, and between them. The focus remained, instead, on trying to resolve these conflicts or prevent further rounds of violence.

The agreement granted a six-year period of autonomy for Southern Sudan, leading to a vote for independence, which passed with an overwhelming majority. After a few short years, another civil war broke out in the newly independent South Sudan, beginning a new round of vicious violence. When a peace agreement was first brokered in that civil war, exactly ten years after the 2005 agreement between the north and south of Sudan, the issue of responding to past crimes was approached very differently, with a detailed chapter setting out plans for criminal justice, truth, and reparations. This is addressed below.

Congo

In the Democratic Republic of Congo, there have been a number of peace or disarmament agreements with various armed groups over many years, beginning in the early 2000s. Issues of justice were always present. At several points, international representatives—from the UN, EU, or U.S.—successfully pushed the armed groups to exclude serious crimes from a proposed amnesty clause. In some cases, a UN representative traveled deep into rebel-held territory to broker demobilization agreements with rebel groups. These were simple, one-page, handwritten agreements—completed in a rush so that the visitors could return to their base before nightfall. Even in these contexts, the UN representatives were able to persuade the rebel leaders to specifically state that an amnesty would not cover international crimes.

Excluding amnesty from these agreements did not, by any means, ensure justice. The only serious attempt to prosecute Congolese warlords was by the ICC, which eventually was able to detain several persons for trial in The Hague. But in any case, the ICC wouldn't have been constrained by an amnesty included in a peace agreement. Some of the agreements, including arrangements to integrate rebel forces into the army, worked directly against the pursuit of accountability; these forces were incorporated with no screening to remove those complicit in serious abuses, despite a well-known record of atrocities. The most extreme example was the incorporation into the army, at officer level, of a rebel leader who had already been indicted by the ICC, Bosco Ntaganda.[27]

Nepal (2006)

At the start of the peace talks with the Maoist armed opposition in Nepal, the government granted a pardon to some 500 prisoners who were detained for opposition activities. It was an important example of a targeted amnesty serving as a useful confidence-building measure.

The talks themselves were fairly unstructured, and the consideration of human rights issues and dealing with past crimes was likewise imprecise. The final language of the agreement, reached in 2006, said that the state would "withdraw accusations, claims, complaints, and cases under consideration against various individuals due to political reasons and to make immediately public the state of those in detention and to release them immediately."[28]

The international community was not directly present in the talks themselves, and there was no independent mediator or facilitator between the parties. But the UN maintained a peace mission in the country, and it considered whether this language in the accord would violate international standards. In the end, the UN decided that although the language was ambiguous, it should not be taken to cover international crimes.[29]

Those who signed the document, however, apparently understood it to be relatively broad and inclusive.[30] The full reach of this amnesty provision remained unclear as implementation of the agreement slowly moved forward over the next years. The final agreement also included both a truth commission and a commission on the disappeared, which resulted in confusion on the overlap between the two bodies. The legislative process to establish these bodies continued for many years, and regardless of the language in the peace agreement the issues of amnesty and truth remained both politically and legally contentious.

Agreeing to New Tribunals

It is rare that peace agreements include a provision for a new special court, or other proactive measures to prosecute crimes of a war.

Some ad hoc tribunals have been established soon after a war ended (Sierra Leone and Rwanda) or even many years later (Cambodia), but these have not originated from a peace agreement. Often established in conjunction with the UN and incorporating both national and international judges, prosecutors, and staff, and given a mandate to investigate crimes of both national and international law, these are usually referred to as "hybrid" or "mixed" tribunals. They are born of the great difficulty of bringing high-level, sensitive cases to trial within national courts.

Most of these are contexts where the ICC does not have jurisdiction, usually because the crimes were committed before 2002. However, there are some examples whereby a new war crimes tribunal is agreed even where the ICC is present and actively monitoring the situation; this may be to strengthen the prospect of criminal justice and expand the number of cases that could be brought to trial (beyond the very few cases ever likely to come before the ICC) or to evade the reach of the ICC by creating an alternative system of accountability.

As the pressure against impunity and for accountability has increased, and especially where the ICC has jurisdiction, simply leaving an amnesty out of an agreement is no longer seen as sufficient. In 2015, peace negotiators in two very different contexts agreed to create a new special tribunal for serious crimes that took place during the war. This is a new and unexpected development, since (as already noted) those negotiating the agreements have a strong personal interest in avoiding trial or any risk of jail. But there is a stark difference between these two agreements, in South Sudan and Colombia, and in their likelihood of being implemented. A few years earlier, the talks in Uganda also concluded that a specialized approach to prosecutions at the national level was the best approach, in part to respond to the ICC's engagement.

Uganda

The 2008 peace agreement in Uganda intended to create a special mechanism to prosecute war crimes within the national judiciary. The rebel leadership abandoned the agreement in the ultimate hour, failing to show up for the signing ceremony. Nevertheless, the government of Uganda committed to implement what it could of the unsigned agreement, and moved forward to create an International Crimes Division of the Ugandan High Court to prosecute serious crimes of the war.

The first attempt to try a former Lord's Resistance Army combatant in the new court was stymied by an existing amnesty law; the Ugandan Supreme Court ultimately ruled that the trial could go forward and the amnesty would not apply in this case. Meanwhile, other LRA combatants continued to receive amnesty and were actively encouraged to defect and to be reintegrated into their communities. Ugandan civil society and religious leaders worried that a repeal of the amnesty would endanger future peace efforts and deter combatants from demobilizing, but international rights groups pushed for a repeal (or a significant limiting) of the amnesty regardless of the views of national victims' advocates.[31]

South Sudan

The only peace accord that included provisions for a new special court with no restrictions on the crimes to be prosecuted, or the possible punishment that might result, was in South Sudan in August 2015. This intended to end a year and a half of brutal civil war whose abuses deeply implicated the political leadership on both sides. This Hybrid Court for South Sudan would be created by the African Union, cover international and national crimes, and include judges from South Sudan and elsewhere in Africa. In addition, the agreement included a Commission for Truth, Reconciliation, and Healing and a Compensation and Reparations Authority.[32]

The government signed the agreement ten days after the opposition and only after strong pressure was exerted by the international community, including the threat from the UN Security Council that it was ready to impose an arms embargo and targeted sanctions. While signing, the government released a lengthy list of reservations to the text, disagreeing with many specific aspects that it said would infringe on national sovereignty or that were otherwise unacceptable. None of these reservations pertained to the hybrid court or the truth commission. One reservation focused on the stipulated Compensation and Reparation Authority, saying this was inappropriate and unrealistic.

Within a day of signing, both sides said the agreement was an "imposed peace" and not to their liking.

It is not clear why the two principals in the peace talks—President Salva Kiir and the former vice president and head of the armed opposition, Riek Machar—agreed to accountability mechanisms, and in particular a special tribunal, that would clearly investigate crimes in which they were implicated. Some people close to the negotiations thought the parties simply hadn't focused on these details. Or perhaps the parties were just acceding to the international community's interest in human rights, knowing that their resisting accountability would look suspect. The parties might also have presumed that once in power, they could easily block the tribunal. In any case, even after signing the agreement, human rights observers said that both sides continued to commit serious crimes.[33]

When I visited South Sudan in November 2015, armed attacks against civilians continued, the leader of the opposition had not yet returned to the capital, and there was worry that the agreement might not take hold. But there was quiet optimism that the hybrid court spelled out in the agreement would be implemented, and international donors were making plans for funding and support. The agreement does not require the involvement of the national government to establish the hybrid court. It could be created outside the country and with foreign funding, with the African Union acting independently, theoretically even if the overall peace agreement were to break down.

South Sudan has suffered deep impunity, especially during the recent civil war when there was reportedly little pretense, by either side, of trying to halt the widespread atrocities against civilians. To break this cycle of extraordinary violence and impunity, it may well be necessary to rely on a fully independent criminal justice mechanism. The leadership has seemed impervious to other pressures.

Colombia

The Colombian armed opposition, FARC, deeply distrusted the Colombian judiciary. The FARC also understood that some form of criminal justice would be necessary for the war's crimes, given the oversight of the International Criminal Court, strict national laws, and indeed the existing Colombian arrest warrants for the FARC leadership.

The parties ultimately concluded that the only solution to these justice dilemmas was to create a new tribunal. They decided on a national tribunal, and a new special prosecutor, that would work independently from the normal judiciary. The new system would vet cases and encourage full confessions in exchange for vastly reduced and alternative sentences.

The initial agreement for this new tribunal was announced in September 2015. This was just a month after the South Sudan peace agreement had included its own new hybrid tribunal, but in many ways the two plans couldn't have been more different. While there was to be some international involvement in the Colombian tribunal, such as in the appointment of judges, it would be led by Colombians. The final Colombian agreement was very detailed, complex, lengthy, and would be quite difficult to implement. The agreement for the South Sudan tribunal was only a couple of pages, would be led by internationals and probably based in a neighboring country; it also provided no system of incentives or alternative punishments, thus giving it an air of unreality.

The Colombian agreement had the buy-in of the parties and an expectation that it would be implemented. The practical constraints of a very large number of cases to be processed would be its main challenge, as well as the possibility of political resistance from those who were ultimately charged.

The Colombian tribunal is set out in much more detail below, especially in the chapter on Colombia in Part II.

Victim Reparations and Vetting

Justice is not just about holding individuals to account for crimes or investigating the truth about what happened. It is also about responding to victims' needs and making changes to prevent further abuses.

In most peace processes, the subject of victim reparations is discussed only briefly. Both sides see it as a relatively easy subject, so long as no commitments are required on the source of funding, how beneficiaries will be determined, or the amount that is due. Certainly, both parties would want their own victims to receive compensation. But the questions of who, how, how much, and especially "who pays" immediately raises the uncomfortable dilemmas that will eventually have to be confronted to carry out such a program.

These difficulties, against the pressures and pace of the peace process, often leads to a generic commitment to a reparations fund with little indication of process, time, amount, or specific aims. This makes implementation difficult, and the reparations elements of peace agreements have often been ignored during the first years of implementation. The government and international community's focus instead is on disarmament, reintegration, refugee return, elections, and other security-related issues. Regrettably but perhaps unsurprisingly, those handed the massive task of implementing a wide-ranging and complex peace accord almost never prioritize victim reparations. Adding to the challenge is the fact that the international community is rarely willing to pay for victim compensation.

In some places, the issue of victim reparations has been even more contentious than that of criminal justice. In the talks for Darfur, Sudan, the most intense negotiations centered on victim compensation, with lengthy back and forth between the parties on the specific amount to be paid to victims. This was the issue that ultimately threatened a breakdown of the talks.

But reparations should not be addressed solely as cash payments to survivors. Apologies, memorials, or health or trauma services for victims may also be important. These have not yet been commonly included in peace agreements, although some of this can be completed with little financial cost.

The minimal attention to reparations in the peace implementation period often means that those who suffered the brunt of the conflict receive scant attention in these first critical post-war years. There is a risk that the public sees the peace process, like the war itself, as centered on the interests of the most powerful, rather than on society as a whole and specifically the war's victims. The creation of a truth commission can help to counter that impression, but this will also highlight the dire needs of many survivors.

Some of the most recent agreements, such as in South Sudan and Colombia, have offered more details of a reparations provision, going well beyond the one-sentence commitments seen in many earlier peace agreements. But the improved language has still left many details wide open, leaving the hard work on designing a workable program and finding sufficient financing to those involved later.

The chapter on transitional justice in the 2015 South Sudan peace agreement was divided into three parts: in addition to the hybrid court and truth commission, it includes a section spelling out a Compensation and Reparation Authority that would assist persons whose property was destroyed in the conflict and oversee a fund for direct victims. There is no mention of how this would be financed. As noted, the government of South Sudan took the unusual step of formally protesting the inclusion of a victim reparations program when it signed the overall agreement. "This provision is inappropriate, unprecedented and susceptible to abuse because the whole country would quality," the government wrote.[34] Experience with reparations agreements elsewhere showed it was impractical, it added. It proposed that priority should instead be given to general reconstruction and rebuilding, as well as to economic recovery through an Enterprise Development Fund.[35]

The agreement in Colombia also included a section on reparations, agreeing to psychosocial support, rebuilding, and other victim support. A point of contention was whether the FARC would pay into a national reparations fund or instead directly control a program of reparations and services for victims. In the final agreement, the FARC committed to putting its resources directly into a national victims fund.

It might be effective in future peace processes to set out a specific process that will follow the signing of an agreement, to work out the details of a reparations program. While the parties' political commitment to victim-centered programs is very important, this is clearly insufficient. Appointing a committee or working group tasked with this responsibility could lead to more success.

There are also few good examples of peace agreements that set out terms to screen and remove those persons in the security service who were involved in serious abuses during the war, often referred to as "vetting" or "lustration." El Salvador provides the best example: the 1991 agreement set out terms for an Ad Hoc Commission—so called because the parties couldn't agree to any other name. This body was comprised of three independent Salvadorans, and it reviewed the files of the top echelon of the military, about one hundred officers. It concluded that the majority of these should be removed from their position due to credible allegations of human rights violations; these were mostly forced into early retirement over the next months. In Liberia, the parties also agreed to a vetting process. But since victims were usually unable to identify specific soldiers, the impact of the review was limited.

Overall, much more could be done on noncriminal justice in peace agreements. In those contexts where warring parties simply don't prioritize the needs of victims or the need to reform security forces, both the mediator and victims groups may need to push to bring more attention to the issue.

Conclusion

Several conclusions emerge from the above.

First, perhaps unsurprisingly, process matters. The timing of when justice is broached will affect the result. Usually the most difficult issues of justice—in particular criminal liability and truth seeking—are not addressed until very late in the talks, often in the ultimate hour. The combination of very high self-interest from the parties, intense passion on these issues from victims and often the public at large, and pressure from international sources makes for a treacherous negotiation. Trying to conclude these agreements before trust has been built between the parties may suffer the consequences, resulting in a weaker outcome and the potential to do damage to the process as a whole, as we saw in Guatemala.

Peace processes have certainly been more attuned to international standards on human rights as these standards have become more widely accepted in the international sphere. The language especially on amnesty has largely been driven by outside pressures: the mediator's insistence (El Salvador, Guatemala); the stated policy of the UN (Sierra Leone); the policy of various international institutions or states (as seen in Congo and Sudan); or the threat of the ICC's intervention, as we shall see in a later chapter. In some cases, national civil society has played the most important role in pushing justice proposals, in part because internationals were not at the table (Nepal) or because civil society participants were fully empowered as delegates (Liberia), but the resulting language in these agreements has sometimes been less clear. Often, of course, there is a mix of national and international pressures.

Where victims are least organized or have the least access to the talks, and where internationals are for whatever reason not very focused on justice for past crimes, peace agreements even very recently have been sparse on the subject. For example, a February 2015 agreement in Minsk, which intended to stop the fighting in Eastern Ukraine, included a promise for a broad pardon and amnesty that prohibited prosecutions "in relation to events" in the region (although putting this into Ukrainian law would not prove to be easy).[36]

The very few peace processes that have tried to institute a proactive accountability mechanism, through some form of special tribunal, have found this difficult to bring into reality. The Colombia agreement is far more complex than is any other to date and still too new to judge; observers expect that it will be challenging to carry out on both legal and operational grounds. South Sudan soon descended back into horrific violence after its 2015 peace agreement; many internationals considered the agreement to still be in force, hoping the violence could be stopped, but the development of the agreed hybrid tribunal was moving slowly in the African Union. Uganda's new Serious Crimes Division has had minimal application to former combatants.

While international standards, or at least international policies, are relatively clear on what can be granted amnesty in the course of peace negotiations, such specific guidance is still lacking in relation to truth commissions, reparations, and vetting. Most of the best-practice guidance relates to the operation of these mechanisms, not the powers and attributes that negotiating parties should agree in order for the institutions or processes to be respectable, effective, and fair. On amnesty, so far it has been simple: no amnesty for international crimes. For the other areas, there is less clarity.

The role of international human rights advocates has been important in strengthening human rights standards, but their almost-exclusive focus on criminal accountability and on perpetrators is now out of balance with the needs. International rights advocates too often approach a peace process with the singular question of whether an amnesty will be included, whether any amnesty applies to serious international crimes, or whether there are any other restrictions on criminal prosecution and punishment.

This narrow focus has two problems: first, it misses or significantly undervalues the nonprosecutorial justice components of a peace agreement, which may lead to mistakes or significant weaknesses in the mandates for a truth commission, victim reparations plan, vetting, or other reforms to lessen future abuses. From a victim's perspective, such initiatives may be much more important and impact their lives much more directly than will a small handful of high-level prosecutions. Second, a focus on excluding amnesty for serious crimes has simply been ineffective as measured by the degree of criminal justice that follows. It is clear that exclusion of amnesty in no way assures that criminal prosecutions will take place. In most cases, the only war-related prosecutions after a peace agreement have come from an international court, which would be unrestricted by a national amnesty in any case. Even where there is ample evidence of crimes and no amnesty in place, national-level prosecutions have been rare, and usually not until many years later. The next chapter will look more closely at this record and why this is true.

Thus, in a nutshell: human rights issues are becoming a more prominent agenda item in peace negotiations; the resulting agreements are increasingly more detailed on these subjects and in most cases more careful to comply with developing international standards; and creative and country-specific solutions to these difficult issues have been found even where it was thought to perhaps be impossible. But there are two main areas of weakness that remain: first in the approach to nonprosecutorial justice issues, and especially victim-focused programs; and second in the actual implementation of the agreements as written. The next chapter looks at the post-agreement record, in particular in the arena of criminal responsibility, where so much of the advocacy attention has focused.

Notes

1 The concept of "undoing" the past was suggested by Christine Bell in *Peace Agreements and Human Rights* (Oxford: Oxford University Press, 2000), 233.

2 Ibid. See also *Negotiating Justice? Human Rights and Peace Agreements* (Versoix, Switzerland: International Council on Human Rights Policy, 2006) and the case studies linked to this report, at www.ichrp.org. Another good resource, including texts of past agreements, is peacemaker.un.org.

3 Bell, *Peace Agreements*, 194–196.

4 A good analysis of the forward-looking human rights components in the Good Friday Agreement and the lack of measures focused on the past is provided by Maggie Beirne and Fionnuala Ní Aoláin, "Rights After the Revolution: Progress or Backslide After the Good Friday Agreement?" in Eileen F. Babbitt and Ellen L. Lutz, eds., *Human Rights and Conflict Resolution in Context: Colombia, Sierra Leone, and Northern Ireland* (Syracuse: Syracuse University Press, 2009), 210–229.

5 Comments by MILF leader, Oslo, Norway, June 2014.

6 "Annex on Normalization," section H, para. 1, 25 Jan 2014, an annex to the "Framework Agreement on the Bangsamoro," 15 Oct 2012, and incorporated into the "Comprehensive Agreement on the Bangsamoro," 28 March 2014. See also "Terms of Reference for the Transitional Justice and Reconciliation Commission," signed by the parties on 28 March 2014.

7 There has been extensive writing and debate on the question of whether amnesties can be extended to serious crimes. For a critical discussion of the history and legal basis of a narrow interpretation of this amnesty language in Protocol II to the Geneva Convention, see William Schabas, *Unimaginable Atrocities: Justice, Politics, and Rights at the War Crimes Tribunals* (Oxford: Oxford University Press, 2012), chapter 7, 173–196. See also Transitional Justice Institute, *The Belfast Guidelines on Amnesty and Accountability* (Belfast: Transitional Justice Institute, University of Ulster, 2013). For a general overview on the subject, see Office of the United Nations High Commissioner for Human Rights, *Rule-of-Law Tools for Post Conflict States: Amnesties*, 2009.

8 Mark Freeman, *Necessary Evils: Amnesties and the Search for Justice* (Cambridge: Cambridge University Press, 2009).

9 See the fascinating account in Allister Sparks, *Tomorrow Is Another Country: The Inside Story of South Africa's Negotiated Revolution* (Sandton, South Africa: Struik, 1994), 122–123. The ANC "feared they were being led into a trap" and might be seized and imprisoned, writes Sparks.

10 During the several early years of peace talks for Aceh, Indonesia, trust between the parties was thin. At one point in this rocky dialogue process, armed opposition (GAM) members on the "monitoring teams," which had been created through the talks, were arrested by the Indonesians and held for a number of weeks. An internal assessment of these ultimately failed talks by the mediator, the Centre for Humanitarian Dialogue, notes, "In addition, other GAM Committee members, as well as the Centre's own international and local staff, were harassed and threatened by police, and provocative statements were made in

the press about the end of the dialogue process." See "Aceh Initiative: Internal Review," Centre for Humanitarian Dialogue, Nov 2003, www.hdcentre.org.

11 Alvaro de Soto, interview by author, 28 Nov 2012, Amsterdam.

12 Chapultepec Peace Accords, Article 5, signed 16 Jan 1992.

13 Comments by Alejandro Diaz and Leonor Arteaga, "Human Rights Prosecutions and El Salvador's Justice System," panel at the Washington Office on Latin America, 4 Nov 2015, www.wola.org/video/human_rights_prosecutions_and_ el_salvador_s_justice_system.

14 U.S. authorities found that one of these officers was living in the U.S. He was convicted for lying on his visa application in relation to his military record, and given a twenty-one-month sentence, long enough that he might be extradited to Spain. See, generally, Geoff Thale, "Amnesty under Fire in El Salvador: Legal Challenges and Political Implications," Washington Office on Latin America, 21 Oct 2013, www.wola.org.

15 See Aryeh Neier, "Shutdown of Salvadoran Human Rights Office Disturbing in Light of War Atrocities," *National Catholic Reporter*, 24 Oct 2013, www. ncronline.org.

16 Hector Rosada, interview by author, 18 Apr 1996, Guatemala City.

17 Comments by a senior member of the URNG team, New York, Nov 2014.

18 "Agreement on the Establishment of the Commission to Clarify Past Human Rights Violations and Acts of Violence that have Caused the Guatemalan Population to Suffer," UN Doc. A/48/954/S/1994/751, Annex II, 23 June 23 1994.

19 Francisco Goldman, "In Guatemala, All Is Forgotten," *NY Times*, 23 Dec 1996. This op-ed suggests that "Guatemala has opted for ignorance . . . The agreement is not a peace treaty, it's a surrender. And what has been surrendered, after a fruitless and horrifying war, is the truth." In the end, most of the restrictions built into the commission's mandate were seen to be open to interpretation.

20 Larry Rohter, "Guatemalan Amnesty Is Approved Over Opponents' Objections," *NY Times*, 19 Dec 1996.

21 Jean Arnault, "Legitimacy and Peace Processes: International Norms and Local Realities," in Alexander Ramsbotham and Achim Wennmann, eds., *Accord #25: Legitimacy and Peace Processes: From Coercion to Consent* (London: Conciliation Resources, Apr 2014), 25.

22 Sierra Leone President Ahmed Tejan Kabbah explained this to a visiting diplomat prior to the beginning of the talks.

23 Accra Peace Agreement, 2003, Article 8.

24 The final agreement also indicated that the transitional government would consider the possibility of an amnesty. This was never taken up by that government. (Article 34 states that the transitional government "shall give consideration to a recommendation for general amnesty to all persons and parties engaged or involved in military activities during the Liberian civil conflict that is the subject of this Agreement.")

25 Accra Peace Agreement, Article 2(a).

26 Sarah M.H. Nouwen, *Complementarity in the Line of Fire: The Catalysing Effect of the International Criminal Court in Uganda and Sudan* (Cambridge: Cambridge University Press, 2013), 267, and interview with Nouwen by author, Florence, 17 May 2017.

27 The details of the Bosco Ntaganda case are explored in Chapter 6.

28 Comprehensive Peace Agreement for Nepal, Section 5.2.7, 21 Nov 2006.

29 Interviews by author.

30 Interviews by author. For further information see Priscilla Hayner and Warisha Farasat, "Negotiating Peace in Nepal: Implications for Justice," International

Center for Transitional Justice and Initiative for Peacebuilding, June 2009, www.ictj.org.

31 Kasande Sarah Kihika and Meritxell Regué, "Pursuing Accountability for Serious Crimes in Uganda's Courts: Reflections on the Thomas Kwoyelo Case," International Center for Transitional Justice, Jan 2015, www.ictj.org. ICTJ found it "surprising" that national civil society organizations were in favor of the amnesty for the sake of peace and to encourage combatants, including abductees, to defect. But this has been the consistent position of Northern Ugandan community leaders and victim advocates for many years.

32 Intergovernmental Authority on Development (IGAD), *Agreement on the Resolution of the Conflict in South Sudan*, 17 Aug 2015, Chapter V: Transitional Justice, Accountability, Reconciliation, and Healing, 40–45.

33 Jehanne Henry, "In South Sudan's Brutal Chaos, Civilians in the Middle," *Huffington Post*, 23 Dec 2015.

34 "Reservations by the Government of the Republic of South Sudan to the 'Compromise Peace Agreement in the Resolution of the Conflict in South Sudan,'" Juba, 26 Aug 2015, 8.

35 Ibid.

36 Paragraph 5 of the "Minsk II" agreement commits the parties to "Provide pardon and amnesty by way of enacting a law that forbids persecution and punishment of persons in relation to events that took place in particular districts of Donetsk and Luhansk oblasts of Ukraine." Signed 11 Feb 2015.

4 After a Peace Agreement

It would be a mistake to think that the signing of a peace agreement—even an agreement with detailed provisions on justice, truth, or amnesty—closes the issue, settling things for good. On the contrary, experience shows that these contentious issues effectively continue to be negotiated for months and years to come, and there are often unexpected changes to the original agreement.

Experience also shows that despite the intensive (and largely successful) efforts of human rights advocates to keep amnesties out of peace agreements, it is rare that there are prosecutions and trials for the many serious crimes of a war, even when it may be well-known who (allegedly) committed such crimes, there is ample evidence against them, and they have no legal protection from prosecution. So what is happening here?

Do Trials Follow?

First, a look at the interesting paradox about amnesties, and specifically the prohibition against amnesty for serious crimes. There has been a strong push for mediators and peace negotiators to stand by this prohibition. But the experiences described in the previous chapter show clearly that keeping an amnesty out of a peace agreement does not often lead to prosecutions. In fact, trials for serious crimes of a war are rare, especially after a negotiated peace agreement. In very few cases have trials for war crimes followed a negotiated peace agreement.

The few trials that have occurred were generally very limited and usually took place many years later; some have been in international courts where national amnesties don't apply in any case. Indeed, there are numerous examples where a blanket amnesty was successfully kept out of an agreement, but where no serious movement towards prosecutions has yet taken place at the national level.

It cannot be concluded, however, that this is caused by the negotiated nature of the transition. That would be a natural suspicion: whether explicitly in the agreement or not, one might assume that the negotiations must be bargaining away the rights of victims. In fact, the evidence suggests otherwise: the scarcity of justice is not the result of a negotiated agreement per se, but rather reflects political and other unmovable realities in each context, usually including weak or compromised judicial institutions.

While it might be expected that an outright military victory would result in a better record of justice for crimes of the war, in these cases too such trials are limited in number and often suspect in other ways. National prosecutions following military victory are usually one-sided, raising the specter of "victor's justice," and often raise questions about basic due process and fair trial guarantees. If one considers the record of Sri Lanka, Libya, and Rwanda, for example, these very concerns have been clear.

The few cases where national-level trials have made some progress only highlight how limited these are, and the difficulties associated with successfully prosecuting these quite atrocious crimes, especially for those at senior levels of responsibility. South Africa and Colombia are cases in point.

In South Africa, many high-level perpetrators chose not to apply for amnesty through that country's truth commission, and it seemed there was plenty of evidence to support successful trials. The commission concluded its work by providing a list of 300 persons that it recommended for criminal investigation. But the prosecutorial authority made little movement on this list, and in the end only six people have been prosecuted for apartheid-era crimes—and several of these were acquitted. Those closely watching these developments concluded that a level of political resistance blocked further progress.

In Colombia, paramilitary forces agreed to disarm in 2002 under an unwritten understanding of full impunity. However, the combination of public pressure and decisions by the national courts forced this impunity arrangement to be reversed. Ultimately, a Justice and Peace Law was instituted that required an individualized review of serious crimes cases and offered a reduced sentence of five to eight years for those who told the full truth about their crimes. Each person was to be heard in court, in a process managed by magistrates; those who didn't comply with the terms risked forty to sixty years in jail. In many respects, this was the most complex and far-reaching justice program for demobilizing combatants to date. But the cases moved slowly, the role of victims in the peace and justice hearings was limited, and both the procedure and outcome of the process were strongly criticized. In advance of the peace talks with the FARC that began in 2012, the record of how justice for the paramilitaries was handled raised more questions than it answered about what the best approach to justice might be.

Given the rarity of successful prosecutions for crimes of war, particularly in national courts, some observers quietly ask what, really, is explicitly gained by so adamantly insisting on excluding international crimes from any peace-agreement amnesty.

Human rights advocates offer two arguments in response. First, it is important to protect and strengthen the norms of international law and core human rights principles. In time, these norms will become more solid and those perpetrating abuses will know they cannot expect impunity for their crimes. This argument is based on principle, but also on the hope of a deterrent effect in future conflicts. (Chapter 6 will return to this question of deterrence.)

Second, they say, even if trials may not be possible immediately, it is important to keep the door open for future action. In fact, there are a number of examples where national amnesty laws have been overturned or reinterpreted by national courts, unexpectedly allowing prosecutions even when a departing regime thought it had put protections in place. For example in Argentina and Chile, in the early 2000s, ten to fifteen years after their respective transitions from authoritarian rule, previously untouchable amnesty provisions were overruled or reinterpreted by the national courts, and several hundred former regime officials were subsequently arrested and put on trial for killings, disappearances, and torture.[1] It was a remarkable turn of events. But while laws or agreements can sometimes be overturned later, such a step usually takes time and can considerably hinder progress. It is preferable to keep such a blanket amnesty out of a peace agreement altogether, and to respect the highest international standards in the language of such a founding national document.

These are legitimate points, and indeed any backsliding on the amnesty question—if the international community were to give its support for blanket amnesties even for the most serious crimes—would be seen as a major step backwards in the struggle to advance rights protections worldwide. We should also recognize, however, that it is not the fact of amnesty that prevents prosecutions in most contexts.

Continued Negotiation of Justice, Long After a Peace Agreement

What happens in relation to justice after a final peace agreement has been signed? Usually, the conversation continues, but with a broader group of participants, over a longer period of time.

There are two interesting trends here. First, what is in the agreement is rarely the final word on justice. On the contrary, the issue usually continues to be hotly discussed and new proposals debated, and the constraints and possibilities change over time, as the veto power of perpetrators may decline, and victims might become organized and less fearful.

Second, perhaps as a logical result of the above, the strongest justice programs have been worked out after the conclusion of a foundational peace agreement. The countries that required the most from accused perpetrators have concluded the details of their justice programs after a peace agreement, after a transition, and after the power of the perpetrators was reduced.

These two trends are intimately linked, in fact.

The "un-settle-able" nature of justice, accountability, and reconciliation is a common thread when comparing many peace negotiations. Clear tensions between seeking justice for past crimes and seeking a peaceful end to a conflict usually continue to play out long after a peace agreement is signed. These continued tensions sometimes generate significant international attention and concern because of the threat to the peace that is often implied. Political dynamics and popular pressure may push in either direction—either for greater assurances of impunity or for greater justice—but it is unlikely that the issue will go completely quiet.

The nature and strength of these demands can also change over time. For example, robust measures of accountability may bring a strong reaction, even quite specific threats, if accused perpetrators believe they can stop justice (as was seen in Liberia, described below). This underlying resistance may continue for years. Further, there may be attempts to control or compromise justice initiatives before they are able to gain momentum, sometimes through formalized political maneuvers (as in Aceh, Nepal, and Kenya). And finally, the victims themselves may react with anger and even violence in response to blatant impunity and continued denials, especially if the post-war political dispensation includes significant perks for persons well-known for serious crimes (also seen in Liberia, for example).

There are many examples of the slow and winding development of justice initiatives as they take shape in the years after a framework peace agreement. Let's turn to South Africa, Liberia, and Kenya to see some of these patterns.

South Africa

The issue of accountability for the apartheid years received little attention during most of the negotiations in the early 1990s. A detailed, book-length account of the South African talks makes no mention of the possibility of a truth commission or other post-accord justice issues.[2] The question was intended to be on the agenda, but it wasn't addressed until the very end "because nobody knew what the solution might be," according the government negotiator Roelf Meyer.[3] After the final text was complete, with all other issues settled, two negotiators were tasked to come up with a solution on amnesty.

The government pushed for an amnesty for past crimes; it was understood that the armed forces were making their support conditional on receiving amnesty. After urgent consultations with experts by phone, the parties finally agreed to include mention of an amnesty, in general terms, without going into any detail. This was included as a "post-amble" to the interim constitution, the document that would form the basis for the transitional period. The Truth and Reconciliation Commission (TRC) was not discussed at this time.

The TRC was first formally proposed by the new minister of justice in the first year of the Mandela government. This proposal responded in part to an idea put forward by a South African scholar two years earlier. Eighteen months of intense debate and discussion followed, with international conferences to look at the experiences of Chile and Argentina, many hours of parliamentary hearings looking at the draft bill for a TRC, and strong lobbying from human rights and victims groups to strengthen its terms. This broad public engagement resulted in a significant strengthening of the procedures and substantive coverage of the Commission. Among these, for example, was the agreement to hold any amnesty hearings in public, rather than in private as initially proposed.

These core components of the TRC, which ended up being so critical to South Africa's transitional period, could not have been worked out at the peace table. The breadth of voices was too limited, the power of those accused of abuses was too great, and the complexity of the model that was ultimately crafted could not have been worked through in such a tight time frame and out of view of public scrutiny. The post-agreement period of consultation was critical.

Liberia

The Comprehensive Peace Agreement in Liberia included a truth commission and excluded an amnesty. But it pushed to the future the unsettled question of individual accountability for well-known war criminals.

As with many truth commissions, the Liberian truth commission's detailed terms of reference were only worked out through a fairly broad and consultative process; this led to yet another round of public consultations for the selection of commission members. Altogether, there was over two year's delay in the commission starting work, but this allowed for much more public input into the process.

Meanwhile, the tensions around any individual accounting for the war's abuses remained just below the surface. In one public hearing of the truth commission, an unrepentant rebel leader flaunted his past deeds, boasting about a long record of killings. As the hearing concluded, the crowd rushed him, angry and ready for revenge. It was probably only the presence of United Nations peacekeeping troops that prevented a serious attack, as the former rebel leader was whisked away.

When the truth commission concluded its work by urging prosecutions and publicly listing the names of primary suspects, it again touched a nerve. As outlined in the previous chapter, the former warlords strongly resisted even the suggestion of criminal prosecutions. In Liberia, it was clear that judicial accountability would have to wait.

Kenya

The peace negotiations in Kenya followed a two-month period of intense interethnic violence after the controversial elections of December 2007. The initial agenda for the talks envisioned a truth commission, but the parties only turned to the issue after the fundamental power-sharing agreement was brokered. With the violence so recent and explosive, neither party felt that a nonjudicial truth inquiry was a sufficient response. The quickly agreed to a "two track response," as they announced after the first day on the issue, which was to include a special commission that would report quickly on the post-elections violence, as well as a truth commission to look into the roots of rights violations over the last decades.

Engaging the ICC was neither envisioned nor discussed during the talks, despite the fact that the ICC became such a major element over the next years. The commission on post-election violence recommended that its evidence be forwarded to the ICC if the national system did not respond to the crimes. The parties had pushed for clear accountability measures during the talks, focused on their own victims, but each party resisted any advances for judicial accountability when they realized they were also legally vulnerable for serious crimes.

Much of the political class, including a majority of Parliament, seemed intent on thwarting efforts at criminal justice, first through stifling the initiative for a Kenyan special tribunal to address post-election violence, then trying to block ICC jurisdiction in the country. There were also serious problems with the person Parliament appointed to chair the truth commission, who was widely perceived as compromised.

It became clear, in the years following the 2008 agreement, that the question of accountability was hardly a settled matter and would not be for some time. Indeed, these issues would help define the political arena, as well as the risk of further violence, given the very high positions of those the ICC intended to put on trial. Many worried that any perception that the ICC was prosecuting members of one ethnic group more than another, or if one side was found guilty and the other was not, could be the spark for much more violence.

These three examples are typical of the long-term attention demanded by these justice challenges. In each of these cases, rather than closing the question of justice, the negotiated peace naturally opened up space, over time, for further discussions of justice, almost always including a greater range of participants in the discussion. This has tested the political limits of accountability, the level of inherent risk, and the changing power structures that could open possibilities in unexpected ways. These changing dynamics can play out over many years.

It is for these reasons that the strongest justice results have come out of post-agreement negotiations and arrangements. This also has other positive effects: these discussions are based in the political arena, or a more public arena of consultation, NGO advocacy, and direct or indirect pressure that may come from an international court or other international entities. This allows for a much more inclusive and democratic process, with victims and other independent actors given a much greater role in the debate as compared to the narrower discussions between warring parties that are typical of formal peace talks.

As the Liberia and Kenya examples show, the power and continued threats from accused perpetrators may continue long after a war or conflict ends, and the "tests" of the political and juridical space for accountability might continue to show significant de facto restrictions. Democratic leaders and national prosecutors are quick to understand these realities, and may bide their time before trying to take proactive measures. Complaints from human rights advocates and others may well be absolutely correct—impunity continues for very serious crimes, even where the culprits are easily identifiable. But sometimes those who live in the country, and who would suffer the consequences of further violence, are cognizant of the realities that may require further passage of time and, ultimately, a reduction in the power of those who obstruct justice, before this impunity can be broken.

From the perspective of warring parties who are carefully negotiating what kind of arrangement they are willing to sign, it may at first seem unfair or even unacceptable that the well-considered terms of the peace may change over time. But these are political processes, in which a negotiated agreement composes one part. It is in the nature of such a process that political factors and influences are not frozen in time. They fluctuate, always. And ultimately, any successful political project, if it would be based on the tenets of democracy or fairness, or a basic foundation in the rule of law, should gain the support of the public and cannot be dictated by the short-term power of the gun.

In this sense, the defining parameters that give shape to any peace agreement naturally shift. Issues of justice—including truth, reparations, and individual criminal accountability—are clearly among the issues that continue to mature. They will demand further debate, under pressure from victims and others, for months and years after the conclusion of a peace agreement, despite the intention of that agreement to define exactly what will happen and to limit what might be possible.

Conclusion

Those countries that have worked out the details of their justice program after a peace agreement has been concluded have ended up with much more robust accountability. The spoilers have less power, civil society and victims have a greater voice, and there is more time to delve into more sophisticated options. It is useful if a peace agreement sets out basic parameters or first steps; these can open the door to other justice measures. Even a very general agreement for an amnesty in the South African interim constitution led to the design of a truth commission with important conditions attached to the amnesty.

But even in the best cases, and regardless of the language in the accord and the typical exclusion of amnesty for serious crimes, criminal prosecutions for crimes of war remain rare after a negotiated peace agreement. Other forms of accounting, such as a national truth commission, are much more common.

Notes

1 Argentina and Chile both ended dictatorships in the 1980s, but did not do so through negotiations and a peace accord. These cases are therefore not covered in any detail here.
2 Allister Sparks, *Tomorrow Is Another Country: The Inside Story of South Africa's Negotiated Revolution* (Sandton, South Africa: Struik, 1994).
3 Roelf Meyer, interview by author, Oslo, 19 June 2015.

5 The Impact of International Courts on Peace Negotiations

As international courts have gained prominence, the issue of justice is no longer solely in the hands of the mediator, the negotiating parties, or other national authorities. Many human rights advocates have welcomed this. But this new reality has raised concerns. When the threat of justice is wielded at the wrong time, or in the wrong way, certainly this will affect a peace process. It might also directly affect—negatively or positively—ongoing violence or the threat of violence. There are clear examples of all of these experiences. Whether the impact is indeed negative or positive, however, is not always predictable.

This chapter will analyze a number of cases where an international or "mixed" court has engaged in contexts of ongoing peace negotiations, or where formal negotiations were expected to begin shortly. The intention is to identify what the impact has been on peace processes, and why and how this effect took place.

When the texture and detail of these cases are investigated more closely, some interesting trends emerge. In most cases, investigations or warrants by an international court did affect the course of peacemaking—its pace, content, the exclusion of key participants, or its ultimate success or failure. The quality of this impact has been mixed, however. In many cases, the impact has been different from what was expected (or feared, or hoped for) by the mediator or others. In at least one case, the ultimate success of peace negotiations was credited to the well-timed indictment of a key leader or leaders.

While the impact of an indictment is hard to predict, it is equally difficult to control. In the context of a dynamic process on the ground, with shifting alliances of power and intentions, no one person can determine how such an indictment will play out, be it the mediator, the prosecutor bringing charges, the parties to the talks, or often even the person or persons targeted by warrants. But the way that an indictment, or even the threat of an indictment, is handled by the mediator and others engaged in the process can help shape the quality of this impact.

From a legal perspective, those accused are innocent until proven otherwise. But the political reality is that an indictment from an international court usually immediately delegitimizes a leader, often sidelining him or her from a leadership role until the charges are cleared. Some manage to avoid arrest and continue to govern, but their international access is greatly reduced: they are unable to travel easily and they are often shunned in the diplomatic and international arena.

Meanwhile, international courts, including the ICC, have often described their mandate as not only prosecuting past crimes, but also preventing future crimes. There are now many examples where the ICC Prosecutor has publicly threatened prosecution of those who appear on the verge of escalating political violence; these threats have sometimes been surprisingly effective. Thus, direct deterrence does sometimes result. But in other circumstances, or with a different kind of threat or manner of engagement, the ICC has worsened a situation, even causing greater entrenchment of intransigent leaders or sparking further violence. This aspect of the impact of international courts—that of prevention, deterrence, or otherwise affecting ongoing violence—will be explored in the next chapter.

While the record varies, it is clear that international justice does have an impact on peacemaking efforts and on local violence and conflict.[1] Before exploring specific cases to assess the different ways this has played out, the following pages review the views and intentions of international justice advocates, as well as mediators who have struggled with this relatively new element in peace talks.

Differing Perspectives

The perspective of those working to promote international justice is understandably different from mediators who are trying to shepherd along a difficult process of peace negotiation. Those who champion international justice, including international prosecutors, insist that their efforts are largely positive for peacemaking. The ICC, for example, describes itself as contributing to peace and the peaceful resolution of conflict, as a force that promotes stability and helps prevent war. As the ICC Chief Prosecutor said in a speech to the Council on Foreign Relations in late 2012:

> I would like to discuss with you how the preventive impact of the court's work could be maximized. How can we stop the current genocide in Darfur? How can we prevent a cycle of violence during the next elections in Kenya? How can we support Colombia's efforts to end half a century of violence? And I would say one word: institutions. In our countries, the congress, the police, the prosecutors and the courts are the basic institutions to establish and enforce law and order. The Rome Statute, which establishes the ICC, is building the same idea internationally. Judicial institutions are created to contribute—to prevent and manage massive violence.[2]

Elsewhere, the Prosecutor wrote in 2013 that the ICC has a "capacity to diffuse potentially tense situations," and it has helped to "isolate individuals . . .

or kick-start negotiations." The suggestion that the ICC could serve as an obstacle to peace is narrow and shortsighted, she wrote, as the ICC has "never precluded or put an end to any peace process."[3] Staff in the Prosecutor's office have explained that they hope their actions will indeed affect peace agreements, helping to assure that any language on justice is in compliance with the Rome Statute.[4]

These general views are echoed by many other smart minds in the human rights field. Juan Méndez, a long-time advocate with vast international experience, wrote a long and thoughtful paper on this subject in 2010. He said:

> [T]he stigma and political isolation brought about by prosecution can act to separate those actors who, in addition to being international criminals, are also the real spoilers of any serious agreement. . . . Conversely, a bad agreement can lead to further fighting and further atrocities. . . . [P]rosecutions often have the effect of pushing reluctant parties to the bargaining table, even if in the belief that they can obtain amnesty through peace negotiations.[5]

Human Rights Watch also argues that sustainable peace requires justice, and specifically criminal justice. Any deal that does not include judicial accountability "may prove costly in terms of lives and long-term stability," and will "set the stage for further abuses." Conversely, they believe that international justice "promotes the rule of law and long-term stability."[6]

Peace mediators, in contrast, see the simple fact that powerful commanders or combatants who are threatened with a jail term are not likely to sign on to peace or give up their weapons.

The executive director of the largest NGO involved in peace mediation, David Harland of the Centre for Humanitarian Dialogue, notes that, "The getting to yes is harder the more seriously you take the human rights normative framework. It's certainly seen as an impediment to our work." In his experience, the justice question is one of the first issues to be raised as a priority from fighting parties, who usually want amnesty. At the same time, he describes his own personal experience in the Balkans, where he observed how the threat of international prosecutions had a positive effect on perpetrators' behavior during the fighting.[7]

James LeMoyne, who has engaged in peace mediation for two decades, says that many mediators are now sensitized to the justice issue. While they recognize that this issue must be confronted, and in fact that it is better for a peace process to address the subject directly, "mediators also know that this may prove hard to do—and that it could easily become a stumbling block. Mediators today are well aware that justice is not a small issue; addressing it in negotiations is a major challenge."

"The ICC is a reality that can't be avoided," LeMoyne says. "There is little question that before the ICC it would have been easier to broker peace" in those countries where the ICC now has jurisdiction.[8]

Case Experience

A review of peace negotiations over the past twenty years shows that there is considerable variation in how international courts have affected these processes. The six cases set out below reflect the range of these experiences.

The experiences of Liberia, Uganda, and the former Yugoslavia are important reference points in trying to understand what the impact of international justice might be on an ongoing (or imminent) peace process. These situations relate to three different international courts (the Special Court for Sierra Leone, the ICC, and the International Criminal Tribunal for the former Yugoslavia [ICTY]), but they raise similar questions. In each case, indictments or arrest warrants were announced just as peace talks were about to begin, and the leaders who were indicted were seen as critical to any successful negotiations and stable peace. In each case, there was a fear that the indictments might bring the peace process to a halt or make it impossible to reach a final settlement. While the peace talks did continue in each of these contexts, from there the stories diverge.

In two of these cases (Liberia and Uganda), the international indictments profoundly affected the nature—and ultimate outcome—of the negotiations, although in very different ways. In retrospect, the Liberian peace process was seen to have been considerably strengthened by the involvement of the outside court, while the Ugandan process perhaps saw more negative than positive flowing from ICC engagement. Despite the first fears, the Dayton talks on the former Yugoslavia were not weakened by the ICTY's indictments, and some argue they had an important positive effect, but there are differences of views here.

Darfur, Libya, and Congo provide very different kinds of examples. The impact of the ICC was mixed in both Darfur and DRC, as will be seen below; over time, the effect in each context changed, sometimes viewed as positive and sometimes negative. In Libya, many observers believed that any slight possibility of a negotiated end to the war came to a close when the ICC arrest warrants were announced.

Liberia

After fourteen years of war and over a dozen failed peace agreements, the Liberian fighting groups agreed to new peace talks in early 2003. As they gathered in Accra, Ghana, to open the talks, Liberia President Charles Taylor was informed of an indictment against him just hours before the opening ceremony. The indictment, by the Special Court for Sierra Leone, had been held under seal for several months, and the prosecutor intentionally chose this moment to make it public.[9] But instead of arresting him, the Ghanaian authorities sent him back to Liberia, reportedly in the comfort of the Ghanaian presidential plane.

Before he left Accra, however, Taylor attended the opening ceremony and offered to step aside if it would be in the best interests for peace in Liberia. Until that moment, there had been broad skepticism that the peace conference would yield much of a result, including among those attending the talks. His opponents expected him to manipulate the outcome so that he remained in power, as he had done several times before, whether through a fraudulent election, an initial and then broken agreement for shared power, or other trickery. In the coming days, as his representatives who remained in Ghana obtained his formal agreement to leave the presidency, the nature of the negotiations fundamentally changed. Most delegates had planned for a two-week visit to Ghana for the peace conference; three months later, they finally concluded their negotiations with a successful agreement.

As the talks continued in Ghana, back in Liberia West African leaders visited Taylor to put pressure on him to keep his commitment to step aside. Finally, with a formal hand-over ceremony witnessed by several African heads of state, he transferred power to the vice president (until a National Transitional Government was inaugurated at the conclusion of the Ghana talks). Taylor then boarded a plane for asylum in Nigeria.

The decision to unseal the indictment against Taylor was controversial, with most West African states and some persons in the U.S. government (whom the prosecutor consulted in advance) strongly opposing this move. For African leaders, it was seen as a violation of the diplomatic principles inherent in a peace conference. Some feared a violent response in Monrovia. In the hours before it was clear whether Taylor would be arrested, observers reported threats of violence by Taylor's supporters, including possible revenge against the large Ghanaian population in Liberia. But others who were present insist that the main reaction by Taylor's armed supporters, in these uncertain hours, was confusion and a slackening of their weapons—"like a snake whose head was cut off," as one person described it—unsure of whom they should follow.[10]

In retrospect, most participants in the Accra peace conference, even some who were wary of the Special Court's actions at the time, felt that a peace agreement and transition would not have been possible without the indictment of Taylor, which directly resulted in his giving up the presidency and leaving the country. Was there a risk of a more negative outcome? Certainly serious violence might have been possible if he had been arrested, at least some people argue. But in this specific case, and in the mix of very unpredictable events, the timing and the fact of the Special Court's indictment was ultimately very positive for peace.

Uganda

The story of the ICC impact on the Uganda peace talks is more mixed, and it remains controversial.[11] There were many at the time—and particularly Ugandans, including those in the north who had suffered most from the conflict—who felt that the manner, timing, and nature of the ICC intervention in the country was ill-advised and a risk to the possibilities of a serious peace process.

In contrast, ICC supporters argue that the infamous rebel leader Joseph Kony agreed to peace talks because there was an arrest warrant from the ICC, which he was keen to have lifted. It is true that the Lord's Resistance Army (LRA), and Kony himself, repeatedly raised concerns about this issue, and the question of justice became the most difficult substantive agenda item of the talks. While the arrest warrants helped to draw attention to accountability issues, they also made it very difficult to persuade the LRA leadership to finally accept the proposed peace deal.

The ultimate failure of the talks, after two intense years and many interim sub-agreements, was rooted in a number of interlinking factors, some of these entirely independent of the challenges around justice and the threat of arrest of the LRA leadership. But this factor loomed large. It was not the only reason, and perhaps not the primary reason, that the final agreement collapsed—which happened spectacularly with a no-show signing ceremony deep in the forests, with dozens of international witnesses waiting for days, without success, for Kony to appear. But it was clear then, as it was during the full two years for the talks, that the justice element was one of the greatest hurdles for the process to overcome, and in the end it was never fully resolved.

The frustration with the ICC expressed by northern Ugandans was not only, or primarily, because the Court released arrest warrants against the LRA leadership and did so very early in the peace process. Many Ugandan leaders supported the work of the ICC and saw justice as ultimately important. But their greatest disagreements were in the manner in which the ICC engaged: the exact timing of the announcement of the warrants, the fact that there was no public outreach (for the first two years) to explain the Court's role, the sense that ICC staff fundamentally misunderstood the local context and undertook little consultation, and the perception that the ICC Prosecutor was one-sided and unquestionably supportive of the government—which was itself also accused of serious abuses in the north.

Community and religious leaders traveled to The Hague in mid-2005 to meet with the ICC Prosecutor, while investigations were under way and before warrants were announced, hoping to avoid negative repercussions and pleading that, at least, the timing of any warrants be carefully considered in light of the imminent peace negotiations. Despite a positive reception, Ugandans were disappointed that arrest warrants were nevertheless announced soon thereafter.

Ultimately, the agenda and shape of the peace talks, and who could directly participate in them, were greatly influenced by the arrest warrants, which hung over the LRA leadership like a dark cloud—never fully understood, from all accounts, but also very much feared.

Those who spoke with Joseph Kony during this time described his preoccupation with the ICC and the threat of justice reaching him. He listened to the BBC regularly, and he drew lessons. He told visitors that he would not follow the path of former Liberian President Charles Taylor, who was granted asylum in Nigeria only to be arrested and put on trial two years later. He took note of how Saddam Hussein was detained, quickly tried, and hanged shortly after he left power in Iraq. And ever since Angolan rebel leader Jonas Savimbi was killed in 2002, Kony was extremely careful about using a mobile or satellite phone, assuming his exact location could be tracked.

The Ugandan talks began just three months after Charles Taylor was arrested in Nigeria, and this precedent stood prominently in many people's minds. President Museveni told a visiting envoy in Kampala, "It's important that Kony knows: I will not do an Obasanjo on him"—referring to the former president of Nigeria, Olusagun Obasanjo, who had granted Taylor asylum and then allowed his arrest.

Kony wanted guarantees that he could stay in Uganda, even if he would face justice there. After many months, a creative solution was worked out by the mediator's legal team, in conjunction with the parties. This depended on a national solution (a special war crimes court) that should have ultimately lifted the threat of the ICC warrants, based on the complementarity principle (in which a credible national prosecution would overrule ICC jurisdiction). Alternative penalties and sanctions would replace prison sentences, with an emphasis on confessions, cooperation, traditional justice, and contributing to reparations for victims. Indeed, this agreement reflected many elements that would be included in the Colombian accord eight years later.

But a final agreement also depended on good will and trust between the parties, which by this time had all but disappeared. A solution to the justice challenge was possible, even in this most challenging of cases, but it could only have been carried out under different overall circumstances. While Kony may have ultimately concluded that there was no reliable path to fully escape justice, according to persons close to the talks, the failure to conclude an agreement was largely a result of other problematic aspects of the talks, which worsened in the last months.

But there are still many lessons for the ICC from this case. The Ugandans' concerns, and their interest in preserving space for a peace process, were underappreciated. The goal of the ICC cannot be simply to target perpetrators for arrest, at any cost, ignoring other factors and setting aside local wisdom on the matter, including the views of victims. When local advocates for justice and those pushing for peace are both strongly critical of the ICC Prosecutor's manner of engagement, then the Prosecutor should perhaps take a second look at his or her procedures, presumptions, and strategic priorities.

There is a final element in the overall calculation of the impact of the ICC on the Ugandan conflict. At the start of the Juba peace talks, the LRA relocated to a national park in Congo, on the border of Southern Sudan. This was far from northern Uganda, and thus virtually ended the LRA's threat against the civilian population there. The then-ICC Prosecutor Luis Moreno Ocampo believes it was the ICC arrest warrants that pushed them to move. He describes an informal, verbal agreement with the government of Sudan (which was then supporting the LRA and was also still cooperating with the Court), under which Sudan would remove the rebels from the territory of Southern Sudan at the moment that the Prosecutor released LRA arrest warrants. While there is apparently no written documentation on this, Moreno Ocampo was convinced that the relocation of the LRA was a direct result of the ICC's engagement, and thus should be credited with containing the LRA and significantly reducing its violence, at least temporarily.[12]

Others who were close to this situation had a different understanding of this development. This took place very shortly after the Comprehensive Peace Agreement between Sudan and Southern Sudan, which granted the southern region operational and territorial autonomy from Sudan. Participants recall that the LRA moved their base to Congo as a precondition to starting the talks, as stipulated by the government of Southern Sudan, whose vice president was to lead the talks.

Former Yugoslavia

Some analysts have argued that the peace conference that took place in Dayton, Ohio, in 1995 was another clear example of peace negotiations that were explicitly strengthened by the actions of an international court, akin to the Liberia case.

Key indictments from the International Criminal Tribunal for the former Yugoslavia indeed provided a well-timed intervention, shaping who was able to attend the peace conference and thus ultimately what kind of agreement was possible.[13] The Tribunal announced indictments for Bosnian Serb leaders Radovan Karadzic and General Ratko Mladic shortly before the Dayton talks were set to begin; the U.S. then barred them from attending the peace conference, under threat of arrest. It was fairly clear at the time that a peace agreement would not have been possible if Karadzic and Mladic were present in the talks, and thus their exclusion was indeed critical. Human Rights Watch often cites this case as showing that "criminal indictments of senior political, military and rebel leaders can actually strengthen peace efforts by delegitimizing and marginalizing those who stand in the way of resolving conflict."[14]

Richard Holbrooke, the U.S. representative at the talks, agreed that "their removal from negotiations helped greatly in our success," but he also noted that the U.S. "had already decided to marginalize General Mladic and Mr. Karadzic" before the indictments were announced, since the U.S. strongly preferred to have Serbian President Slobodan Milosevic represent Serb interests in Dayton.[15] The indictments were thus very convenient in supporting a political decision that had already been taken. In his book on the peace process, Holbrooke described the Tribunal as "a valuable instrument of policy."[16]

Other analysts and key participants have questioned whether the ICTY significantly affected the Dayton conference. Scholar Leslie Vinjamuri studied the available documentation from this period and concluded that it is an "erroneous assumption" that the exclusion of the Bosnian Serb leadership from Dayton was due to the indictments.[17] European Union Representative Carl Bildt, a co-chair of the Dayton conference, told me that he felt that the ICTY actions had virtually "no effect," neither negative nor positive, on the ultimate outcome.[18]

Equally important is that the original fears—that badly timed indictments might upend the planned Dayton conference before it even began—turned out not to be true. UN Secretary-General Boutros Boutros-Ghali complained forcefully to the ICTY Prosecutor after the indictments were announced, arguing that peace must be prioritized and that threatening the arrest of possible participants in the peace conference would be an impediment to this aim.

A plausible scenario exists in which the ICTY could have spelled significant trouble for the Dayton talks. If the prosecutor had also indicted Serbian President Milosevic at that time, then all the calculations would have changed. A peace conference wouldn't have been possible without Milosevic, at least not in that place and at that time.

Ironically, the ICTY Prosecutor, although certainly aware of this political context, says he felt more driven by the internal pressures and politics of the UN system, and in particular the need to assure the Tribunal's future. There was strong pressure to have indictments announced quickly in order to assure the Tribunal's future budget, and separately there were rumors that the Tribunal might become a bargaining chip at the Dayton talks, with a potential risk of being closed down to satisfy the parties (Dayton participants deny this). The Prosecutor, Richard Goldstone, said that he pushed very hard to get the Karadzic and Mladic indictments released before Dayton. From his perspective, the immediate effect of the indictments was to "put the Tribunal on a firm footing, immediately: its legitimacy went up in leaps and bounds."[19]

As the Dayton talks were under way, Prosecutor Goldstone released a second indictment against both Karadzic and Mladic, this time on charges of genocide. He was worried that an amnesty might be on the table, and he thus added the second indictment "to remind the mediators of the horrific crimes for which these two men were accused."[20] Ultimately, there was no amnesty, and Holbrooke later insisted that it was never discussed.

The final agreement signed at Dayton included an important provision that anyone "who is under indictment by the Tribunal and who has failed to comply with an order to appear" would be excluded from public office.[21] With this provision, the existence of the Tribunal fundamentally shaped the political realities in the region going forward.

Leaving aside the possible impact on the Dayton conference and the immediate aftermath, the ICTY certainly has helped to shape the nature of the peace in the years since. This became most clear over fifteen years later, in 2012, when several key cases were decided in a manner that significantly worsened and further polarized relations between the various ethnic communities in the region. The Serbs felt increasingly and unfairly targeted, and the Croats vindicated, by several key decisions by the ICTY. As David Harland wrote in late 2012,

> The lack of legal reckoning will once again channel grievances into the political process, laying up plenty of ammunition for further rounds of conflict. It is the opposite of what the war crimes tribunal for the former Yugoslavia was created to achieve.[22]

Darfur, Sudan

A different concern overshadows the experience of Sudan, and in particular the impact of the ICC arrest warrant for its president, Omar al-Bashir. In the months after the Prosecutor requested an arrest warrant for Bashir, but before the ICC Pre-Trial Chamber confirmed the request, Bashir was relatively constructive and cooperative in the national and international arena.

But his posture suddenly changed in March 2009, when the Pre-Trial Chamber announced their confirmation of the arrest warrant. Bashir immediately expelled a dozen humanitarian organizations from the country, understood by all as an act of vengeance, which significantly disrupted food and other humanitarian support to many of the tens of thousands displaced in Darfur.

With the confirmation of warrants for Bashir and others, analyst Sarah Nouwen writes:

> The environment became more hostile. For the first time since the initial years after the 1989 coup, the National Intelligence and Security Service resumed the practice of torturing human rights defenders, now on allegations of cooperating with the ICC. In court, people were convicted for such cooperation. International humanitarian NGOs were expelled and national human rights NGOs were closed on the same allegations fifteen minutes after the ICC's decision on an arrest warrant against Bashir came out.[23]

The arrest warrant for Bashir also seemed to consolidate his power base, and, as Sudan experts have noted, made it virtually impossible for him to step aside at the next round of elections; rather, he stayed in power to protect himself.

The effect on the on-and-off peace talks for Darfur is less certain. The rebels first thought the warrants would strengthen their hand, and thus hardened some of their demands. But over time this perception faded, and the ICC warrants seemed to play less of a role. Ultimately, many Sudan experts described the effect on Darfur peace talks as largely neutral.

As conflict picked up again between the north and south of Sudan, in particular after the referendum for the independence of South Sudan, the outstanding warrants had another effect: it made it more difficult for the international community to engage directly with the person who had the greatest power over the quite serious and increasing violence between the north and south. The United Nations and European Union worked under clear directives for their representatives that prohibited "non-essential" contact with persons under an ICC arrest warrant. The U.S., perceived as a critical actor in the country and region, has said it would not meet Bashir directly, but only send messages through intermediaries. One U.S. diplomat described this inability to speak with Bashir—which was a direct result of the arrest warrant—to be a major impediment to peace efforts.[24]

Meanwhile, Bashir pushed for the warrant to be lifted, as one of his implicit conditions for peace. But lifting an ICC arrest warrant is not possible, as such, and Sudan was apparently not interested in a temporary reprieve by means of a one-year Security Council deferral, under Article 16 of the Rome Statute. The arrest warrant remained in place, and became the first point of resistance and protest by the African Union, which insisted repeatedly that the ICC was an impediment to peace in Darfur.

Libya

The UN Security Council's quick referral of Libya to the ICC, in the very early days of the Libyan war in February 2011, raised questions. Even more questions were raised when the ICC Prosecutor moved very quickly to request arrest warrants for three top Libyan officials, and then the Pre-Trial Chamber of the Court gave its approval to the warrants less than six weeks later. Many worried that the warrants for the arrest of President Gaddafi, his son, and his intelligence chief could make it even more difficult to reach an end to the conflict.

There were many efforts at peace mediation—some cite as many as ten independent tracks of attempted negotiations with Gaddafi during the war—but they found little traction. The rebel leadership refused any proposals that did not include the precondition that Gaddafi give up power. There was little on which to build a starting point for serious talks.

Meanwhile, Gaddafi was under increasing military pressure as the months went on, especially after the fall of Tripoli in August, when he fled the capital with the loyal core of his government and security forces. Those who had contact with him at different moments in 2011 describe how he did not initially take the ICC involvement as much of a threat. He largely used it, at the beginning, to try to rally support from the public, mocking the interventionist policies of the international community. When the arrest warrants were confirmed in June, he first began to see the potential seriousness of the situation, these accounts suggest.

A telling perspective comes from a close confidant of Gaddafi, former Security Chief Mansour Dhao Ibrahim, who was with Gaddafi until his last hours. I interviewed Dhao in a detention center in Misrata, Libya. In his last weeks and months, when Gaddafi knew that he was increasingly under siege, he did not understand what his options might be. Could he still escape to a country that was not a party to the ICC, as was earlier proposed? Could he end the fighting by giving up or fleeing abroad? How could this be done?

Dhao described Gaddafi's frustration. "He kept saying that he expected his friends in the international community to help guide him, to suggest what should be done," Dhao said. "He had this idea in mind until the last minute—that Berlusconi, Blair, or Erdogan, for example, would contact him to help . . . He didn't understand why no one reached out to propose a solution."[25]

These persons—the current or former leaders of Italy, the UK, and Turkey—were under constraint themselves, in the context of ICC warrants backed by a UN Security Council referral. They (especially Italy and the UK, as ICC States Parties) could not have facilitated Gaddafi's escape from ICC arrest, for example. But this was not understood by Gaddafi at the time.

Some within the main opposition body, the National Transitional Council (NTC), thought a compromise solution would have been better, especially after Tripoli fell, in order to avoid the costs in deaths and destruction that came from a full military victory. While they welcomed the ICC referral by the

UN Security Council, the situation was more difficult once the arrest warrants were confirmed. With that announcement, the NTC sensed that Gaddafi dug in his heels and decided to fight to the end.

Congo

The engagement of the ICC in the Democratic Republic of Congo (DRC) has spanned more than a decade and touched on several different armed opposition groups. Its impact has been on many levels: international facilitators have disallowed broad amnesties by relying on the ICC Rome Statute as their primary reference point, and some rebel groups have, at least for a period, turned away from using child soldiers once they saw a rebel commander on trial for this crime. In one case, during the Goma peace conference of 2008, the ICC Prosecutor postponed the announcement of an arrest warrant of an important rebel leader at the urging of persons involved in the peace talks, who feared that this would derail the final conclusion of a peace deal. Meanwhile, the Congolese government waited several months for a strategic moment to arrest former warlords, acting on the orders of an ICC arrest warrant. This warrant had been kept under seal—with only certain officials in the government informed—and thus the accused could be fairly easily arrested when they were least expecting it.[26]

Thus, the relationship in the DRC between the ICC and local processes of demobilization and peace talks has sometimes been subtle and smart. But ultimately, the ICC impact on the conflict in Congo is mixed. I will return to the Congo story in the next chapter when looking at the deterrent effect of the ICC.

The Colombia Approach: Proactive vs. Reactive

The peace processes or conflicts described above were directly affected by actions of an international prosecutor, forcing the parties of a conflict to react. There was some level of surprise when a prosecutor first intervened, and often an unwelcome surprise, at least initially, for those trying to broker peace. In each case, an arrest warrant either for the head of state or for a leader of the armed opposition directly affected the political dynamics and possibilities in relation to negotiations. This altered who could attend talks, and it also usually changed the agenda of the talks, pushing the issue of war crimes to the center of attention. Mostly, though, this was reactive, and at least for some moments was seen as disruptive. Such international arrest warrants seemed to make a difficult peacemaking scenario even more difficult.

The peace talks that began in Colombia in 2012 were also deeply affected by the ICC, but this was without the ICC Prosecutor even formally opening investigations. Rather, the Prosecutor kept Colombia under a watching brief, threatening to open an investigation against either side of the civil war if the national justice system did not do enough. When the Colombian president first contemplated peace talks, he began with a decision that the country could and would avoid ICC prosecutions by meeting all international requirements for justice through national processes. This premise fundamentally shaped the nature as well as the content of the forthcoming negotiations. This also reflected the political reality that all parties to the talks would insist on "legal certainty" so that they would run no risk of unexpected and unpleasant legal surprises in the future. The only way to do this was to institute justice at home, setting out clear parameters as to what this would entail, and thus keep the ICC out. The existing national laws in Colombia in fact already set firm requirements, prohibiting certain forms of amnesty, for example, but the ICC factor removed the option of simply adjusting national law in order to avoid these justice quandaries altogether.

The key components of the Colombian accord reflected these intentions, even if the question ultimately remained open whether the ICC would be satisfied that the regime of alternative punishment was sufficient. The parties agreed to no amnesty for international crimes, to a judicial process for all accused of serious crimes (or for those "most responsible," this was unclear), and to a form of restricted liberty and reparatory actions, outside of prison, for those who confessed to their crimes. The agreement makes repeated reference to the Rome Statute in defining crimes and in other respects.

The seventy-page agreement on justice for Colombia is detailed and complex, reflecting the very legal political culture of Colombia, and unlikely to be repeated in many other countries. But the general approach both by Colombia and by the ICC may suggest a better model for the future. Where it is possible that justice can be done nationally, the ICC should prefer this. Its own caseload is already high, and in principle it supports the idea that national systems carry out justice.[27] Most countries also prefer to keep justice at home.

It's possible that some of the other countries looked at above also would have worked to avoid intervention by an international court and to meet the accountability requirements domestically, but the international arrest warrants were out before talks even began. The mediation team for Uganda included significant expertise on the ICC, and they were actively exploring creative sentencing alternatives that would comply with ICC requirements, for example.

Conclusion

A real threat of prosecutions makes a peace negotiation more difficult and more complicated, and sometimes it makes a solution seemingly impossible. But if an arrangement on justice can be found, it is likely that the final agreement will also be more durable. A proper accountability regime would not only respond to an international court's demands, but should also take into account the needs of victims. It would increase public support for the agreement. And it might help protect against universal jurisdiction claims, such as if a country's leaders travel to Europe. All of these elements help protect and strengthen the durability of the accord.

It is possible that early indictments of high-level perpetrators can strengthen peace talks by removing spoilers, as turned out to be true in Liberia and to some degree in the Dayton talks for the former Yugoslavia. But this is by no means assured, and even in these two cases, no one was sure in advance what the effect of indictments would be. Releasing ICC arrest warrants for the Lord's Resistance Army leadership only made it more difficult to negotiate with them, partly because there was no one who could well represent them at the table.

The experience in Sudan suggests that it is the period in which there is a threat of prosecution where the leverage is greatest. Once an arrest warrant is released, those who are targeted have little room to maneuver. President Bashir changed from seemingly cooperative to aggressively obstinate at the moment that the warrant for his arrest was confirmed.

But it is also true, despite the mixed record summarized in this chapter, that no peace negotiations have come to an end solely over the issue of justice or as a reaction to specific indictments. Rather, the result has been to intensify the difficulty of the negotiations. If this can be overcome in a way that respects the requirements for justice set out in international law, and in particular satisfies the international tribunal threatening to intervene, the end result is likely to be more resilient in the short and long term.

The idea that a president or the leader of an insurgency would voluntarily give up power in exchange for a long prison term has never been credible, anywhere. As the Colombia case suggests, the resolution to the reality of international justice might be found in a careful consideration of the justice that is required, and especially the sentencing regime. The final chapter of this book will return to this specific idea.

Notes

1 There are not many close, comparative studies of this question to date. For two useful reflections, see Paola Gaeta and Lyne Calder, "The Impact of Arrest Warrants Issued by International Criminal Courts on Peace Negotiations," in Laurence Boisson de Chazournes, Marcelo G. Kohen, and Jorge E. Viñuales, eds., *Diplomatic and Judicial Means of Dispute Settlement* (Leiden: Nijhoff, 2013), 47; and Payam Akhavan, "Are International Criminal Tribunals a Disincentive to Peace? Reconciling Judicial Romanticism with Political Realism," *Human Rights Quarterly* 31 (2009): 624.

2 Fatou Bensouda, "The International Criminal Court: A New Approach to International Relations," Address at the Council on Foreign Relations, New York, 21 Sept 2012, www.cfr.org/courts-and-tribunals/international-criminal-court-new-approach-international-relations/p29351.

3 Fatou Bensouda, "International Justice and Diplomacy," *NY Times*, 19 March 2013.

4 Interview by author with staff of the ICC's Office of the Prosecutor (OTP).

5 Juan E. Méndez, "Transitional Justice, Peace, and Prevention," Address at University of Baltimore Law School, Center for International and Comparative Law, 26 Oct 2010 (on file with author).

6 Sara Darehshori, in a Human Rights Watch press release, "Shortchanging Justice Carries High Price: Prosecuting Abusive Leaders May Help, Not Hinder, Peace Efforts," 7 July 2009, www.hrw.org. See also Human Rights Watch,

Selling Justice Short: Why Accountability Matters for Peace (New York: Human Rights Watch, July 2009); Richard Dicker, Human Rights Watch, in *The Economist* online debate on peace and justice, 6 Sept 2011.

7 David Harland, interview by author, Geneva, 27 Apr 2013.

8 James LeMoyne, interview by author, Geneva, 28 Nov 2013.

9 David Crane, interview by author, Aug 2006.

10 As described by Conmany Wesseh, then a civil society leader and later foreign minister, interview by author, 2010.

11 See Mark Kersten, "Peace, Justice and Politics in Northern Uganda," International Justice and the Prevention of Atrocities Project (European Council on Foreign Relations, London, Nov 2013), www.ecfr.eu/ijp/case/uganda.

12 Luis Moreno Ocampo, interview by author, Sept 2013.

13 A useful exploration of this question is provided in Joyce Neu, "Pursuing Justice in the Midst of War: The International Criminal Tribunal for the Former Yugoslavia," *Negotiation and Conflict Management Research* 5:1 (Feb 2012): 72–95.

14 Balkees Jarrah, Human Rights Watch, "The United States Should Support ICC Involvement in Syria," 19 Mar 2014, www.jurist.org.

15 Richard Holbrooke, "The Arrest of Sudan's Bashir Should Proceed," *The Financial Times*, 21 Sept 2008.

16 Richard Holbrooke, *To End a War* (New York: Random House, 1998), 190.

17 Leslie Vinjamuri, "Justice, Peace and Deterrence in the Former Yugoslavia," International Justice and the Prevention of Atrocities Project, European Council on Foreign Relations, London, Nov 2013, www.ecfr.eu/ijp/case/bosnia_herzegovina.

18 Carl Bildt, interview by author, Oslo, June 2012.

19 Richard Goldstone, interview by author, 25 Nov 2014.

20 Neu, "Pursuing Justice," 83, citing Chris Stephen, *Judgement Day: The Trial of Slobodan Milosevic* (New York: Atlantic Monthly Press, 2005).

21 Dayton Peace Agreement, signed 21 Nov 1995, Article IX, "General Provisions."

22 David Harland, "Selective Justice for the Balkans," *International Herald Tribune*, 7 Dec 2012. Over the next months, other ICTY cases were also overturned on appeal, serving other communities' interests. Many of these decisions had significant political ramifications in the region.

23 Sarah Nouwen, "Darfur," International Justice and the Prevention of Atrocities Project, European Council on Foreign Relations, Nov 2013, www.ecfr.eu/ijp/case/sudan.

24 U.S. official, comments at a conference in Oslo, June 2012.

25 Mansour Dhao Ibrahim, interview by author, Misrata, Libya, 26 Jan 2012.

26 For a more detailed exploration, see Laura Davis and Priscilla Hayner, "Difficult Peace, Limited Justice: Ten Years of Peacemaking in the DRC," International Center for Transitional Justice, Mar 2009; and Laura Davis, "The Democratic Republic of Congo," International Justice and the Prevention of Atrocities Project, European Council on Foreign Relations, Nov 2013, www.ecfr.eu/ijp/case/dr_congo.

27 There have been important critiques, however, of the ICC's record in relation to supporting versus supplanting national justice. See Sarah M.H. Nouwen, *Complementarity in the Line of Fire: The Catalysing Effect of the International Criminal Court in Uganda and Sudan* (Cambridge: Cambridge University Press, 2013), 43–62.

6 International Justice and Deterrence

While the previous chapter focused on the impact of international courts specifically on peace negotiations, a second and different question is whether and how the actions of international courts impact on ongoing violence, or the threat of violence, or on reducing or deterring human rights abuses. This may or may not be in the context of peace negotiations.

This is another angle for understanding the impact of international justice on conflict and on peace. The international human rights field has framed this issue as a question of preventing or deterring human rights violations or war crimes, and the analysis below will in part focus on that aim and on the degree to which we see that effect. From a peace mediator's perspective, however, almost the same question can be understood as the possibility of deterring violent conflict, or having an impact on the peace vs. war equation itself. Having a direct impact on war—or preventing the outbreak of fighting more generally—is not usually among the stated ambitions of human rights advocates.[1] However, as we interrogate specific cases below, we will see that the impact (and intention) of ICC engagement has been not only to affect the manner and method of warfare, but also to directly deter the outbreak of violence in a situation teetering on the edge.

The question of this chapter is how, whether, and in what circumstances international tribunals have helped to deter or prevent abuses or have directly affected a conflict itself. While this has been a question of concern for those engaged in international justice for years, relatively little has been published that offers an overview of experience to date and assesses this impact in multiple different cases.

The Idea of Deterrence and Prevention

Can the threat of justice, even from a far-away international court, persuade local actors to fight a clean war? And how would this best be done?

The idea of international tribunals having a deterrent or preventive impact was a central part of the argument in favor of the development of the ICC in the 1990s. Previously, for example in the context of the Nuremberg and Tokyo trials after World War II, there was no stated expectation that international justice would have a general deterrent effect on such crimes taking place elsewhere.[2] Legal scholar Kate Cronin-Furman reviewed the record of the ICC's founding and concluded that "the concept of general deterrence was directly invoked in the creation of the ICC" and that in particular, "[t]he prospects for deterrence were a major consideration in negotiations of the penalties to be included in the Rome Statute."[3]

Another writer concluded in 2001 that general deterrence "is one of the main reasons (perhaps the main reason) underlying the creation of the ICC: the idea is to ensure punishment and, through punishment, to deter."[4]

These scholars note, however, that the theory behind the idea was never spelled out, even by those convinced by the argument. "Rather, deterrence optimists seem to take for granted that more trials will mean more deterrence," Cronin-Furman concludes dryly.

However, there is some suggestion in the literature that this preventive effect might take place in a very specific as well as a much more general manner. A 2009 review summarized the various ways in the ICC is thought to help prevent atrocities:

> In what ways may the ICC contribute to preventing the occurrence of genocide, war crimes, and crimes against humanity? The literature on the subject suggests five primary mechanisms. First, the court's operation may provide a general deterrent effect, convincing those who contemplate orchestrating atrocities that such actions will harm more than help them. Second, the court's unique regime of complementary jurisdiction may allow it to leverage national jurisdictions into action—an effect here referred to as 'complementary deterrence.' Third, the ICC may sideline specific perpetrators so that they cannot commit further crimes. Fourth, the ICC may end cycles of violence by displacing private justice, individualizing collective guilt, and developing a reliable historical record of atrocities. Finally, and most ambitiously, the court may serve as a tool of global moral education that helps shape the norms of combatants and state leaders.[5]

Many analysts have expressed skepticism that deterrence can actually be measured and have cast considerable doubt on a "general deterrence" effect as a result of international criminal prosecutions. By "general deterrence," writers are usually referring to "the idea that punishing criminals reduces crime by deterring other potential offenders"; in relation to the ICC, this suggests deterring potential offenders in other very different contexts elsewhere in the world.[6]

One of the first quite skeptical analyses was published in 1999, by scholar David Wippman, just a year after the Rome Conference. He also noticed the great weight that was being given to the deterrence goal:

> Of course, supporters of the ICTY, the ICC, and Pinochet-style prosecutions have many reasons other than deterrence on which to base their advocacy of international criminal prosecutions, including considerations of justice, respect for international law, retribution, avoidance of personal

vengeance, de-legitimation of indicted war criminals as political leaders, and national reconciliation. But for many, deterrence is the most important justification, and the most important goal.[7]

"Unfortunately," Wippman continued, "the connection between international prosecutions and the actual deterrence of future atrocities is at best a plausible but largely untested assumption." Historically, he proceeded to show, it doesn't hold up well.

Scholar David Bosco further concluded,

> The ICC's drafting history indicates a strong desire on the part of many drafters to create an institution that would deter and prevent future crimes. But the Rome Statute and the subsequently adopted Rules of Procedure and Evidence offer little guidance on whether and how the court should seek to maximize that effect.[8]

These negative assessments continued. In 2013, a commentator analyzed the minimal impact of the ICC on the increasing violence in the Central African Republic, where the ICC was already engaged. He noted that "the ICC's intervention hasn't prevented—or really had *any* effect—on the country's slide into political violence and slaughter," despite the fact that the Prosecutor had released public warnings, and the atrocities taking place in the CAR were exactly those that would be of interest.[9]

However, human rights advocates continue to assert the deterrent effect of the ICC. For example, in 2013 Balkees Jarrah, International Justice Counsel at Human Rights Watch, made a case that the UN Security Council should refer Syria to the ICC based primarily on a deterrence argument:

> (N)obody claims that the court's involvement will stop the killing overnight . . . But a U.S. decision to get behind an ICC referral would signal that the administration is serious about its commitment to end impunity in Syria. Crucially, bringing the court into the picture would send a clear message to all parties to the conflict that grave crimes will carry serious consequences. Indeed, raising the price on today's abuses has real potential to influence tomorrow's behavior and help deter further atrocities.
>
> . . . (T)he failure to hold those responsible for the most serious crimes to account can fuel future abuses. In Syria, we see this playing out in excruciating terms as abuses continue, aggravated by a complete and utter climate of impunity.[10]

The idea is clear: impunity leads to more abuses. Accountability, or the threat of accountability, even for a few critical cases, deters further atrocities.

Some research has evaluated whether mere membership in the ICC has led to reduced violations by the state or armed opposition groups. A study published in 2014 concluded that a state's ratification of the ICC Statute resulted in a considerable reduction of violence against civilians during armed conflict.[11] Another study suggested that the ratification of the ICC Rome Statute "tended to be correlated with a pause" in conflict hostilities. And a third showed an increase in domestic prosecutions once the ICC became engaged, due in part to increased international support for independent actors pushing for justice.[12] But the methodology of these studies has raised questions, as have their conclusions on specific cases.[13] These kinds of studies, which rely on a statistical analysis of large numbers of states rather than a close understanding of the dynamics in each case, don't quite answer our core questions.

The ICC itself defines a central tenet of its mandate as "crime prevention," which is to say an assumption that an effective justice system and the threat of prosecutions will deter further serious crimes. The first Chief Prosecutor, Luis Moreno Ocampo, firmly believed in this deterrent effect, claiming in a 2007 conference that "Experience has taught us that . . . law is the only efficient way to prevent recurrent violence and atrocities."[14] The 2013 strategic plan of the ICC's Office of the Prosecutor (OTP) defines its mission as comprising four overall goals; one of these is "promoting peace by preventing the commission of such crimes."[15]

My conclusion, as reflected in the cases described below, is that a deterrent effect does sometimes result from the ICC's work. There is no question that the engagement of an international court can have (and sometimes has had) a direct and positive impact on political violence. It is clear that local political and military actors become quickly aware of the ICC when it is focused on their country and go to some ends to avoid being a target of its prosecutions.

But again, as we have seen on other questions, the impact in this area is not uniform. There are also cases where the ICC threat has arguably worsened a conflict or apparently led to further violence. The ultimate effect, positive or negative, seems to depend on two critical elements of a court's engagement: the timing of its involvement and, more broadly, its manner or strategy of engaging. As we will see further below, this immediately raises the question of whether an international prosecutor should in part shape his or her actions (including whom to indict and when) on an assessment of how this will affect the broader conflict. Needless to say, this is a complicated—and controversial—question.

A parallel idea to the direct-deterrence argument is that the mere existence of the ICC will strengthen national judicial systems, given the obligations of a state after it joins the ICC, and that this will help prevent crimes. This idea of prevention implies a longer-term strengthening of state institutions and laws and instilling a culture of accountability, so that human rights abuses are less likely to occur. For example, many ICC member states have added international crimes (such as crimes against humanity) to their criminal codes. This can be important when there is a need to investigate "system crimes"—those crimes that take place in a pattern and appear to be planned or authorized from the top. But where national judicial systems are weak, which is often true in conflict and post-conflict contexts, much more is needed than changes in the criminal code before the national judiciary will be able to respond effectively. The ICC, however, has made clear that it has no intention to engage in judicial reform or training at the national level.

Needless to say, this notion of prevention is harder to measure and will take much more time to develop. It is fair, however, to accept the argument of some ICC advocates who say that the better hope for the ICC is to have a long-term preventive effect, rather than a short-term deterrent effect, which has been the subject of such criticism.

Before setting out those factors that may result in deterrence, let us first consider specific examples where international courts have apparently had a deterrent effect in some shape or manner, or have otherwise affected the calculations of those involved in conflict or war.

Case Experience

Congo

First, a return to the Democratic Republic of Congo (DRC). One interesting and immediate impact of the ICC's engagement was seen in the response to the early indictment and arrest of a rebel commander on charges of recruitment and use of child soldiers, which the ICC statute defines as a war crime. Other rebel commanders, suddenly understanding that this was considered a crime in the international system, reacted quickly to try to rid their own troops of the children within their ranks. Some were demobilized through children's services agencies, but this ran a risk of implicating the commanders in what was clearly an ongoing war crime. Other commanders therefore abandoned their child soldiers in the bush, leaving them to find their own way out (some did; others probably perished). It was an ironic outcome of the Court's effectiveness: the children, whom the Court was intending to protect, became the very evidence that the groups needed to hide. But it is also a clear example of how local military commanders respond, and change their behavior, if they perceive that the ICC might be watching.

On the other hand, this ICC threat and resulting deterrent effect did not seem to have had a long-term effect. Within two years, violent conflict was brewing again in eastern Congo, after a period of relative quiet. These same militia groups, which had only recently cleared their forces of child soldiers, began again to forcibly recruit civilians into their forces, including many children, according to international humanitarian organizations tracking these movements. The initial alarm that there might be further ICC arrests over the use of child soldiers had apparently already waned.

On a more worrying level, turning to a different part of the DRC story, the outstanding arrest warrant for one powerful warlord was suspected of further entrenching him in war, and perhaps even helped to trigger another round of violence. Bosco Ntaganda was indicted by the ICC under a sealed warrant in 2006, and the warrant was made public in 2008. He was nevertheless integrated into the national army under a peace deal in 2009. By 2012, the pressure on the government for his arrest (from the UN, international and national human rights organizations, and foreign states) was considerable, and he was reportedly increasingly worried about possible arrest. Many cite this as one of the primary factors that sent him back to war against the government in early 2012—taking many soldiers with him into the bush (his former rebel contingent had largely remained intact when it was absorbed into the structure of the national army). By the end of 2012, Ntaganda's new rebel movement, the March 23 Movement (M-23), had taken control of a large part of eastern Congo, including occupying the major city of Goma for over a week, with reported rapes, targeted killings of activists, and looting.

It is not clear exactly why the warrant for Bosco Ntaganda was made public. Human rights organizations ask a different question: why did the government fail to arrest him during the several years he was in the national army, when his whereabouts were well-known? Ultimately, in 2013, Ntaganda turned himself in to the U.S. Embassy in Rwanda—apparently fearing that his life was at risk.

One careful analysis of these specific developments in the DRC concluded that the effects of ICC action

> seem to vary across stages of the legal process, even with respect to the same armed group. ICC action can contribute to prevention, but it can also exacerbate atrocities . . . The logic of deterrence in ICC action may sometimes backfire, generating perverse incentives for leaders to escalate violence.[16]

The looming arrest warrant for Bosco Ntaganda pushed him to mutiny, but his arrest in the end significantly weakened his M-23 co-mutineers.

Another critical moment in the history of the ICC in the DRC was the 2008 arrest, in Brussels, of the former Congolese vice president, Jean-Pierre Bemba. He was charged with crimes that took place in the Central African Republic, but there was no question that the political fall-out would be in Congo, where he still had a strong following. When the sealed arrest warrant was sent to the Belgian authorities and he was unexpectedly arrested, in accordance with Belgium's obligations as a state party to the ICC, many worried that violence would erupt back in Congo, in particular in the capital, Kinshasa, where his following was the greatest. Just two years earlier, there had been street battles in Kinshasa between Bemba's supporters and those backing the elected president, Joseph Kabila, after a close election. After Bemba's arrest, it was tense for a few days. But in the end, the tensions did not erupt into violence.

Three years later, in late November 2011, Congo again faced the threat of increasing violence after turbulent presidential elections that raised many questions about the credibility of the official results. In the following days, dozens of people were killed or disappeared, tensions were high, and many were worried that they might reach the tipping point of a serious escalation of violence.

In early December, the Chief Prosecutor put out a statement to warn that he was watching and threatened instigators with prosecution:

> Leaders from all sides must understand this: my Office is watching the situation in the DRC very closely. As we have shown in both Kenya and Cote d'Ivoire, planning and executing attacks on civilians for electoral

gain will not be tolerated. This Court can investigate and prosecute you if you are responsible for committing ICC crimes, irrespective of position, and irrespective of political affiliation. I urge leaders, commanders, and politicians on all sides to calm your supporters. Electoral violence is no longer a ticket to power, I assure you. It is a ticket to The Hague.[17]

Internationals in Congo felt that this statement had an immediate effect. The UN head of police met the next day with the chief of police of Congo. The police chief was eager to keep himself clear of ICC attention. He said, "You're my witness: I'm doing everything I'm supposed to be doing—everything you've asked me to do I've done. I'm making sure my people are doing right. I don't want to be the next one going up to The Hague."[18]

Violence did not increase. One Congo expert working with the UN in Kinshasa at the time, who like others felt that the ICC statement definitely helped, explained how the Court was perceived:

> The government—and others—in Congo are quite aware of the ICC; it makes them sit up straight and take notice. The ICC didn't just go after warlords in the far-away East, it also went after Bemba. People think: 'If you can get Bemba, you can get anyone—certainly little old me who is not as big as Bemba.'

He continued, "People in Congo say: 'When the ICC coughs, the DRC gets uncomfortable.' Nobody wants to end up in The Hague."[19]

Kenya

After the intense violence following the 2007 presidential elections in Kenya, there was a worry that this level of violence might erupt again in the presidential ballot of 2013. But in the end, the 2013 elections were considerably less violent than other presidential elections in the country over the last twenty years. There was some rioting after the results were announced, but it was a major improvement as compared to the past.

Most observers agree that the ICC's engagement in the country was an important factor in keeping things calm. The ICC had brought charges against six persons in relation to the 2007 post-electoral violence, including two persons who became candidates for president and vice president in the 2013 elections. The ICC was prominent in the political sphere and in the minds of Kenyans: its role in the country was certainly very controversial, but it was at least strongly felt.

However, the ICC was not the only factor. Analysts noted several reasons why the elections were comparatively peaceful. An analysis by the *New York Times* pointed to a number of factors: the candidates urged their supporters to stay calm and to trust in the decisions of the courts; the public had a greater degree of confidence in the neutrality of the courts, following significant vetting of judges and other judicial reforms since the last elections; public protests were outlawed during the 2013 election period, and the police were out in great numbers to respond to any dissent; and Kenyans were generally fearful of returning to the difficult months after the 2007 elections, when the violence descended into a terrible and frightening spiral that became almost impossible to stop. Finally, there was the ICC, which was "hanging over Kenya like a thick, black cloud . . . Many Kenyans said this has served as a brake, making politicians of all stripes fearful of inciting any violence and then being hauled away."[20]

At the same time, another dynamic took root. The candidates who were under indictment by the ICC used this fact to effectively rally political support, feeding on public sentiment against international invention into Kenya's affairs. Thus, observers say, while the ICC's engagement in the country reportedly helped prevent political violence, it also helped to secure the victory, as president and vice president, of two of the men most implicated in the violence that followed the 2007 election.[21]

Guinea

The Congo example is not the only time that the ICC has intentionally taken steps to try to deter violence around difficult elections. In Guinea, in 2010, the ICC played a similar role, but rather than through a public statement, it acted through direct warnings delivered in person to all of the relevant parties.

The ICC Prosecutor sent a high-level team to Guinea during the week of the run-off presidential election in November 2010. Many feared the possibility of violence as the election results would likely be contested. The ICC team spent the week visiting candidates, their supporters, and others. "We warned them of the risk of ICC action if serious violations took place, and made it clear that we were watching," said an ICC staff member. The elections came off without violence. The OTP believes, credibly, that its input contributed to preventing crimes, although they acknowledge that there were many efforts by other actors as well.[22]

Côte d'Ivoire

The threat of ICC prosecution was also explicitly used to calm down a treacherous situation in Côte d'Ivoire. In November 2004, the national radio and television stations began airing a barrage of inflammatory messages, seemingly intended to activate the many armed militias and mobs that were roaming the streets. It was "eerily reminiscent of the days preceding the Rwandan genocide," noted then-UN Special Advisor on the Prevention of Genocide Juan Méndez.[23]

Trying to halt the rising threat of violence, Méndez issued a statement saying that those responsible for this hate speech could be prosecuted by the ICC for "incitement to violence" leading to possible genocide. "My press release was widely publicized in Abidjan," Méndez reported.

After 48 hours, expressions of racial hatred in radio and TV ceased. Calm returned. It was established later that the prospect of ICC prosecution was carefully analyzed by persons in authority and their legal advisers. The conflict receded and the incident is evidence that threat of prosecution can stay the hand of perpetrators.[24]

Six years later in Côte d'Ivoire, the ICC Prosecutor warned the parties again of the risk of prosecution, after the election of 2010. But the kernel of the message—and the timing in relation to national events—was quite different, and it may have had the opposite effect on those it was hoping to influence.

After the presidential elections in late 2010, Côte d'Ivoire was in crisis, with the outgoing president, Laurent Gbagbo, refusing to accept election defeat and eventually bunkering down in his residence. While Gbagbo continued to claim victory, his opponent, Alassane Ouattara, was widely recognized internationally as the legitimate victor. The standoff lasted for months, with violence increasing between the supporters of the two parties and escalating into serious fighting.

In early April 2011, with the crisis at its peak, the ICC Office of the Prosecutor released a statement that it was "very concerned about the deteriorating situation" and was actively collecting information on alleged crimes, including mass killings, by different parties.[25]

This only had a negative effect on the entrenched standoff, according to close observers. West African expert Mike McGovern called it "dangerously counter-productive," noting,

> When Gbagbo was hiding and refusing to give up power, one can think of few statements more unhelpful than the declaration by Luis Moreno-Ocampo, the International Criminal Court's chief prosecutor, that no one in Côte d'Ivoire could receive amnesty from war crimes prosecution. With one sentence, Moreno-Ocampo ensured that Gbagbo would reject any negotiated solution and instead fight to the end.[26]

Timing, strategy, and context: these two examples from the same country make it abundantly clear why an international prosecutor must not operate blind to national context and should consider the likely impact of his or her actions.

Libya

As described in the previous chapter, the referral of Libya to the ICC by the UN Security Council raised many questions about the impact on the possibility, however slight, of a negotiated end to the conflict. It is also important to consider whether the ICC's engagement in Libya had any effect on the abuses or threatened abuses of the Gaddafi government or the opposition.

In brief, it seems there was little deterrent effect, despite the very prominent engagement of the Prosecutor and the very fast development of cases and announcement of arrest warrants. There is no evidence that the ICC involvement in Libya affected the fighting tactics of the regime's forces. They committed serious abuses throughout the conflict.

Many in the opposition, meanwhile, perceived the ICC as only interested in the government's crimes, and there is little indication it had much impact on rebel actions. Some officials or force commanders in the opposition National Transitional Council (NTC) were aware that the ICC had jurisdiction over both sides of the conflict and tried to relay this message, but it did not seem to reach others. Communication from senior commanders to fighting forces, and between different militia groups, was very weak. Some, and perhaps many, opposition commanders were urging respect for the laws of war and gave lectures to their troops emphasizing this subject; however, this message was based primarily on religious and cultural foundations and generally did not make reference to the ICC or international obligations.[27]

In the end, the opposition's record on abiding with the laws of war was inconsistent, at best. Even in those cities where there was a professed commitment by the rebel forces to respect international humanitarian law (and human rights law from the time they took over power), there were significant reports of abusive practices, such as torture of detainees, by these very forces. By this time, several months into the war, it seemed increasingly clear that the focus of the ICC Prosecutor was exclusively on the Gaddafi regime. There was no response or reaction from the ICC Prosecutor to the increasing reports of these abuses.

The former chair of the NTC, Mahmoud Jibril, remembers receiving two or three emails from NATO, urging respect for human rights, but there were no messages from the ICC or any indication from the ICC Prosecutor that the opposition might also be a target of investigation.[28] The ICC of course held jurisdiction over both sides of the conflict, and the Prosecutor made this clear in his reports to the UN Security Council in New York. But this did not seem to be generally understood in Libya.

Thus, while there may have been a possibility of having a deterrent effect on the rebel forces (and ultimately the new post-Gaddafi government of Libya), especially given the initial interest and apparent good faith from the opposition leadership, the one-sided nature of the Prosecutor's attentions weakened this prospect almost to zero.

Other Accounts of Deterrence

I have heard various other stories of possible deterrence resulting from ICC action or the threat of prosecutorial action. Some of these accounts are more speculative than evidence-based, and I have been unable to document their veracity sufficiently to include them here. However, the following accounts do show this effect and how it can play out in very different ways. While none of these resulted in perfectly clean wars without war crimes, they show how combatants respond at least in the short term to a perceived threat of justice for their crimes.

Afghanistan

Human Rights Watch describes how a report on atrocities in Afghanistan, and the implicit threat of prosecution for those responsible, was reported to have directly affected an important warlord in Afghanistan. As described by Human Rights Watch:

> In May 2002 the *Christian Science Monitor* reported that a key warlord in northern Afghanistan, Gen. Abdul Rashid Dostum, forced more than 90 commanders to listen to a reading of a 52-page Human Rights Watch report alleging atrocities committed by his forces after the fall of the Taliban. The report, entitled 'Paying for the Taliban's Crimes,' described widespread abuses including killings, sexual violence, beatings, and extortion committed against Pashtuns . . . The report called for Afghan commanders and combatants responsible for war crimes to be held to account.
>
> During the meeting, the warlord warned his men, 'You must be careful in the future. These [investigators] are very dangerous men. They can take you to an international court of justice if they can prove your actions.' He also said, 'I am dying of these accusations from the international community . . . If any one of my commanders commits these kind of acts, I will kill him tomorrow.'[29]

Perhaps this specific outcome—a warlord threatening to kill his own commanders without due process—was not what HRW hoped for. But it was clear that he took note of the ICC threat, at least in the short term.

However, given the continued widespread abuses in Afghanistan, including by the very General Dostum quoted above, this story does not suggest any long-lasting deterrence or prevention.

Mali

After the 2016 conviction and sentencing of Ahmad Al Faqi Al Mahdi, an Islamic militant, on charges of destroying fabled shrines in Timbuktu, other armed groups in Mali took notice.[30] Several armed group representatives contacted the UN mission's human rights division to ask for a briefing on the concept of war crimes and crimes against humanity, and to find out whether their own past military actions could be at risk of ICC prosecution. The UN organized briefing sessions to inform them of the specific constraints set out in the international laws of war.[31]

Demobilization of Child Soldiers

One of the most frequently cited anecdotes by those who argue for a deterrent effect is based on a comment by Special Representative of the Secretary-General for the Protection of Children in Armed Conflict Radhika Coomaraswamy, in her testimony before the ICC in 2010. In the context of the trial of Thomas Lubanga, who was charged for the conscription and use of child soldiers in the DRC, she said that the ICC's prosecution for conscripting child soldiers had led several armed groups around the world to approach the UN in order to negotiate the release of child soldiers. When Lubanga was convicted, she again said that she expected the sentence would have a deterrent effect globally. She has unfortunately never clarified further details about these comments.

Elsewhere

In early 2016, I visited one of the countries that was under ICC preliminary examination. I met with the deputy minister of justice to discuss their general plans for accountability and transitional justice. He described how the ICC's attention to his country had affected him and others in government, raising concerns for possible war crimes. "I say to my colleagues in other ministries, including the Ministry of Defense, 'Be careful: the ICC can come after you. Be sure your manuals are up to date on international humanitarian law, for example.'" When the ICC asks questions, this sends signals, he said, and he and others take notice.[32]

What Determines the Deterrent Effect of International Justice?

The above examples indicate that the ICC's impact on the violence or human rights abuses can vary significantly between different countries, and even within one country at different moments in time. However, it seems very clear that when local actors feel the direct engagement and oversight of the ICC Prosecutor, it gets their attention, and they do change behavior as a result.

Analysts to date have largely focused on whether there is a generalized, global deterrent effect from the ICC, or whether mere ICC membership changes state practice, or perhaps whether specific prosecutions have affected perpetrators' actions. But the accounts above suggest that the better questions may be elsewhere. The ways in which we are seeing a deterrent effect, or otherwise seeing an effect on perpetrator behavior, seems to be different from what was first expected.

There are several interesting indications. First, the ICC's greatest deterrent effect sometimes emerges from specific actions by the Prosecutor other than investigations or prosecutions. It is the clear and specific threat of action that potential perpetrators seem to respond to—statements and warnings, rather than rolling out arrest warrants that are difficult to pull back once they are released. Second, this impacts the behavior of those closest to the situation, usually in the same country context, rather than having a dispersed or global effect. Third, deterrence is most clear where the ICC threat is perceived as real and present and immediate; the influence on perpetrator choices and actions lessens with time, as this threat is dispersed or forgotten, usually because the Prosecutor no longer shows any signs of investigating new cases in the country. Fourth and finally, the impact on the behavior of perpetrators or potential perpetrators is not always positive: ICC engagement has sometimes had unexpected, negative consequences in the reaction of those targeted.

To understand all this better, we must look at the factors that help explain the impact of international prosecutions.

Deterrence is based on threat, implicitly or explicitly. If the threat of consequences is real and effectively delivered, and the person targeted can do something to avoid the threat, then the likelihood of a positive result is greatest. The police commander in Kinshasa, the rebels in eastern Congo who quickly rid their forces of child soldiers, and the party-aligned militias in Guinea heard the message from the ICC Prosecutor, and these warnings or threats seem to have had a directly positive effect on reducing or deterring violence or rights abuses.

It is not so clear, however, that abuses were deterred in the medium to long term in those same contexts or on a more global level. When the threat of prosecution is real and present, the deterrence effect is highest. Further, when the ICC is perceived to target only one side of a conflict, the potential deterrence of crime only apparently affects that one side.

Unfortunately, there is little yet to suggest that the existence of the ICC is deterring abuses generally around the world. Some clearly hope that one day the international justice system might be ever-present and efficient enough to have such a deterrent effect everywhere (or in the countries that are members, if the ICC does not reach universal membership). But the reality of the ICC is that it can only act on a relatively small number of cases, in a relatively small number of countries, at any one time. It is really not clear how it might extend a more general "threat" over virtually everyone, everywhere.

Thus, deterrence is apparently limited in time, limited in whom it affects, and limited in the type of behavior affected.

As we saw in the previous chapter, perpetrators usually react to the ICC in a fairly rational way. When a person has already been indicted, and this is publicly announced, then his or her room for maneuver is limited. The examples of Bashir in Sudan, Kony in Uganda, Bosco in Congo, Taylor in Liberia, Kenyatta and Ruto in Kenya, and Gaddafi in Libya all tell this story: as would seem logical, they did their best to avoid any possibility of arrest and adapted their strategy with respect to peace negotiations and their engagement with the international community accordingly. In Côte d'Ivoire, the message from the Prosecutor to besieged President Gbagbo, even before he was indicted, was: you cannot escape, and no amnesty is possible. In many of these cases, the public release of arrest warrants or direct threats against targeted individuals only reduced the possibility of a negotiated solution, and in some cases led to further violence.

Indeed, as suggested above in the cases of Congo and the former Yugoslavia, the behavioral impact of the threat of ICC prosecution is not always what we might hope: rather than ceasing abuses, some perpetrators decide instead to hide any evidence—by removing or covering up mass graves, for example, or abandoning children to avoid demobilizing child soldiers whose very existence represents evidence of a war crime.[33] And sometimes perpetrators react to an arrest warrant with more abuses, as was the case of Sudanese President Omar Bashir in 2009. Strongmen who are pushed into a corner can react badly.

For those whose primary interest is preventing or deterring serious crimes, it would not make much sense to limit one's attention to prosecuting and punishing violators or even strengthening the threat of prosecutions. Needless to say, political and military leaders have a variety of motivations for changing behavior, and they may respond better to incentives, rather than threats, to prevent or halt abusive practices. In some cases, especially for rebel groups, it may be a question of providing information, training troops, and putting appropriate oversight systems in place.[34] The international credibility and respect that may result from doing this correctly (or making every effort do it correctly) can be a strong positive incentive in itself.

Many armed political movements claim (or claimed, when they were founded) a strong commitment to the idea of human rights and the rule of law—and may in fact have first taken up arms to oppose serious abuses on the part of the state. In this respect, trainings in the laws of war have been quite effective in changing the behavior of some armed groups.[35]

Conclusion

The minimal conclusion that can be reached based on the above review is that the ICC Prosecutor is not likely to accomplish her stated aim of "promoting peace" and "preventing future crimes" unless she considers not only the crimes committed and the evidentiary base for prosecution, but also the likely impact of her actions. The belief that *any* form of criminal justice for serious crime will have a deterrent or preventive effect—regardless of timing, the indictee targeted, or sensitivity to the local political context—does not appear credible. Indeed, it may be dangerous.

The unfortunate results of a blind faith in a deterrent effect are two-fold: first, there is a greater risk of having a negative, rather than positive, impact on perpetrator behavior. And second, opportunities to increase the likelihood of having a positive impact will be missed.

The next chapter shows how prosecutors, and international prosecutors especially, have choices to make. There is an important opportunity for the Prosecutor to deploy her existing prosecutorial discretion to improve the impact of the Court, increasing the likelihood of deterring further violations and decreasing the possibility that the ICC may unintentionally do damage to credible efforts towards peace.

Notes

1 Indeed, as noted above, the policy of some human rights organization is to avoid taking any position on conflict or peace, as long as the war is being fought in a manner that respects the laws of war.

2 See the historical review of the idea of deterrence in international criminal law in Kate Cronin-Furman, "Managing Expectations: International Criminal Trials and the Prospects for Deterrence of Mass Atrocity," *International Journal of Transitional Justice* 7:3 (2013): 434–439.

3 Ibid., 437.

4 Jan Klabbers, "Just Revenge? The Deterrence Argument in International Criminal Law," *Finnish Yearbook of International Law* 12 (2001): 251.

5 James F. Alexander, "The International Criminal Court and the Prevention of Atrocities: Predicting the Court's Impact," *Villanova Law Review* 54:1 (2009): 9.

6 Cronin-Furman, "Managing Expectations," 434.

7 David Wippman, "Atrocities, Deterrence, and the Limits of International Justice," *Fordham International Law Journal* 23 (1999): 474. This was also the conclusion of David Bosco, writing that in the ICC Rome Conference, "Other preventive theories were discussed during the negotiations, although far less frequently . . . (I)n general, deterrence displaced discussion of broader preventive theories, including incapacitation, rehabilitation, education, stigmatization, and moral pressure." David Bosco, "The International Criminal Court and Crime Prevention: Byproduct or Conscious Goal?" *Michigan State Journal of International Law*, 19:1 (2011): 174.

8 Bosco, "Crime Prevention," 175.

9 Mark Kersten, "The ICC in the Central African Republic: The Death of Deterrence?" *Justice in Conflict* (blog), 11 Dec 2013, www.justiceinconflict.org.

10 Balkees Jarrah, "Why U.S. Should Back ICC Role in Syria," *CNN Global Public Square* (blog), 25 Sept 2013, www.globalpublicsquare.blogs.cnn.com.

11 Hyeran Jo and Beth Simmons, "Can the International Criminal Court Deter Atrocity?" 18 Dec 2014, ssrn.com/abstract=2552820.

12 Geoff Dancy, Bridget Marchesi, Florencia Montal, and Kathryn Sikkink, "The ICC's Deterrent Impact: What the Evidence Shows," *OpenGlobalRights* (blog), 3 Feb 2015, www.opendemocracy.net/openglobalrights. For deterrence and national prosecutions, see Hunjoon Kim and Kathryn Sikkink, "Explaining the Deterrence Effect of Human Rights Prosecutions for Transitional Countries," *International Studies Quarterly* 54 (Dec 2010): 939–963.

13 States that ratify the Rome Statute are more likely in any case to be in a transitional moment where a reduction of human rights atrocities can be expected, for example. Two of these studies suggest Uganda as a case where abuses by the Lord's Resistance Army decreased when the ICC warrants were released, but this does not take into account the context of peace negotiations being launched or the increase in violations once again when the peace talks broke down. See, for example, Jack Snyder and Leslie Vinjamuri, "To Prevent Atrocities, Count on Politics First, Law Later," *OpenGlobalRights* (blog), 12 May 2015, www.opendemocracy.net/openglobalrights.

14 Luis Moreno Ocampo, "Building a Future on Peace and Justice," address at Nuremberg, 24–25 June 2007, www.icc-cpi.int.

15 ICC Office of the Prosecutor, "Strategic Plan June 2012–2015," 11 Oct 2013, www.icc-cpi.int.

16 Michael Broache, "Beyond Deterrence: The ICC Effect in the DRC," *OpenGlobalRights* (blog), 19 Feb 2015, www.opendemocracy.net/openglobalrights.

17 Rebecca DiLeonardo, "ICC Prosecutor: DRC Election Violence Will Not Be Tolerated," *Jurist: Paper Chase* (blog), 6 Dec 2011, www.jurist.org.
18 As recounted by a UN staff member in Congo at the time.
19 Interview, UN staff member, 2012.
20 Jeffrey Gettleman, "Spurts of Violence Punctuate Calm After Kenyan Vote Is Upheld," *NY Times*, 31 March 2013.
21 See, for example: Michela Wrong, "Indictee for President!" *NY Times Latitude* (blog), 11 Mar 2013, latitude.blogs.nytimes.com.
22 Interview with ICC OTP staff.
23 Juan E. Méndez, "Transitional Justice, Peace, and Prevention," address at the University of Baltimore Law School, 26 Oct 2010, 13 (on file with author).
24 Juan E. Méndez, "The Importance of Justice in Securing Peace," Review Conference of the Rome Statute, 30 May 2010, ICC Doc. RC/ST/PJ/INF.3, para 18. See also "Statement by the Special Advisor on the Prevention of Genocide," 15 Nov 2004, www.un.org/News/dh/infocus/westafrica/mendez-15nov2004.htm.
25 ICC Office of the Prosecutor, "Widespread or Systematic Killings in Côte d'Ivoire May Trigger OTP Investigation," 6 Apr 2011.
26 Mike McGovern, "The Ivorian Endgame: Can Ouattara Rebuild a Shattered Country?" *Foreign Affairs*, 14 Apr 2011. Gbagbo was subsequently arrested in his residence by military forces and later in the year transferred to The Hague on an ICC warrant.
27 Interviews by author of former NTC commanders and political leaders, Tripoli and Misrata, Libya, Feb 2013.
28 Mahmoud Jibril, interview by author, Tripoli, Feb 2013.
29 Human Rights Watch, *Selling Justice Short: Why Accountability Matters for Peace* (New York: Human Rights Watch, July 2009), 123–124. It cites Ilene Prusher, "Battling Warlords Try Civility," *Christian Science Monitor*, 9 May 2002, and its own HRW report, *Paying for the Taliban's Crimes: Abuses Against Ethnic Pashtuns in Northern Afghanistan* (New York: Human Rights Watch, Apr 2002), www.hrw.org.
30 This was the only ICC prosecution to date solely on charges of cultural destruction as a war crime. Specifically, Al Mahdi was convicted of deliberate destruction of the historical and religious monuments in Timbuktu, Mali, in 2012. He pled guilty and was sentenced to nine years in jail.
31 UN staff member, citing internal UN briefing on Mali mission.
32 Comments made in a private meeting by author, 2016.
33 In the case of the Srebrenica massacre in Bosnia Herzegovina, for example, there was evidence that the Serbian forces began to move and disguise mass graves after the ICTY announced that it might look at this case.
34 For example, the independent organization Geneva Call works with non-state armed groups to obtain commitments to respect specific norms of international humanitarian law. Geneva Call provides intensive training to each group that is ready to make such a commitment, working closely with force commanders, and monitors compliance thereafter, publicly reporting any violations. (I served on the Board of Directors of Geneva Call from 2006 to 2015.)
35 Ibid.

7 A Prosecutor's Discretion in Contexts of Conflict

International courts work in intensely political contexts. Their actions affect local politics, and they are fundamentally affected by local political dynamics. It is clear that they can also directly impact on peacemaking or on violence; at some times this has been their aim, at other times this effect is unintentional.

The obvious question before us, therefore, is to what degree contextual factors or dynamics, and an assessment of likely impact, should be taken into account in the decisions of a prosecutor? This chapter, and the next, attempt to assess how, whether, and when international courts should try to balance a host of factors and interests in its decisions, beyond simply evidentiary questions.

Focusing especially on the ICC, this chapter will argue the need for a strategic approach that takes advantage of the existing powers of the prosecutor to exercise discretion. Employing discretion and making choices are necessary and inescapable for a prosecutor whose jurisdiction covers the majority of countries of the world.

Context and Choice

Justice advocates have often warned of the risk of the ICC being politicized or vulnerable to political pressures if it were to consider factors other than purely evidentiary and case-specific elements when it takes decisions. If it tries to prejudge the likely impact of its actions, it would surely go wrong, given the complexity of each context and the fast-moving changes in the local context, advocates argue. If the Prosecutor made it clear that she was open to changing her approach based on non-evidentiary factors, this could expose her to lobbying, including by those who have personal or political interests at stake.

While the aim of being "non-political" and "non-politicized" would generally be accepted as the correct standard to ensure fair justice in generic terms, these intentions are quickly challenged under the glare of ICC realities. How is it possible to work free of influence of a multitude of local factors that are central to building a case and that are, at the end of the day, essentially political, or at least directly impact on political actors and interests? The challenge of sustaining neutrality in its operations is that the very nature of the work of the ICC runs directly into forceful political interests, and the Court is unlikely to be successful if it fails to recognize and understand these, and in some cases adjust the prosecutorial strategy to take this into account.

In fact, the ICC Office of the Prosecutor (OTP) itself, as well as independent advocates for the interests of the ICC, recognize that it is impossible to work free of political forces. The OTP three-year strategic plan published in 2013 explicitly acknowledged that its results would be influenced by "the political dynamics surrounding each situation."[1] This is inescapable, given the realities inherent in its mandate.

One prominent analyst of international justice, Carsten Stahn, who previously worked in the office of the ICC judges, notes that the work of the ICC cannot be compared with prosecutions in domestic contexts:

> International criminal courts are almost a different species. They involve highly political cases, but accountability structures are typically less developed . . . Moreover, [prosecutors] tend to downplay the political dimensions of their decisions. They are forced to make highly sensitive and political decisions in the context of the investigation and prosecution of international crimes. But they prefer to label their courses of action by reference to the application of enforcement of the law.[2]

Many ICC proponents acknowledge that the prosecutor's actions will affect politics, and her office will likewise be affected by politics. But they are wary of the threat of undue "political" influence. The director of the International Justice Program at Human Rights Watch, Richard Dicker, says that the cardinal rule for the prosecutor is to be "firmly grounded in independence from political influence or pressures." But the prosecutor "should not be oblivious to the political environment—just not driven or influenced by pressures of the environment in making key prosecutorial decisions."[3] His colleague, HRW Legal and Policy Director James Ross, argues that "Every single thing you do, as a prosecutor, will be looked at with a political lens, and it would be naïve not to recognize that." But a prosecutor should try to minimize this to the degree possible. One must not only be impartial, but be seen to be impartial.[4] Human Rights Watch has elsewhere criticized the ICC Prosecutor for being insufficiently rooted in the local environment; they argue that the OTP should increase its in-country presence so that it better understands the contexts where it is engaged.[5]

Certainly, it should serve the interests of the prosecutor to understand the political context where she or he is working. The results of being more politically attuned are evident in some of its cases. It is not coincidental that the Prosecutor brought charges against three persons from each side of the tense political divide in Kenya; many Kenyan experts had warned of a violent reaction if one "side" was targeted by the ICC more than the other was. International human rights advocates are nevertheless uncomfortable that prosecutorial decisions might be affected in this way; it somehow feels contrary to the fundamental principle of working free of political influence. But shouldn't it be a priority for the prosecutor not to be the cause of further violence, if such a threat is foreseen?

The ICC Prosecutor's actions have been criticized as lacking understanding or appreciation of the local context in some countries. In Sudan, Uganda, Colombia, and elsewhere, the timing or manner of the prosecutor's engagement has at times been seen as unhelpful, even damaging, and seemingly unaware of local realities. As suggested below, this may be improving.

With a mandate strongly focused on trying to prevent violations, as outlined in the previous chapter, it seems even more difficult to ignore these contextual considerations.

Under a different court—that of the Special Court for Sierra Leone, in reference to the Liberian peace talks—we see an example of an international prosecutor who was quite intentional in trying to impact the political (and therefore human rights) context. He decided to release the warrant against Liberian President Charles Taylor at the time and in a manner that would have the greatest political effect. He explained his reasoning: "I wanted to embarrass and delegitimize Taylor in front of his West African colleagues and make it impossible for him to continue as head of state," he told me.[6] Likewise, the choices of former ICC Prosecutor Luis Moreno Ocampo, including his frequent public statements, were often perceived as aiming for a political effect, such as trying to discredit, sideline, or threaten senior officials, and thereby affecting what they could or could not do. He denied such intentions.

It is important to protect the independence and credibility of the Prosecutor and ensure that the institution as a whole retains public trust. But this cannot mean that the Court should be oblivious to factors outside of specific evidentiary considerations for prosecuting a case. Many questions that must be considered from a prosecutorial perspective will be affected, and the analysis strengthened, by a close understanding of local context and political realities. These factors may affect OTP decisions on timing (when to engage), pace (how fast to move forward on investigations or indictments), public outreach (informing the local population of the Court's work), targeting decisions (whom to indict, when), and public posture (when and whether to make public statements or warnings). The Prosecutor has the power to exercise discretion in all of these areas, as set out further below. Her work, and the effect of the Court as a whole on both justice and peace, could be strengthened by fully employing this prosecutorial discretion.

The ICC Prosecutor's Posture Towards Peace

Part of strategy, evidently, is understanding context. This would seem a natural point of departure in any national context: prosecuting leaders of organized crime networks at the domestic level might be futile—and may well exacerbate the problem—if undertaken without understanding the structures and the likely effect of the targeted prosecution of certain leaders. In war contexts, one point of analysis should be the expected impact on the conflict and on the stranglehold on power that the targeted person may hold. This does not imply that criminal justice should be held off for the most powerful. Rather, context, timing, and strategy should be considered carefully when determining how a prosecution is done.

Contexts of active peace mediation, such as Colombia and Uganda, have highlighted the tensions that develop when the actions of the ICC Prosecutor are perceived as hindering a peace effort. Both government officials and civil society advocates have expressed discomfort, sometimes profound discomfort, with ICC interventions that seem to be unaware of local dynamics and the impact its engagement may have. The discomfort is not so much with the fact of the ICC Prosecutor investigating, or even the release of arrest warrants. Rather, the frustration with the ICC is usually a response to the Prosecutor's making public threats, sometimes ill-timed, as well as with the OTP's explicit intention to influence national court decisions or the wording of a peace agreement. This level of intervention has felt inappropriate to both nationals and non-nationals who have worked hard to stop a raging war or who are trying to advance human rights protections on a broader level.

The policy and practice of the ICC Prosecutor's office seems to be evolving on these questions. The first Chief Prosecutor, Luis Moreno Ocampo, started with a fairly broad understanding of his mandate, but later settled on a relatively hardline position against acknowledging or taking into account local contextual factors, such as an assessment of conflict dynamics. He insisted that he would follow justice "blindly," pursuing accused war criminals "solely based on the evidence," with no other factors influencing his decisions, the timing of his actions, or how public he would be with arrest warrants. He argued at an international conference in 2007 that "As the Prosecutor of the ICC, I was given a clear judicial mandate. My duty is to apply the law without political considerations."[7] But this only raised further questions: was it possible, and was it indeed preferable, to ignore the political context when prosecuting a country's highest leaders, and especially in the midst of a war? Probably impossible, and probably unwise, even for the Prosecutor's own interests: after all, how an arrest warrant is handled will directly affect the likelihood of arrest, for example.

Fatou Bensouda became the second Chief Prosecutor in 2012. She has clearly grappled with how her work might affect conflict and peacemaking. Although she has defined one of her primary aims as "promoting peace" through preventing and deterring crimes, she at least initially rejected the idea that she could take into account the interests of peace in her decision-making or prosecutorial strategy. "As the ICC is an independent and judicial institution, it cannot take into consideration the interests of peace," she wrote in the *New York Times* in 2013.[8]

Over the next years, the Prosecutor continued to emphasize that the Court had a central role in promoting and achieving peace, and her position seemed to evolve somewhat. When I interviewed her in 2016, she told me that "The very reason for establishing the Court was to contribute to peace and security in the world."

In this respect, she said, her operational decision-making was attuned to local conflict dynamics and constantly evaluating the risk of aggravating violence. "Yes, we take into account the interest of peace," she said. "Why are we intervening? To bring back peace. We are sensitive to that: we are not spoilers. Our intervention should not aggravate the plight of victims." This issue was constantly on her mind, she said, and was evaluated throughout her assessment and engagement in any particular context.[9]

In this sense, she saw that there is a risk in peace and justice actors working on parallel and separate tracks, and she called for better communication and understanding between these two groups. Her office was trying to be sensitive to the interests of peace mediators, she told me, just as peacemakers should be careful not to do damage to the prospects for justice.

Still, in operational terms, the Office of the Prosecutor continued to define their options narrowly. In a major speech in Oslo in 2015, the Prosecutor explored these tensions in detail.

> We are of course fully aware of the political realities and sensitivities involved, and indeed, we are keen to play a constructive role within the prescribed limits of our mandate . . . For instance, we will inform political actors and mediators of our actions in advance, so that they can factor investigations into their activities.[10]

But the idea of adjusting her own work in response to the realities of a peace process clearly remained uncomfortable. In the same Oslo speech, she set out the line that she would not cross. "Political considerations relating to peace and security . . . certainly do not and will never form part of the decision-making in the Office of the Prosecutor," she stated. Prosecutions lead to deterrence, and thus promote "sustainable peace," she said. "Law and justice will *not* be sacrificed at the altar of political expediency to the detriment of victims. Violence left untamed by the virtues of justice will beget a cycle of violence."

In this evolving landscape, challenges remain. The Prosecutor's explicit recognition of the tensions between the overlapping aims of justice and peacemaking is a step forward, as is her openness to regular communication with those working at a political level. But there is more room for maneuver on the part of the Prosecutor than she seems ready to accept.

The resolution to some elements of the peace-justice dilemma can be found in a strategic approach by an international prosecutor, attuned to timing, understanding local dynamics, and an appreciation that justice extends beyond criminal prosecutions. Justice interests should be considered in the long term, and with a holistic understanding of the broader interest of victims. Such an approach should incorporate all tools at the Prosecutor's disposal, using the discretion that is inherent in her mandate.

Prosecutorial Discretion

With a vast array of possible situations and cases to focus on, an international prosecutor must make choices. The U.S. Law Library defines prosecutorial discretion as the "power to choose whether or not to bring criminal charges, and what charges to bring in cases where evidence would justify charges."[11]
Legal scholar Carsten Stahn further notes that:

> Discretion extends to various types of decisions, such as the decision whether or not to investigate or prosecute, the selection of charges, the timing of charges, and the determination of the forum of adjudication.[12]

Stahn describes such prosecutorial discretion as "a necessity in international criminal tribunals like the ICC," noting that they must choose "whom to prosecute, when to prosecute, and how to sequence cases."[13] These aspects of the prosecutor's work are not well regulated by the Rome Statute, leaving many aspects open. However, "discretionary powers are not arbitrary or unchecked powers. The very concept of discretion is based upon the assumption that there are rules and limitations which define the boundaries of discretion."[14] Legal scholars agree that such discretion is not only allowed but is a necessity in international tribunals.[15]

The discretion of the Prosecutor can serve both internal and external goals. James Goldston, executive director of the Open Society Justice Initiative, highlights aspects of the Prosecutor's discretion that could strengthen the Court's own effectiveness:

> It is essential to be guided by 'the law' and 'the evidence.' But in many situations doing so may not sufficiently narrow the range of possible charges or perpetrators. The prosecutor may have to consider other factors as well in deciding how to proceed.
>
> These might include the need to demonstrate the court's viability (for example, by charging at a level or in a manner that prevents states from simply ignoring the court's orders); its efficacy (by charging persons who may readily be apprehended); its efficiency (by limiting the number of charges, and thereby the length of trials); or its independence (in appropriate circumstances, by charging officials of governments which have referred situations to the court).[16]

But strategic considerations should go beyond the internal interests of the Court, such as efficacy and independence. The Court should also consider the impact of its actions in the places where it works.

International human rights organizations that have argued for limited prosecutorial discretion have met with criticism from legal scholars. Solicitor Henry Lovat writes,

> while it may well be a challenging task, there is no reason why it should not be possible to construct a set of guidelines which would preserve the

discretion of the Prosecutor, as well as ensure the legitimacy and credibility of the OTP and of the ICC.[17]

Stahn takes a similar position, suggesting:

> The most compelling argument in favour of prosecutorial discretion in the initiation of investigation, the choice of perpetrators and prosecutorial strategy is not the quantity and nature of crimes, but the political ramifications of indictments and selection. Prosecutorial discretion may be defended on the ground that it involves certain political choices which the Prosecutor's office is best placed to make in light of its presence on the ground and its close ties to domestic and international authorities.[18]

Discretion is relevant to an international prosecutor in a number of different ways. These include, but of course are not limited to, the following:

Timing

Whether opening an investigation, requesting an arrest warrant, unsealing a warrant that may have been sealed, or making general public statements, the question of "when" has to be considered. While the ICC OTP is already aware of timing in many of the steps that it takes, it is useful to ask whether it is using this de facto flexibility to the maximum effect. In some cases, this directly confronts the question of impact on an ongoing peace process.

Prescribing a general strategy on the timing of ICC action would be impossible. For example, while it is commonly assumed that peace would be best served by avoiding a confrontation with international arrest warrants during peace talks, we have seen one clear case (Liberia, in relation to the warrant for President Taylor by the Special Court for Sierra Leone) in which the impact on reaching a peace agreement was unexpectedly positive.

The OTP's policy has been to especially take local security or political factors into account when timing its visits, in consideration for the safety of its staff. If there were ongoing violence or other evident security risks, the OTP would hold off on a visit to the country or avoid traveling to certain areas. But at least some of its senior legal experts have felt that these factors should not be part of an analysis in taking prosecutorial decisions.[19]

The difficult question of timing is relevant well beyond the ICC. Prosecutions based on universal jurisdiction laws, such as exist in a number of European countries, should also consider these questions. Does it serve a country's interests, or victims' interests, for a person to be arrested while partaking in peace talks, if this would damage the talks and perhaps limit the prospects for peace? Might it be more effective to wait for a better moment a bit later? How much weight should legal and human rights advocates give to such political processes? It seems clear that a focus on victims' interests would grant considerable respect to the need to stop the fighting. A strategic delay in prosecutions might allow a peace process to move forward.

Should an Arrest Warrant Be Public or Sealed?

One important decision for the Prosecutor is whether to publicly announce a request for an arrest warrant or to put this under seal, so that it is shared selectively when and if a government is in a position to make an arrest. In such cases, even the existence of the arrest warrant would be kept confidential until the arrest takes place.

After the ICC confirmed the arrest warrant for Muammar Gaddafi, analyst Alison Cole argued that the prosecutor made a mistake in not keeping the warrant sealed. Looking at the ICC's record to date, she concluded, "In all cases where arrests were achieved, the arrest warrants were first issued under seal for several weeks or months, then unsealed and made public on the day of the arrest."[20] In contrast, warrants in many high profile cases, including President Gaddafi and President Bashir of Sudan, were released publicly from the start. Others, such as for the Lord's Resistance Army leadership in Uganda, were initially sealed but then unsealed after a few months, losing the opportunity that might have come with confidentiality. A sealed arrest warrant provides a greater possibility of securing arrest. It is also friendlier to a peace process, in most cases.

In considering how to handle the case of President Bashir, former Prosecutor Moreno Ocampo told me that his office reviewed past experiences in other contexts, and they concluded that a sealed warrant for a head of state was not practical.[21] Staff within the Prosecutor's office described a process of consultation with a number of states parties; most states did not think it would be appropriate to arrest a visiting head of state based on a surprise, sealed arrest warrant. The Prosecutor's office was also skeptical that a sealed warrant for a head of state would remain confidential. It was for these reasons that ICC warrants for the highest level of state power were made public, they explained.

But there are strong critics of the decision to go public with this arrest warrant, as well as the decision to target the head of state in Sudan rather than other senior officials where success may have been more likely (addressed below). The public nature of the indictment made it virtually impossible to gain Bashir's arrest; it halted any prospect of cooperation with the ICC by the Sudanese state in relation to this or other cases; it aggravated a revengeful response from Bashir against human rights and humanitarian actors; it entrenched Bashir and his cohorts in power, as they closed ranks and dug in, in order to protect themselves from the ICC; and all of this ultimately weakened the credibility of the Court.[22] Thus, it seems that the public arrest warrant against Bashir worsened any prospects for peace in relation to a number of difficult conflicts in the country.

It may be that an arrest warrant for a head of state should be evaluated differently than for other officials. But experience to date challenges the wisdom of announcing the warrant publicly from the start. President Charles Taylor traveled to Ghana to preside over the opening of the Liberian peace talks without knowing that there was a warrant for his arrest; the government of

Ghana also did not know. He fled back to Liberia as soon as the warrant was unsealed. It is highly unlikely Taylor would have traveled if the warrant had been announced earlier; it is also unlikely he would have agreed to a peace conference if he knew in advance that he would be written out of any future role. As outlined elsewhere in this book, Gaddafi also reportedly felt cornered by the indictment against him.

Under Fatou Bensouda, the second Chief Prosecutor, there appears to be a greater reliance on sealed rather than public warrants, although it continues to evaluate each case on its own merits. The question of sealed versus public arrest warrants is most often considered in relation to the likelihood of obtaining the arrest of an individual.[23] It is equally important, however, in relation to the ICC's impact on a braoder array of issues pertaining to stability and peace.

Targeting: Deciding Whom to Prosecute

International tribunals have taken into account political and other local factors—including a calculation of whether its actions could spark further violence—in identifying targets for prosecution. As noted above in Kenya, the prosecutor charged three persons on each side of the political divide, having been duly warned that prosecutions perceived as targeting one side of the ethnic and political divide more than the other could easily trigger violence. In Sierra Leone, the prosecutor indicted three people from each of the three main fighting groups, even though the rebels were thought to be much more complicit in serious crimes.

The OTP strategic plan for 2012–2015 opened the possibility of prosecuting lower-level persons before moving to the most senior level, moving away from past practice of only targeting the highest-level persons from the start. The OTP wrote,

> a strategy of gradually building upwards might . . . be needed in which the Office first investigates and prosecutes a limited number of mid- and high-level perpetrators in order to ultimately have a reasonable prospect of conviction for those most responsible.[24]

This may be a response to a critique of the office over previous years.

Sudan experts saw the arrest warrant for President Bashir of Sudan, for crimes in Darfur, as counter-productive in several ways. Targeting persons directly complicit in the crimes at the second tier of the security apparatus, instead, might have engendered continued cooperation from the president and the government as a whole and helped build a foundation for higher-level indictments later. Rather, the arrest warrant for Bashir entrenched him in power as he prioritized protecting himself from arrest. Waiting until he left power would also have increased the likelihood of an arrest warrant being carried out. Instead, President Bashir remained in power, unlikely to leave his post and resisting the ICC at every turn.

Assessing Complementarity: What Is Sufficient Justice at the National Level?

What is sufficient national action to comply with state obligations to investigate and prosecute, as required by the Rome Statute? And how much flexibility should be allowed, so that a state has some leeway in crafting a national strategy on justice and punishment? In the parlance of the ICC, this is a question of "complementarity": the principle set out in the Rome Statute that the ICC only holds jurisdiction where national authorities have not fulfilled their obligation to investigate and prosecute.[25]

Interpreting this "complementarity" provision of the Rome Statute is difficult on both legal and operational grounds, and there have been volumes dedicated to its many interrelated questions. Clearly, this provision leaves considerable room for the ICC Prosecutor's discretion in deciding whether to act. It is particularly tricky when national authorities do take steps to prosecute, but the ICC Prosecutor concludes the intended punishment is insufficient. To date, the OTP has taken a fairly narrow stance towards this question.

This became evident and met strong national resistance and even anger in the context of Colombia, when the OTP intervened on the question of national sentencing requirements. A confidential letter from the ICC Prosecutor to the Colombian Constitutional Court, which was quickly leaked to the public, advised that a full suspension of a sentence—even if balanced with other contributions such as reparations—was unacceptable and could result in the ICC opening prosecutions in the country.[26] In response to the letter, a few weeks later the Constitutional Court included this restriction—no suspension of sentences—in its preliminary decision, announced in August 2013, that set out the parameters for justice in the peace talks with the FARC. (The final Constitutional Court decision, released in December 2013, was more nuanced on this question.[27])

Both the government of Colombia and many national human rights advocates were sharply critical of this level of ICC intervention into Colombian affairs. Commentators saw the ICC's involvement as making the prospects for peace more difficult. Further, as noted by rights advocates in Colombia and internationally, the Rome Statute provides no guidance on sentencing, and international law is otherwise not clear on the question.[28] One prominent Colombian rights expert suggested that this kind of intervention in the Constitutional Court's decision-making would be an impeachable offense if done by a national-level prosecutor.[29]

The OTP saw the situation differently.[30] For the ICC, this was, first, a question of precedent. How could the Prosecutor allow minimal, symbolic, or suspended sentences in Colombia—perhaps in exchange for truth or reparations—unless they accepted the same for Congo, Sudan, or Kenya? Other countries might conclude that an alternative justice arrangement, with no prison time, was a means to escape the ICC's reach. Thus, the OTP's response to Colombia was partly shaped by its interest in setting rigorous standards for justice and punishment everywhere.

Second, the Prosecutor felt that she must inform the Colombian authorities when she believed that a proposed arrangement would not meet Rome

Statute requirements. In a visit to Colombia, OTP staff had heard of plans to sentence perpetrators based on confessions, in order to meet the obligation to prosecute, but then to immediately suspend the sentences. Colombian authorities had asked that the OTP communicate any concerns that it might have. Thus, the letter from the Prosecutor was sent not just to the Constitutional Court but also to other Colombian authorities whom the OTP staff had met. The OTP felt that it would be better to relay their concerns immediately rather than risk derailing the process after an agreement was reached.

A year and a half later, the ICC Deputy Prosecutor delivered a lecture in Bogota that set out publicly the OTP views on sentencing. While maintaining its rejection of suspended sentences, much more flexibility was offered in the arena of alternative and reduced sentences.[31] This was a valuable contribution that provided national authorities more specific guidance on ICC requirements. The form of presentation was also welcomed: the OTP may indeed have avoided the earlier criticism and anger if it had chosen to relay its views in some public form rather than through a confidential letter that was widely perceived as inappropriately and secretly influencing a national court decision.

After the negative reaction to her letters to the Constitutional Court, as well as other recent statements insisting on criminal justice for all crimes of the war, the ICC Prosecutor was reported to have shifted her stance when she met with Colombia's President Santos a few weeks later. Her words had been misunderstood, the Prosecutor told him. "She showed a strong willingness to support our peace negotiations with the FARC," President Santos said after the meeting. "They do not want to become an obstacle, but rather they want to be an engine of the process."[32]

An important decision by the Inter-American Court of Human Rights, in 2012, may signal the direction of the legal community as it grapples more openly with the dilemmas around justice in peace processes. After years of consistently strict interpretations that limited or overruled national amnesty laws, the Court opened the door to some flexibility in contexts of a negotiated end to conflict. While this decision pertained to El Salvador, it was seen as most relevant and helpful to Colombia, providing guidance on how the Inter-American Court would evaluate an alternative justice arrangement.

The question of whether a sufficient number of investigations and prosecutions have taken place, or if sentences are sufficiently punitive, will remain difficult for those trying to assess this from an international perspective. Ultimately, behind these questions lies the more general, critical issue of whether the ICC Prosecutor specifically, and the international community generally, should grant national actors greater room to maneuver in the timing and reach of its justice programs after large-scale crimes.

The Prosecutor's Bully Pulpit

When should an international prosecutor speak out publicly to warn leaders of possible criminal prosecutions, with the aim of changing behavior and averting a threatened bloodbath? There are a number of important, positive examples where threats from the ICC have helped to deter violence. There are also examples where the Prosecutor has been criticized for intervening inappropriately or unhelpfully. As set out above in Chapter 5 and Chapter 6, these interventions have included well-timed public statements and warnings, direct meetings with local political leaders to convey concerns, and visits to a country with the intention of attracting significant press attention and giving a clear message. The Prosecutor also publishes substantive country reports that set out its expectations for local action with some detail and specificity.

Some of the more effective interventions have relied on the fact of the Prosecutor's power of the bully pulpit. This is and should be seen as an important element in her strategy of prevention. But, as suggested in some of the cases in the previous chapter, this should be used carefully, with full appreciation for timing and intent, and with care not to abuse or overuse. The Prosecutor and her office has shown an increasing appreciation for this difficult balancing.

Conclusion

The above elements of prosecutorial discretion are inherent in the work of an international prosecutor's responsibilities. Most of these are implicit rather than explicit powers and are flexible in how they might be interpreted and applied: that is, of course, the nature of discretion. The ICC Prosecutor has many choices to make and room to maneuver.

In addition, there is another element of discretion that is special to the ICC. The next chapter will look at the notion of the "interests of justice," as set out in the Rome Statute, which gives the Prosecutor a reason to look beyond criminal evidence and further opens the door for her to consider the impact of the ICC on victims and on peace.

Notes

1 ICC Office of the Prosecutor, "Strategic Plan June 2012–2015," 11 Oct 2013, www.icc-cpi.int.
2 Carsten Stahn, "Judicial Review of Prosecutorial Discretion: Five Years On," in Carsten Stahn and Goran Sluiter, eds., *The Emerging Practice of the International Criminal Court* (Leiden: Nijhoff, 2009), 248.
3 Richard Dicker, interview by author, New York, 23 Dec 2013.
4 James Ross, interview by author, Geneva, 15 June 2012.
5 See the useful discussion on how the ICC could increase its impact in Human Rights Watch, *Making Justice Count: Lessons From the ICC's Work in Côte d'Ivoire*, 4 Aug 2015, www.hrw.org.
6 David Crane, interview by author, July 2006.
7 Luis Moreno Ocampo, "Building a Future on Peace and Justice," address at Nuremberg, 24–25 June 2007, www.icc-cpi.int.
8 Fatou Bensouda, "International Justice and Diplomacy," *NY Times* (op ed), 19 March 2013.
9 Fatou Bensouda, interview by author, The Hague, 20 Oct 2016.
10 Fatou Bensouda, "The Peace-Justice Interface: Where Are We Now and What Are the Challenges Ahead?" in Paul Dziatkowiec, Christina Buchhold,

Jonathan Harlander, and Massimiliano Verri, *Peacemaking in the New World Disorder: Oslo Forum Meeting Report* (Geneva: Centre for Humanitarian Dialogue, 2015), 24–27, www.hdcentre.org.

11　See "Prosecution: Prosecutorial Discretion," *Law Library: American Law and Legal Information*, law.jrank.org. This is the definition used by Carsten Stahn, for example, although he notes that others define the concept somewhat more narrowly. See Stahn, "Judicial Review," 247, note 1.

12　Stahn, "Judicial Review," 247.

13　Ibid., 252.

14　Ibid.

15　For example, a review by scholar Jens David Ohlin concludes that "The standard view in the literature recognizes wide prosecutorial discretion to the ICC Prosecutor." Jens David Ohlin, "Peace, Security, and Prosecutorial Discretion," in Stahn and Sluiter, eds., *Emerging Practice*, 187.

16　James A. Goldston, "The International Criminal Court: Justice and Politics," *OpenDemocracy* (blog), 13 Jan 2010, www.opendemocracy.net.

17　Henry Lovat, "Delineating the Interests of Justice," *Denver Journal of International Law and Policy* 35 (2007): 286.

18　Stahn, "Judicial Review," 256.

19　Interview with ICC OTP staff, Nov 2013.

20　Alison Cole, "Gaddafi Might Have Been Arrested by Now If the ICC's Warrant Had Been Sealed," *Open Society Blog* (Guardian Legal Network), 31 Aug 2011, www.theguardian.com.

21　Luis Moreno Ocampo, interview by author, March 2010.

22　Kai Sheffield, "Speak Softly and Carry a Sealed Warrant: Building the International Criminal Court's Legitimacy in the Wake of Sudan," *Appeal: Review of Current Law and Law Reform* 18 (2013): 163–175.

23　See, for example, "Report on Arrest Strategies by the Rapporteur," Annex VII to the Report of the Bureau on Cooperation, 21 Nov 2014, ICC-ASP/13/29/Add.1.

24　ICC Office of the Prosecutor, "Strategic Plan June 2012–2015," 11 Oct 2013, www.icc-cpi.int.

25　This is set out in Article 17 of the Rome Statute, which addresses admissibility.

26　The letters from the Prosecutor to the Colombian Constitutional Court are provided in a link to the following story: "Una Carta Bomba: La Fiscal de la Corte Penal Internacional se le atraviesa al Marco Jurídico para la Paz," *Semana.com*, 17 Aug 2013, www.semana.com/nacion/articulo/una-carta-bomba/354430-3.

27　"Demanda de inconstitucionalidad contra el artículo 1° del Acto Legislativo 01 de 2012 (parcial)," Constitutional Court of Colombia, Decision C-579–2013, 28 Aug 2013 (released Dec 2013).

28　For example, see comments by Rodrigo Uprimny, Executive Director, Centro de Estudios de Derecho, Justicia y Sociedad (DeJusticia), "IX Conversatorio de la Jurisdicción Constitucional: Diálogo para la Paz," Medellin, Colombia, 19 Sept 2013.

29　Comments by a Colombian human rights advocate, at a conference at Greentree, New York, 14 Nov 2013.

30　The following views were expressed in numerous conversations and interviews with OTP staff.

31　James Stewart, "Transitional Justice in Colombia and the Role of the International Criminal Court," 13 May 2015, www.icc-cpi.int.

32　Radio Caracol, "CPI respetará autonomía judicial de Colombia en proceso de paz," 24 Sept 2013, and "ICC respects Colombia's peace process: Santos," *Colombia Reports*, 25 Sept 2013.

8   Acting in the Interests of Justice

The Rome Statute directs the Prosecutor to take into account the "interests of justice" when deciding to initiate an investigation or to proceed with a prosecution after undertaking investigations. Experts disagree as to how this phrase should be understood, but the ICC Prosecutor's office has interpreted it quite narrowly, setting out its position in a policy paper in 2007.

While the OTP has suggested that the issue is now settled and that it is not interested in reconsidering the policy, this has not stopped the debate. Many experts outside the ICC argue that the language in the Rome Statute on the "interests of justice" calls for much greater flexibility, in particular when working in contexts of peace negotiations. The following reviews this debate and asks whether there may be more room to maneuver in ICC engagements than currently granted by the OTP's chosen policy.

The Rome Statute and the Interests of Justice

The Rome Statute states that the Prosecutor shall open an investigation where evidence is sufficient, the Court holds jurisdiction, and the case is otherwise admissible, unless:

> Taking into account the gravity of the crime and the interests of victims, there are nonetheless substantial reasons to believe that an investigation would not serve the interests of justice.[1]

The Statute further states that the Prosecutor may decide not to proceed with prosecution, after its investigation, if she or he concludes that:

> A prosecution is not in the interests of justice, taking into account all the circumstances, including the gravity of the crime, the interests of victims and the age or infirmity of the alleged perpetrator, and his or her role in the alleged crime.[2]

But the "interests of justice" is left undefined. Some diplomats who participated in the Rome negotiations understood this to be intentional: this wording would allow room for any number of unforeseeable factors to be considered and avoid creating an inflexible institution that was blind to context. Surprisingly, those creating the ICC did not foresee that it would work primarily in contexts of ongoing conflict. As this reality has taken shape, many have argued that the prosecutor should consider contextual factors, such as peace negotiations, before deciding to act. The logical place to do this would be through an "interests of justice" analysis.

There has been considerable discussion by legal scholars about the breadth and possible meaning of the interests of justice. Some see this language as equivalent to the "public interest" test found in British law, for example, which allows prosecutors to consider the broader impact of prosecutorial decisions, beyond the narrow question of whether there is sufficient evidence to prosecute.[3] The narrow interpretation by the OTP on understanding the "interests of justice," many analysts argue, is a choice rather than any requirement of the Rome Statute.

At the heart of the difference of views is the question of whether the concept of "justice" reaches beyond criminal prosecutions of a few high-level perpetrators, and whether the OTP should take into account other factors that will, among other things, affect the possibility of justice being carried out at the national level in the future.

This question was only briefly addressed during the discussions to establish the ICC. Some participants worried that there would be limited space for sovereign national decisions during difficult transitional moments.[4] After the Rome Statute was agreed, this issue quickly became a question in the public debate about the role of the Court. Kofi Annan, then UN Secretary-General, was asked about this just a few weeks after the Rome Statute was adopted, during a visit to South Africa. He responded, "It is inconceivable that . . . the Court would seek to substitute its judgment for that of a whole nation which is seeking the best way to put a traumatic past behind it and build a better future."[5]

Two years later, former ICTY Prosecutor Richard Goldstone and Nicole Fritz were among the first to address this at more depth in an academic article. They acknowledged that justice is "a concept which is tremendously contested—meaning different things to different people." They continued that "Democracy offers the most credible, secure basis for ordering social relations justly—it acts as a safeguard to justice," and, therefore, that "On occasions the interests of justice might compel that the transition to democracy not be imperiled and that the threat of prosecutions and punishment not be brought to bear."[6]

Another early contribution came from Darryl Robinson, a former legal officer with the Canadian Department of Foreign Affairs and International Trade, who had served on the Canadian delegation to the 1998 Rome Conference. He had been directly involved in the negotiations around Article 53, including the "interests of justice" phrasing, and recounts the spirit of the discussion at that time. He argued in 2003 that the ambiguity in the Rome

Statute in this and other articles was an intentional means of resolving strong differences of views between states during the negotiations.[7] He continued,

> A fundamental preliminary question is whether the notion of 'interests of justice' is confined only to the interests of *retributive, criminal* justice, or whether broader considerations of 'justice' can also be taken into account. The latter appears to be the only supportable interpretation. . . . [T]he ordinary meaning of this text, examined in the light of its object and purpose, suggests that 'interests of justice' is a relatively broad concept.[8]
>
> (italics in original)

Law professor Chris Gallavin, also writing in 2003, went further, suggesting that the notion of the "interests of justice" as set out in Article 53 is "grossly inadequate" for an international court.

> [U]nder international law, where law and politics are fused, it is folly to establish a permanent criminal court under which no appreciation of political realities is allowed. The Court must be politically independent but it must not, through its Prosecutor, be politically unaware.

This aspect of the Rome Statute should be expanded and strengthened, he wrote, "to cater expressly for political issues such as the effect on regional and global stability, the likelihood of retaliation and the re-instigation of hostilities that an investigation or prosecution may, themselves, procure."[9]

Carsten Stahn, writing in his personal capacity but at a time when he was also a legal officer in chambers of the ICC, wrote in 2005:

> The express distinction of the Statute between specific criteria and the general notion of the interests of justice (based on 'all the circumstances, including . . .') in Article 53(2)(c) suggests that the term 'interests of justice' may embody a broader concept, which is not only confined to considerations of 'criminal justice'. The Prosecutor might invoke the concept of interests to justify departures from classical prosecution based on both amnesties and alternative methods of providing justice.[10]

Stahn offered several guidelines to the Court, suggesting that "The Court has judicial autonomy to decide whether an amnesty, a pardon or other alternative forms of justice are permissible under the Statute."[11] The Rome Statute, he continued, "leaves both the Prosecutor and the Judges of the Court some leeway to strike a balance between the needs of a society in transition and the requirements under universal and regional treaty instruments and customary international law."[12]

Kenneth Rodman, professor of government at Colby College, argued in 2009 that law cannot be separated from politics, and that "the Prosecutor should construe his discretion broadly in order to assess the political context in which international criminal law has to operate."[13] Rather than relying on Article 53 and the interests of justice clause, however, he suggests that the ICC Prosecutor should rely on his or her "inherent discretion" in difficult contexts, such as in making choices of timing and targeting, as outlined in the previous chapter.[14]

Likewise, Cornell University Law Professor Jens David Ohlin wrote in 2009:

> One can only assume that the phrase 'interests of justice' was chosen by the Assembly of State Parties because of its broad meaning and application. Indeed, it is difficult to think of a factor that would *not* be relevant under the banner of the 'interests of justice.' One might as well have used the term "all things considered."[15]

In the midst of these academic and policymaker opinions that argue for a more flexible understanding of the interests of justice, the Prosecutor's office was beginning to articulate its own views. In the first writings on the subject, the OTP suggested flexibility in applying an "interest of justice" lens, quite similar to the other legal experts above. These ideas came through in three different documents produced or commissioned by the OTP in 2003 or 2004. The most specific recommendations on interpreting "interests of justice" came from the Expert Group on Complementarity, which was established by the OTP to advise the Prosecutor. The OTP also addressed the issue in draft regulations that were published in 2003. Finally, the OTP released a draft policy specifically on the interests of justice, in 2004. Each of these documents suggests that a context and impact analysis would be advisable.

The Expert Group on Complementarity was concerned that, in the context of the interests of justice language of Article 53, "alternative approaches forms of justice . . . should not be summarily dismissed," and that, while the mandate of the ICC is prosecution, it suggests a long list of factors by which the Court could evaluate national, complementary justice initiatives.[16]

The more general OTP draft regulations also addressed the question of how the "interests of justice" should be interpreted. It suggested that an OTP analysis of the interests of justice might take into account a range of factors. Specifically, the OTP should evaluate whether

> (a) the start of an investigation would exacerbate or otherwise destabilize a conflict situation; (b) the start of an investigation would seriously endanger the successful completion of a reconciliation or peace process; or (c) the start of an investigation would bring the law into disrepute.[17]

These basic criteria seem eminently reasonable, but they were quickly challenged by international human rights organizations, who were beginning to turn their attention to this issue and argued for a much narrower approach. The suggestions of flexibility in these first OTP documents were countered by the NGO concerns that "political" factors should be excluded.[18] Facts such as ongoing peace negotiations or alternative justice arrangements should be entirely excluded from consideration by the Prosecutor, these international human rights advocates argued. Human Rights Watch responded to the OTP draft policies with a long paper that specifically argues that none of the factors suggested by the OTP—including "bringing the law into disrepute" or "exacerbating a conflict"—should be considered by the OTP.[19]

The Human Rights Watch paper turned to the Vienna Convention on the Law of Treaties, which establishes that treaties should be interpreted according to their "object and purpose," to argue that the Rome Statute requires a narrow understanding of the interests of justice. The Rome Statute "does not permit considerations of domestic amnesties, truth processes, traditional mechanisms or peace negotiations," the paper argues, and "political decision-making regarding the impact of an investigation on international peace and security" can only be undertaken by the UN Security Council.[20]

Amnesty International also published a detailed response, primarily worried that "interests of justice" might be used by the Prosecutor to suspend investigations once they had begun. Any decision to suspend an investigation for the purpose of positively influencing peace negotiations would be political, and thus should be avoided, it said. Like Human Rights Watch, Amnesty International insisted that such decisions could only be taken by the Security Council.[21]

Amnesty International wrote that Article 53 of the Rome Statute

> is not designed to permit the Prosecutor to turn on and off criminal investigations or prosecutions to influence the pace or content of political negotiations to end armed conflicts . . . Suspension of an investigation for political reasons would be inconsistent with the spirit of international standards governing prosecutorial duties and discretion.[22]

Other analysts strongly challenged the arguments of these two organizations, particularly those in the Human Rights Watch paper.[23] They especially questioned the wisdom of relying on the Security Council to monitor and calibrate the ICC's engagement in complex and fraught contexts. I will return to the Security Council further below.

The OTP Policy on Interests of Justice

Three years after releasing its draft for comment, the OTP published its final policy paper on the interests of justice in 2007. It pulled back from many of its earlier ideas that suggested the need for contextual analysis, and instead outlined a narrow interpretation that greatly limited the possibility of the OTP relying on "interests of justice" as a reason to halt or delay action. While its position seems to closely align with the arguments of the international human rights advocates, one of the primary drafters of the policy within the OTP says that the NGO papers were not the reason for the change. Rather, the OTP concluded that "it was the most correct legal understanding of the provision in light of the objects and purposes" of the Rome Statute.[24] It also had the benefit of avoiding the unreasonable and unpredictable political pressures that might otherwise arise.

The final OTP policy on the interests of justice starts from a "strong presumption that investigations and prosecutions will be in the interests of justice"; any decision to not act based on the interests of justice, it says, would be highly exceptional.[25]

However, the policy allows that the prosecutor would consider the "interests of victims" in assessing whether investigations and prosecutions would be in the interest of justice. The policy paper does not say how the interests of victims would be determined (which victims, and how to assess their interests?), but OTP staff explain they might look for indications in victim surveys or similar mechanisms to assess whether the great majority of those who suffered the crimes were opposed to prosecutions.[26] In short, it is a very narrow understanding of both the interests of justice and the interests of victims, generally equating justice with criminal prosecutions for the immediate crimes at hand.

The policy paper includes a brief section on peace processes and concludes that interests of justice should not include concerns for peace and security, beyond possible considerations for victim and witness protection. "However, the broader matter of international peace and security is not the responsibility of the Prosecutor."[27] It also recognizes that international prosecutions may be insufficient and expresses support for the complementary approaches to justice such as truth seeking, domestic prosecutions, and victim reparations.

The process of drafting the policy paper was also an important process for clarifying its position internally. Some within the office saw it as a means to limit the expansive tendencies of the first Chief Prosecutor, who was privately signaling an interest in helping to end conflicts and was shaping his work with this in mind, through his public posture, threats, and targeting prominent war-makers. This made OTP staff nervous, and the policy paper on the interests of justice was a means to push against this idea and constrain the Prosecutor himself.[28] The OTP even felt it necessary to state that "the Prosecutor should not assume the role of a mediator," nor should the ICC be seen as a "conflict management tool"—something that would have been self-evident to those in the mediation world.[29]

As of 2016, the ICC Prosecutor has never employed the "interests of justice" clause as a reason not to open investigations or prosecutions. There are accounts of the first Prosecutor referring to the interests of justice in his meetings with interlocutors in Uganda and Colombia, but this was prior to the 2007 policy paper on the matter and was never formally articulated to the Pre-Trial Chamber as a factor in the Prosecutor's decisions.[30]

What Might "Interests of Justice" Mean in the Context of Peacemaking?

We are left in a curious position. As questions continued to be raised on the possibility of thinking beyond the OTP's narrow conception of the interests of justice, including in a high-level expert seminar in 2014 and again in 2017, exploring the subject in depth, the OTP made clear that it had no intention to further review or to change its policy.[31] This was a "settled issue," it said.[32] But the sentiments from in-country human rights practitioners and the analysis from legal experts continue to challenge this position. It is an awkward imbalance, with the OTP position often in a stark minority against strong legal arguments for a broader and contextual view.

It is clear that the Rome Statute does not prevent or discourage the Prosecutor from taking a broader view of the meaning of the "interests of justice." There is even a strong legal case that the wording of the Statute actually requires a broader interpretation.[33] At a policy level, considering the greater aims of the Court, there are also important arguments for such a broader perspective. I outline three of these here:

First, given changes at the national level in the course of a peace process, holding off on immediate prosecutions might lead to more or better justice later. There might be greater space for criminal accountability nationally or perhaps more effective international prosecutions. This is different from a "complementarity" analysis, in which the OTP must assess whether national authorities are unwilling or unable to genuinely carry out proceedings. Rather, the idea is to give space for a national transition that might include a broad justice package, recognizing that such a transition could open the doors to greater justice than is currently possible.

Second, as suggested by numerous commentators above, the concept of "justice" should be understood to be more than the criminal prosecution of a few of the worst perpetrators. It is common for peace agreements to include a range of initiatives to strengthen the rule of law and advance nonjudicial forms of justice. These may include reform of the judicial sector; vetting and removal of corrupt judges or abusive police; extending the reach of the judicial system throughout the country, including former rebel-held areas; providing reparations and trauma-recovery programs for victims; or establishing commissions to investigate the full extent of past abuses. If these components are included in the agenda of peace talks—and if, importantly, the plans outlined in any agreement are credible and likely to be implemented—then the "interests of justice" would clearly be served by a successful conclusion of the peace agreement and robust implementation.

When asked about the possibility of greater justice resulting from a peace process, OTP staff were not persuaded. Where a national judiciary has the capacity to respond, then the Prosecutor is more likely to allow the national authorities the opportunity to do so and to hold off on opening an investigation. "But in many cases it's a question of building a national judicial system almost from scratch. This isn't so likely," a senior member of the Prosecutor's staff noted.[34] Thus, the OTP would not assume that a peace agreement would lead to greater criminal justice in the future.

Third, we must ask whether ending war is not inherently in the interests of justice and in the interest of preventing further atrocities, irrespective of new justice initiatives that may be included in a peace deal. War opens space for horrific atrocities. It serves as justification and cover for serious crimes— specifically the kinds of crimes that the ICC Prosecutor has said they most want to stop or prevent. The most effective way to stop war crimes is to stop the war. Logically, the prosecutor's stated priority of prevention should lead to a respect for—or at least a consideration of—credible peace efforts. If a peace agreement might be reached as the result of the ICC Prosecutor delaying or halting prosecutions, would that not be in the interest of justice?

There is no question that there are risks to such an approach. Human rights groups have an important point when they worry about the dangers of a Prosecutor trying to assess and respond to "political" factors, as explored in the previous chapter. If the Prosecutor acknowledges the importance of contextual factors, such as an interest in not disturbing a peace process, she could open herself to political pressures or even blackmail. It is not difficult to imagine such a scenario. The first ICC Prosecutor, Luis Moreno Ocampo, often said that such a stance would simply invite interference from well-intentioned mediators or other interested parties who would plead for his office to hold off on action in order to allow peace talks (or even the exploration of peace talks) to progress on the ground. Any possible progress in a peace process could spark further lobbying of his office, he feared, making it impossible to act independently and subjecting the OTP to political forces that would be impossible to manage.

Worse, warring parties might explicitly condition their willingness to participate in peace talks on a commitment from the ICC Prosecutor to step back or stay out. Most peace negotiation processes begin with a cautious and often lengthy period of exploratory pre-negotiations, in which the parties assess whether they are willing and interested in peace talks, and under what conditions—the location, the agenda, who is acceptable as a facilitator or mediator, and assurances of safety and security. Experience shows us that warring parties are usually well aware of the risks of international prosecutions, including the ICC but also possible universal-jurisdiction cases or being extradited to third countries. If they could reduce some of the most obvious risks, they would surely do so. On a practical level, it may also be too much to expect the prosecutor's staff in The Hague to track enormously complex and quickly changing dynamics in the countries that they cover.

But these risks can be foreseen and mitigated against. There are more advantages to defining the "interests of justice" as including these larger aims of prevention, peace, and victim interests, rather than holding to an unnecessarily narrow interpretation.

The UN Security Council

The ICC Rome Statute grants two specific powers to the UN Security Council. One is the possibility to refer situations to the ICC Prosecutor, which the Security Council did in relation to Libya and Darfur, Sudan. In this manner, states that have not joined the international court can be brought under its jurisdiction.

The second power granted to the Security Council is the possibility of stopping action by the ICC on any specific country situation.[35] Such a deferral can only be given for one year at a time. Given that the Council is a political body, made up of states that are balancing many different interests, and with Council membership changing every year, there is no way to assure that an Article 16 deferral would be extended each year.

As we saw above, international justice advocates argue that the Security Council is the more appropriate body to make determinations regarding peace and security. However, these international rights advocates also worry that a deferral by the Security Council risks politicizing international justice, and they argue that this power should be used only on a very limited basis. Human Rights Watch writes that "A deferral of an ICC investigation risks legitimizing political interference with the work of a judicial institution and could set a dangerous precedent for accused in other situations. Any exception must be extremely rare."[36] International human rights expert Juan E. Méndez, in reference to the use of Article 16, writes, "A political decision to suspend investigations and judicial actions will mostly undermine the credibility of the ICC as an independent and impartial body and will tend to encourage defendants and potential defendants to challenge the ICC's jurisdiction."[37]

A different view is taken by Louise Arbour, another well-known expert with long experience as former judge, ICTY Prosecutor, UN High Commissioner for Human Rights, and president of the International Crisis Group. She is less inclined to reject such a role for the Security Council, depending on the context of the case. For situations that were originally referred to the ICC by the Security Council, she argues, a deferral could be appropriate. "The Council presumably referred because it was seen to be good for international peace and security. If it's then good for peace and security to *lift* ICC action, then that should not be a problem," she says.[38]

Leaving aside these points of principle or appropriateness, the one-year time frame of any Article 16 deferral limits its usefulness, since the Security Council would have to regularly extend the deferral for it to remain in force.

Thus, a Security Council deferral can be seen as problematic both on principle and on practical grounds. It is opposed by ICC advocates; it is subject to de facto political forces that limit how and when it could be employed; and it is a blunt and relatively limited tool, providing only short-term relief from ICC actions and with no guarantee of extension. Despite these limitations, a Security Council deferral could sometimes play an important role and may well be the key to facilitating a peace agreement in some narrow sets of circumstances.

Uganda presents exactly this example. The final agreement in the 2008 peace talks with the Lord's Resistance Army, which was completed but ultimately not signed by the LRA, was built on a gentleman's agreement that the Ugandan government would ask the UN Security Council to provide a deferral of ICC action. This would have allowed time for a special war crimes chamber to be created within the Ugandan judiciary, while Kony was held in modified detention in northern Uganda.[39] If the new court functioned well, national prosecutions would have overridden jurisdiction by the ICC. Such a result would have represented a direct, positive impact of the ICC through strengthening the national response to serious crimes. Because that agreement was not signed and the LRA did not disarm, this example remains hypothetical, but it is easy to imagine a similar scenario in the future.

Some analysts have argued that the UN Security Council should be even more robust in its use of referral and deferral powers, given its mandate to promote peace and security, and should explicitly use the threat of international prosecutions to bring war-makers into line. Scholars Leslie Vinjamuri and Jack Snyder argue that this could be part of a "coercive diplomacy" of the Security Council; for example, through strategically referring situations to the Court and even naming specific individuals for referral, so as to encourage defections from an abusive regime.[40] Such a robust and intentionally coercive use of the ICC has not gained support in the Security Council. However, as I have addressed elsewhere, the Council's referrals to the ICC to date have implicitly had the hope of helping to stop ongoing armed conflict, as part of a broader package of measures.

Assessing the "Interests of Justice"

Given the relatively inflexible options of a Security Council deferral, an "interests of justice" strategy by the ICC Prosecutor could potentially be a much more nuanced and effective tool for promoting national justice and allowing space for a peace process. There are two challenges here: what factors might be taken into account in making an "interests of justice" assessment, and what procedure or structure could best make such an assessment.

Structurally, it is possible to envision an advisory component to assist the Prosecutor, so that she could more comfortably evaluate the likely impact and timing of her actions in each different national context. For example, independent country-specific advisors on the "interests of justice" could offer regular assessments, while leaving all decisions entirely to the Prosecutor. Such advisors could evaluate a host of factors: victims' interests; the credibility of national (criminal and noncriminal) justice initiatives; and whether ICC actions might rattle an ongoing or developing peace process. Admittedly, this may overlap with "complementarity" assessments, but the interests of justice would allow an analysis beyond strictly prosecutorial criteria. This kind of advisory procedure could be established by the Prosecutor without the need for any formal indication in the Rome Statute or otherwise.[41]

Some legal scholars have called for more specific and public guidelines that would set out exactly what factors it will take into account in analyzing the interests of justice. Commentators have suggested a range of factors for consideration. The suggestions include assessments of what has been done or is planned at the national level and the quality of these initiatives; an analysis of circumstances that might justify a departure from strict prosecutorial demands; and the process by which alternatives are approved, especially with input from victims. The most extensive and detailed set of suggested criteria came from the 2003 Expert Group on Complementarity, established by the OTP to advise the Prosecutor. A number of legal experts have also made specific proposals.[42]

Incorporating and expanding on the ideas in these various proposals, the following set out a number of factors that could be assessed in determining whether OTP actions would or would not be in the interests of justice. While it will rarely be possible to know without doubt what the impact would be, it is reasonable to assess and balance a range of factors based on known information and national input. For example:

- Would the start of an investigation or prosecution be highly likely to exacerbate or otherwise destabilize a conflict situation?
- Would OTP action endanger the successful completion of a peace process or reconciliation program?[43]
- Do the "severity of circumstances" justify alternatives to full prosecutions at the national level?[44]
- If there are current peace negotiations under way, are justice issues included on the agenda and are the parties expressing a commitment to international standards?
- If there is a preliminary justice agreement, does it have the support of society as a whole and especially victim communities? What is the process by which alternative justice arrangements are approved at the national level?
- Has the UN or other regional or international bodies expressed support for alternative justice arrangements?[45]
- If there is a nonjudicial investigation into the facts, such as a truth commission, is it of high quality? Is it sufficiently independent and impartial, with the powers and resources necessary for a robust inquiry?[46]
- How many cases of serious crimes will be processed through national mechanisms, even if maximum sentencing is not planned?
- Would delaying OTP action to a later date have a more positive impact, in allowing the space for a cessation of conflict and thus preventing further abuses?

The interests of justice should include an interest in avoiding damage to a peacemaking or peace-implementation process that is real, concrete, and making progress—and that includes a credible justice component.

In some cases, such as Uganda in mid- to late 2005, plans for peace talks were quietly under way, and Ugandan community leaders urged the prosecutor to hold off on any arrest warrants. These pleas were apparently ignored; warrants were released by the ICC not long after a group of community leaders visited The Hague to urge the prosecutors to hold off. In other cases, as in Colombia, the ICC has actively monitored the state of law and national prosecutions while peace negotiations were under way; while this was generally welcomed, many Colombians (and international experts) felt the ICC went too far when it intervened in—and apparently directly influenced—the Colombian Constitutional Court in relation to its decision on an alternative justice legal framework. In cases where a broad range of national actors, including human rights advocates, are urging that a peace process be given breathing space and for international justice to be temporarily quiet or held at bay, this should be taken into consideration.

Conclusion

There are thus two approaches under which the ICC Prosecutor can apply her judgment in taking into account broader interests of peace, conflict, and victim interests. One is through the range of discretionary powers, outlined in the previous chapter, that are inherent in her mandate as an international prosecutor. It is evidently impossible for her to prosecute all the cases that fall under her jurisdiction, and thus choices are necessary. These choices can be made while taking into account national conflict dynamics: questions of timing, targeting, and allowing space for national processes and a context-specific approach to sentencing—these and other aspects can be approached with flexibility.

The second approach to discretion is through the interpretation given to the "interests of justice," as outlined in this chapter. The explicit requirement in the Rome Statute for the Prosecutor to assess the interests of justice in every case, before she proceeds with a prosecution, gives this extra importance and opens an opportunity. To date, the current and former Prosecutors have interpreted this narrowly. While there are smart minds that arrive at different legal conclusions on the intention of this phrase, the great majority of legal scholars and practitioners argue for a much broader understanding than that taken by the Office of the Prosecutor.

The current Prosecutor has articulated her desire to act in a manner that is friendly to peace processes. She may still be working through how this is best done, as new cases bring up new challenges. Perhaps in time the Prosecutor's office will be more open to a strategic approach that more explicitly incorporates an analysis of conflict and prospects for peace (and a peace that includes credible justice). Such a strategic approach should fully respect its own mandate for justice while maximizing its positive impact on peace, on past victims, and on preventing more violations.

Notes

1 Rome Statute, Art. 53(1)(c).
2 Rome Statute, Art. 53(3)(c). The Statute further provides that "The Prosecutor may, at any time, reconsider a decision whether to initiate an investigation or prosecution based on new facts or information." The Prosecutor must

inform the Pre-Trial Chamber if he or she takes a decision not to open an investigation or proceed with a prosecution based solely on interests of justice. The Pre-Trial Chamber may review this decision and may request the Prosecution to reconsider. Rome Statute, Art. 53.

3 See "Code for Crown Prosecutors: The Full Code Test" at www.cps.gov.uk. For an in-depth comparison with the "public interest" test, see Chris Gallavin, "Article 53 of the Rome Statute of the International Criminal Court: In the Interests of Justice?" *King's College Law Journal* 14 (2003): 179.

4 The Rome Statute was discussed as the South African Truth and Reconciliation Commission was under way; this commission had the power to grant individual amnesties, even for serious crimes, to those who told the full truth about their crimes. Delegates to the Rome Statute questioned whether the ICC would make it impossible for national authorities to put in place similar conditional amnesties elsewhere. These questions could not be fully answered, and thus the issue of national amnesty was left unaddressed in any explicit manner in the Rome Statute.

5 Kofi Annan, Address at the University of the Witwatersrand, South Africa. 1 Sept 1998.

6 Richard J. Goldstone and Nicole Fritz, "'In the Interests of Justice' and Independent Referral: The ICC Prosecutor's Unprecedented Powers," *Leiden Journal of International Law* 13 (2000): 662–663.

7 Darryl Robinson, "Serving the Interests of Justice: Amnesties, Truth Commissions and the International Criminal Court," *European Journal of International Law* 14 (2003): 483.

8 Ibid., 488.

9 Gallavin, "Article 53," 179–80, 197.

10 Carsten Stahn, "Complementarity, Amnesties and Alternative Forms of Justice: Some Interpretative Guidelines for the International Criminal Court," *Journal of International Criminal Justice* 3 (2005): 698.

11 Ibid., 700.

12 Ibid., 718.

13 Kenneth A. Rodman, "Is Peace in the Interests of Justice? The Case for Broad Prosecutorial Discretion at the International Criminal Court," *Leiden Journal of International Law* 22 (2009): 101.

14 Ibid., 123.

15 Jens David Ohlin, "Peace, Security, and Prosecutorial Discretion," in Carsten Stahn and Goran Sluiter, eds., *The Emerging Practice of the International Criminal Court* (Leiden: Nijhoff, 2009), 188.

16 Expert Group on Complementarity, "Informal Expert Paper: The principle of complementarity in practice," Office of the Prosecutor of the ICC, 2003, 23.

17 Office of the Prosecutor of the ICC, "Draft ICC Regulations of the Office of the Prosecutor," 3 June 2003, 47, note 79, www.jura.uni-muenchen.de/fakultaet/lehrstuehle/satzger/materialien/istghdrre.pdf.

18 A collection of these submissions can be seen on the website of the Coalition for the International Criminal Court: www.iccnow.org.

19 Human Rights Watch, "Human Rights Watch Policy Paper: The Meaning of 'The Interests of Justice' in Article 53 of the Rome Statute," June 2005, 22–23. Human Rights Watch confirmed that this paper still reflected their position as of early 2017. Richard Dicker, interview by author, 10 May 2017.

20 Human Rights Watch, "Policy Paper," 9.

21 Amnesty International, "Open letter to the Chief Prosecutor of the International Criminal Court: Comments on the Concept of the Interests of Justice," 17 June 2005, AI Index: IOR 40/023/2005.

22 Ibid., 3, 5.

23 See, in particular, Henry Lovat, "Delineating the Interests of Justice," *Denver Journal of International Law and Policy* 35 (2007): 275–286; and Dražan Dukić, "Transitional Justice and the International Criminal Court: In 'The Interests of Justice'?" *International Review of the Red Cross* 89 (2007): 698–700.

24 Interview and correspondence with former OTP staff.

25 "[T]he exercise of the Prosecutor's discretion under Article 53(1)(c) and 53(2)(c) is exceptional in its nature and there is a presumption in favor of investigation or prosecution." ICC Office of the Prosecutor, "Policy Paper on the Interests of Justice," Sept 2007, 1.

26 Interview with OTP staff, Oct 2013.

27 ICC OTP, "Policy Paper," 9.

28 As recounted by former OTP staff.

29 ICC OTP, "Policy Paper on Preliminary Examinations," Nov 2013, para. 69.

30 Article 53 of the Rome Statute opens the possibility of review of the "interests of justice" by ICC judges, or an engagement by ICC member states, only if the Prosecutor decides not to move forward with investigations or prosecutions for this reason, and formally makes such a submission to the Pre-Trial Chamber. Unlike the issue of complementarity, where states can submit a challenge to stop ICC action, the interests of justice issue is left entirely to the discretion of the Prosecutor at this initial stage.

31 For example, see Fatou Bensouda, "The Peace-Justice Interface: Where Are We Now and What Are the Challenges Ahead?" in Paul Dziatkowiec, Christina Buchhold, Jonathan Harlander, and Massimiliano Verri, *Peacemaking in the New World Disorder: Oslo Forum Meeting Report* (Geneva: Centre for Humanitarian Dialogue, 2015), 26–27, www.hdcentre.org. The 2014 expert seminar was hosted by the Dialogue Advisory Group, Amsterdam; the 2017 expert consultation was held at the European University Institute, Florence.

32 James Stewart, ICC Deputy Prosecutor, "Transitional Justice in Colombia and the Role of the International Criminal Court," 13 May 2015, www.icc-cpi.int. Stewart argues, "Notwithstanding continuing academic interest in the interface between 'peace and justice', the relationship between peace and justice is a settled issue under the Rome Statute."

33 See, for example, Robinson, "Serving the Interests of Justice." Many of the other articles cited above also implicitly make this argument.

34 Interview with OTP staff, 28 Oct 2015.

35 Article 16 of the Rome Statute states that: "No investigation or prosecution may be commenced or proceeded with under this Statute for a period of 12 months after the Security Council, in a resolution adopted under Chapter VII of the Charter of the United Nations, has requested the Court to that effect; that request may be renewed by the Council under the same conditions." As of mid-2017, the Security Council has never used this power to defer an ICC investigation or prosecution.

36 Human Rights Watch, "Article 16: Questions and Answers," 15 Aug 2008, www.hrw.org. Human Rights Watch further argues that the two times that Article 16 deferrals have been proposed to date (for Kenya and Darfur, Sudan) were not motivated for reasons of peace and security; extrapolating from practice to date leaves them concerned about the potential for political abuse (Richard Dicker, interview by author, 10 May 2017).

37 Juan E. Méndez, "Transitional Justice, Peace, and Prevention," Address at University of Baltimore Law School, Center for International and Comparative Law, 26 Oct 2010 (on file with author).

38 Louise Arbour, interview by author, Brussels, 13 July 2013.

39 Dylan Hendrickson and Kennedy Tumutegyereize, "Dealing With Complexity in Peace Negotiations: Reflections on the Lord's Resistance Army and the Juba Talks," Conciliation Resources, Jan 2012, 24, citing Barney Afako, senior legal advisor to the chief mediator.

40 Leslie Vinjamuri and Jack Snyder, "ICC Sherriff Too Quick on the Draw?" *Duck of Minerva* (blog), 9 May 2011, www.whiteoliphaunt.com/duckof minerva.

41 Scholar David Bosco suggested a similar, alternative approach: he proposed that either the OTP or the registry should create a "small prevention unit with two principal tasks: assessing the likely impact of possible investigations and recording and analyzing the effects of ongoing investigations and cases." David Bosco, "The International Criminal Court and Crime Prevention: Byproduct or Conscious Goal?" *Michigan State Journal of International Law* 19:1 (2011): 199.

42 A useful overview of many of these specific proposals are provided in Linda M. Keller, "Comparing the 'Interests of Justice': What the International Criminal Court Can Learn From New York Law," *Washington University Global Studies Law Review* 12 (2013): 6–15. See also Allison Marston Danner, "Enhancing the Legitimacy and Accountability of Prosecutorial Discretion at the International Criminal Court," *American Journal of International Law* 97 (2003): 510–552; Philippa Webb, "The ICC Prosecutor's Discretion Not to Proceed in the 'Interests of Justice,'" *Criminal Law Quarterly* 50 (2005): 338–44; and Bosco, "Crime Prevention," 200.

43 The first two criteria are taken from possibilities suggested in OTP draft regulations in 2003. See OTP, "Draft Regulations," note 79.

44 The "severity of circumstances" language was suggested by the OTP Expert Group on Complementarity, "Informal Expert Paper," 2003.

45 Again, this was suggested by the OTP Expert Group on Complementarity, "Informal Expert Paper," 2003.

46 Richard Goldstone and Nicole Fritz were particularly interested in this aspect. See Goldstone and Fritz, "Independent Referral," 664.

9   Unraveling the Paradox

The tension between peace and justice is a natural result of wanting both peace and justice at the maximum level, simultaneously, in a context where logic tells us that this is not possible. Legal requirements and political realities may simply clash, making an acceptable peace deal hard to imagine. The perpetrators with the dirtiest hands in a war may also hold the most power in getting to a negotiated peace. These facts cannot just be wished away.

The resolution to this tension can only be found through a strategic and creative response. The successful national solutions that we have seen to date try to balance the two goals of peace and justice. These usually include an important component of individual criminal accountability, but go well beyond prosecutions to include a range of other nonprosecutorial elements, and carefully take into account timing, as well as the relationship between these measures.

There are several broad lessons that emerge from these experiences.

First, it is now clear that a singular, narrow focus on prosecuting wrongdoers and pushing for long prison terms is shortsighted and likely to be ineffective, in terms both of obtaining accountability and in responding to the needs of victims and of society as a whole. There is, I believe, a slow shift under way in the international human rights community that acknowledges this.

Second, regardless of what a peace agreement says, it's clear that any specific justice policy or arrangement will continue to develop and change over time, long after the signatures have dried on the accord. This is usually not foreseen, given the parties' intentions for clarity and predictability in this area. But the questions left unresolved usually make this inevitable. Even in the most complex and detailed peace accords, such as that of Colombia, there were central elements that could only be worked out in implementation, and the parties themselves recognized this. In other contexts, a much greater part of the accountability package has taken shape only after the peace agreement was signed. This is partly due to the process of turning a peace agreement into legislation, where greater detail and specificity is needed. But it is also clear that as political dynamics and the power of military forces change, so do the possibilities for justice.

Third, to withstand both the legal and political pressures to come, a justice agreement must be clearly grounded in local realities. What was appropriate for Kenya is not right for Colombia, and what was right for Guatemala might be wrong for Liberia. There is no one "model" to follow. In this sense, while the obligations and constraints stemming from international law do provide important guidance in some areas, they do not offer a roadmap. Indeed, on some important issues, international law remains unclear or undefined, providing little specific guidance, as will be explored below. The final resolution to the dilemmas at hand must emerge from the hard work of analyzing the possibilities and limitations of each context.

Fourth, we are not seeing peace agreements that reject international justice, and specifically the ICC. Rather, negotiations are much more likely to acknowledge this reality, try to understand the relevant rules and requirements, and aim to build their own system within these constraints. Uganda and Colombia are the two most obvious examples. Certainly there are governments that have tried to thwart the jurisdiction of the ICC, such as Kenya and Sudan, but this has not originated from nor been reflected in these countries' peace agreements.

The respect for ICC requirements is likely to continue as long as these requirements are seen as reachable, even if very difficult. If the ICC's jurisprudence were to crystalize into unrealistically maximalist obligations, parties might outright reject these standards or simply try to escape the reach of the court altogether.

For those directly involved in talks, either as mediators or negotiating parties, the review throughout this book suggests that a deliberate and considered approach can lead to an acceptable resolution to these inherent peace-justice tensions. But this must begin with a recognition that the tensions are quite real and that working out the best response is not likely to be simple. Papering over differences may not help. Parties have interests and concerns, and these should be addressed honestly.

How, Who, and When to Broach These Issues

When seeking a solution, the "how" is as important as the "what" that is to be discussed and agreed. Basic questions of process, including who is involved in the negotiations, will help determine the legitimacy as well as the legal and operational durability of the outcome. While this is true of a peace agreement as a whole, it has particular resonance on the subject of justice for past crimes.

Peace mediators should assume that issues of justice and impunity will arise and plan for it. Gone are the days when it was possible to largely avoid addressing the issue of past crimes, as was done in the Good Friday Agreement for Northern Ireland in 1998: as a result, the following fifteen or more years suffered political crisis and gridlock stemming from unaddressed past crimes, including accusations against the post-accord political leadership.[1] Most armed conflicts, unfortunately, feature war crimes, and most armed groups today will want to know how far any amnesty protections will reach. The question is not whether, but how and when the issue should be addressed.

Also unlikely are further examples of last-minute crisis brokering in which the entire set of questions related to justice, truth, and victims are confronted and "resolved" with a few words added to an otherwise detailed and long-considered accord. This was the approach in South Africa in 1995, not because the parties were oblivious to the issue, but rather because they knew it was indeed very important but simply didn't know how to resolve the obvious dilemmas. Increasingly, today, the parties want much greater clarity on these questions before finalizing any accord.

It is not always easy to incorporate victims or civil society organizations directly in peace talks, but a mediator and the parties should find some means to include their input into the process. This might be through parallel consultations, side meetings with the parties, or inviting issue papers and specific proposals. Channeling independent views and expertise can be critical on this subject, which can be more complex and contentious than other issues on the table. In Colombia, the engagement of direct victims in the talks was important in shaping how the issue was handled by the parties and the public perception of the negotiations, and it also influenced the assessment of the final agreement by the ICC Prosecutor.

A mediator and the parties will also need to decide the right moment to tackle these issues. Some peace negotiations begin with such difficulty that it is virtually impossible to even broach the subject of war crimes until much later, after the negotiations find their footing. This may even be true, or may especially be true, when a war was well-known for significant atrocities. The many attempts and maneuvering to start negotiations in Syria and in Afghanistan in recent years has left these accountability issues to the side, as the protagonists focused instead on how to even get the parties at the same table and tried to work out which armed groups would be included. But no one could have doubted that this issue would ultimately have to be addressed.

Of course, the provisions pertaining to justice for past crimes will impact other aspects of an accord, such as political participation by former armed groups and disarmament and demobilization procedures. Working out the relationship and sequencing between justice provisions and other parts of the accord can be tricky; in many cases, some areas of overlap can only be worked out in implementation.

Policymaker Dilemmas

For many international policymakers, the tension between peace and justice is felt in a different way. The imperative to uphold clear standards of accountability for human rights crimes can seem to run counter to the same institution's or state's policies to push for an end to violent conflict as quickly as possible. Where a foreign state's own national interests are directly affected by a continued conflict and make a resolution a greater imperative (due to refugee flows, a strong domestic lobby, or broader geopolitical interests, or because it has troops engaged either as peacekeepers or in support of one side), then its commitment to human rights principles may be tested. When the UN or others push against a blanket amnesty proposal (as in Sierra Leone and in the agreement between the north and south of Sudan) or insist on language that specifically limits an amnesty's reach (as in Guatemala and Congo), they know they risk derailing, or at least delaying, a possible end to conflict.

These tensions have been particularly acute when the UN Security Council has considered whether to refer a situation to the ICC for investigation and prosecution. Such a proposal usually would arise while a conflict is raging, and the Security Council might hope that ICC engagement will help stop ongoing atrocities. In the two such examples to date, Darfur and Libya, the referral by the Security Council was accompanied by a plea for a halt to the violence. But this threat of prosecution by the ICC may, soon enough, be seen as an impediment to a possible peace process. These same tensions also arise if there is a proposal for the Security Council to defer action by the ICC, once investigations or prosecutions are under way, perhaps to allow a peace process to move forward.

While some intergovernmental organizations have been crystalizing their positions on amnesty, these policies are still relatively narrowly focused, and they are not yet formally integrated into broader institutional procedures or guidelines, much less a more nuanced legal analysis. The UN policy on amnesty has had a positive effect on the quality of peace agreements and indeed in backing up UN mediators who want to avoid impunity arrangements after atrocious crimes. It has not prevented any peace deals. As this policy has become more widely known both inside and outside the UN system, it has increasingly been accepted as the universal standard, even if the explicit international law on amnesties is still in development. The European Union's adopting the same position as the UN, in 2015, reflects this acceptance.

Based on a broad study, Anthony Dworkin of the European Council on Foreign Relations called for a more "consistent and integrated" policy from the international community in relation to the tensions that emerge when seeking justice in conflict contexts. "By failing to acknowledge these tensions and often formulating policies on justice and peacemaking in isolation from each other, international policy currently does not serve the best interests of either objective," he wrote.[2] This is particularly true in relation to the expectations placed on international courts, if they are not backed up when concerns for peace emerge as a higher priority.

Likewise, scholar Laura Davis interrogated the European Union's policies on peace and justice and concluded in 2016 that these were "extremely thin" on the relationship between transitional justice and peace mediation, and that the EU is "not equipped to deal with the complexities" of the issue, despite its various policies in support of both justice and peace.[3]

More cohesive policies by international institutions and individual states could be very helpful, but these may prove difficult to develop. And there is a real risk that more clear policies would also be more rigid, thus creating unhelpful straightjackets in the messy and unpredictable arena of policymaking. The challenge of balancing the imperatives of ending armed conflict and preventing impunity is now widely recognized. Most institutions and states that are active in peacemaking have firm policies in support of both priorities, but predicting and providing guidance on how to balance them when they are in tension is another matter altogether. Ideally, such policies would ensure that the priority of supporting an end to armed conflict does not run at cross-purposes to the commitment to accountability, and vice versa. This would presumably require an ongoing, multi-faceted, and interdepartmental review process, based on legal foundations but also high principles, and relying on a constant evaluation of each case as dynamics change.

Finding this balance is not easy, and this can have a very practical effect. As noted earlier, the U.S. has had a policy against meeting with individuals who are actively evading an ICC arrest warrant, which prevented direct meetings by U.S. officials with Sudanese President Bashir during difficult years, when several conflicts in the country implicated Sudanese troops. U.S. envoys relied on intermediary states to carry messages to Bashir, which reduced the ability of the U.S. to influence the deteriorating situation, despite its outsized role in the region and the leverage it might have had.[4] The UN policy is more nuanced: the Secretary-General released guidance indicating that "Contacts between United Nations officials and persons who are the subject of warrants of arrest issued by the International Criminal Court should be limited to those which are strictly required for carrying out essential United Nations mandated activities."[5] This has allowed meetings by UN representatives with indicted persons when required to try to reduce ongoing violence or advance a peace process.

ICC Impact

The ICC can have a positive or a negative impact on peace negotiations specifically and on conflict and violence more generally. This depends on many factors, some but not all of which are determined by choices made by the ICC Prosecutor.

However, the argument that the Prosecutor should be blind to these dynamics, or that the peace-justice issue is settled, is neither helpful for the Court nor for local efforts to protect rights and reduce violence. Of course, the Prosecutor has many options in how and when to engage and already considers many of these on an ongoing basis. The resistance that the Prosecutor's office has sometimes shown to taking a broader view, such as in their understanding of the "interests of justice," may reflect the ICC Prosecutor's discomfort in recognizing the impact of the Court on broader conflict dynamics. However, the current ICC Prosecutor has begun to recognize and show more interest in trying to foresee her potential impact on conflict and peace. This is a positive development.

What is certainly clear is that the ICC's engagement in any context is not simply a question of law, as some have argued. The impact of ICC actions on justice, broadly defined and in both the short and long term, can be significant; getting this right requires an analysis of political context and an appreciation for dynamics that go well beyond a narrow reading of evidence and the law. This has been addressed in detail in earlier chapters.

It is also clear that while the ICC's engagement can and sometimes does help to deter crimes, especially in the very short term and in a specific context where the Prosecutor is watching closely, we shouldn't overstate this deterrent effect extending more generally to other places.

Human Rights Advocacy

Independent human rights organizations have been important in shaping this field, but analyzing their impact points to two slightly contradictory conclusions.

On the one hand, they have pushed firmly against the idea that peace deals can be built on arrangements of impunity. In contexts where there is little record of accountability for even the most egregious crimes committed by the powerful, there is always a risk that massive crimes of a war will be granted either implicit or explicit impunity. Human rights organizations are right to be concerned, and there is a very important role for these independent voices to urge a credible accounting for serious crimes of a war.

Indeed, some mediators, as well as experts advising negotiating parties, have noted the usefulness of having clear legal constraints emerging from international law. They may refer the parties to the de facto threat of the ICC intervening or the red line from the UN or others that prohibits amnesty for international crimes. Those advising the parties rely on these clear limitations to deter the negotiating parties from an impunity deal and push them towards a more serious justice arrangement. Having no choice in the matter, as a mediator or legal advisor, is a much easier message than trying to persuade recalcitrant groups based on principles of right and wrong, a respect for victims, or a general commitment to the rule of law. Human rights organizations serve to amplify these legal restrictions and usually make clear that they will be watching carefully and will protest any perceived violation of legal requirements. This outside advocacy can thus be very helpful for those on the inside of the talks.

But a strict and narrow reading of these obligations, put forward as inflexible prescriptions, may go too far. The question is: When does a push for accountability become a serious impediment to peace, and thus ultimately do damage to broader human rights interests? There is no clear and concise answer to this, but the question should echo in the background of any discussion on these difficult issues.

Peace negotiations raise a host of dilemmas that do not fit comfortably with a strategy of uncompromising advocacy and a singular focus on past crimes, and particularly a focus on criminal accountability for these crimes. The very premise of negotiating peace is to halt continuing violence and thus prevent future victims of war, and an agreement may include significant reforms of abusive or nonfunctioning systems (such as the police or the judiciary).

Balancing the costs and benefits of a compromise that may lead to a peace accord can feel uncomfortable to those focused only on preventing impunity and on protecting the highest standards of criminal accountability.

As noted previously, many international human rights organizations have long resisted taking a position in favor of peace over war or even expressing support for a ceasefire during a hot conflict. They consider this to be outside their mandate and want to avoid any risk of appearing partial to one side. Their interest instead is advocating for compliance with the laws of war: that is, focusing on how a war is fought.

Amnesty International has explicitly recognized the importance of ending war and preventing future victims. It was early to note the positive side of the peace process in Colombia before criticizing aspects of the justice agreement, noting that an early partial ceasefire had "alleviated some of the worst effects of the conflict on civilians." However, it was particularly concerned that Colombia prosecute every single person suspected of international crimes, calling this a "non-negotiable obligation, even in the context of a peace process."[6] It was also concerned that the foreseen sentences were too light.

Until recently, Human Rights Watch saw little room for flexibility in what was required for punishment: if serious war crimes were committed, these must be met with significant prison terms, in particular for those at the leadership level, it said. They considered the 2015 justice agreement in Colombia to simply be an arrangement of impunity.[7] By the end of 2016, the position of Human Rights Watch had "evolved" and it no longer insisted on prison terms, so long as there was some form of meaningful punishment.[8]

The position of international human rights advocates has changed over time. In the early 1990s, Human Rights Watch would not necessarily have opposed a peace settlement that included an overly broad amnesty, according to Aryeh Neier, who was then its executive director. The organization refrained from taking a public position on some national arrangements, such as the amnesty-for-truth deal in South Africa. "The National Party and [then-president F.W.] de Klerk said that no transition was possible without an amnesty. Mandela went along with that. Human Rights Watch didn't fault him for that," Neier told me.[9]

Neier explained that the general position of Human Rights Watch at that time was driven by the premise that "you want the slaughter to stop. If they are trading away accountability, you try to get as much accountability as you can." In some circumstances, conflict is winding down in any regard, and pushing for justice won't stop that. "In other circumstances, it may be *the* key issue as to whether conflict continues." Likewise, an international prosecutor should "of course take into account a peace process. If prosecutions might jeopardize a peace process, that should be factored in," he said.

Many international human rights organizations do appreciate the need to take into account the context and local and immediate priorities of ending ongoing violence. In separate interviews, the executive director or secretary-general of the International Commission of Jurists and TRIAL International, both in Geneva, and the International Federation for Human Rights, in Paris, each explored these issues with subtlety and nuance: they were worried about measures that might too quickly grant impunity to powerful perpetrators, but they also recognized that mediation contexts may demand some flexibility, given the plight of victims of ongoing war.[10]

In part, international advocacy organizations are worried about precedent, just as the ICC is: if reduced or alternative sentences are allowed in one country, or a decision is made not to prosecute all international crimes, then other countries might well follow suit. This outcome is difficult from an international advocacy perspective and may be seen as leading to an overall weakening of human rights standards. A desire for consistency thus leads to organizational inflexibility. This makes sense from an international perspective, but makes is difficult for those who are working at the national level to find the best solution for a particular context. As explored earlier, national rights advocates are usually more sensitive to the fact that victims' interests extend beyond the prosecution and imprisonment of perpetrators, and that stopping the conflict, and preventing future victims, must be paramount.

Law and Strategy

International law does not resolve these dilemmas. Even if the parties to talks might wish to comply with all legal obligations, many specific issues have not been clarified with precision, neither in the guidance provided in human rights treaties nor in the jurisprudence of international or regional courts. This allows some flexibility, even if it opens up peace deals to protest from those who take the strictest reading of the law.

Some of these undefined areas of law pertain to issues that would be central to any detailed treatment of accountability in a peace negotiation. Most importantly, the legal requirement for prosecuting and punishing perpetrators of serious crimes is still unclear in two important respects: whether *all* accused perpetrators must be prosecuted (or only those "most responsible" for the most serious crimes), and what minimum sentence or punishment is required.

Many advocates point to the obligations set out in human rights treaties, which require investigation and prosecution of those responsible for grave crimes.[11] But where many thousands of people may have committed serious war crimes, no one reasonably expects that all can be prosecuted. Even if a national judicial system functioned well enough to do so, the intensity of resources required would overwhelm most countries, leaving aside the political difficulties in trying to carry this out. Instead, it is much more likely, and more reasonable, to prioritize among cases and select the most important or most representative for prosecution, or to identify those persons considered the most responsible for the abuses. Many human rights lawyers argue that this approach does not strictly comply with international law. But many of these experts also recognize that a strict implementation of these requirements is not feasible in most post-war circumstances, and that a realistic alternative may be necessary.[12] The International Center for Transitional Justice (ICTJ) has set out why a strategy of selection and prioritization is the correct (and only realistic) response.[13] Indeed, the actual practice where there are national-level prosecutions is almost always some form of selective approach.

International and hybrid courts typically aim to prosecute the most responsible persons for the most serious crimes, assuming that others will be prosecuted at the national level. The ICC Prosecutor warned in the case of Colombia that national prosecutorial strategies should not employ this same selective approach, as this would leave most cases unaddressed.[14] Later, however, she seemed to express support for a modified approach, congratulating the Colombians for agreeing to a system that would "focus on those most responsible for the most serious crimes committed during the conflict."[15] Colombia tried to a large degree to comply with a strict reading of the legal requirements through its plan to create a new special tribunal, intending to process thousands of cases primarily through a confessions-based approach. Skeptics questioned whether this system would be realistic in implementation, given the large number of crimes and accused persons.

Ultimately, basic practical constraints have dictated that the obligations set out in human rights treaties have not been and often cannot be read strictly, in the context of a transition from war to peace and after widespread atrocities. In response to this legal dilemma, one group of legal experts has suggested that the full *investigation* of all cases, not necessarily the prosecution of all those implicated, might be sufficient to comply with legal requirements, leaving to the discretion of a national prosecutor the question of which cases would move forward to trial.[16] But comprehensive investigations would also be a tall order in many contexts.

Equally important is the question of sentencing. The insistence by some human rights advocates that perpetrators of serious crimes must receive prison sentences, and that sentences are "appropriate" and "proportional to the crime," is again grounded in the language of human rights treaties and key court decisions, in particular by the Inter-American Court of Human Rights.

Amnesty International suggests that, while international law provides no specific guidance on sentencing, punishment for serious international crimes should be equivalent to that provided for similar crimes under national law. It opposes the idea that one can reduce the punishment in exchange for telling the truth or for other nonpunitive measures.

But other rights advocates argue that there is no categorical obligation for prison time, and that context plays an important role in regulating what is required. When the Americas Director of Human Rights Watch blasted the agreement in Colombia as a "piñata of impunity," in particular because it did not require prison sentences, his counterparts at Colombian human rights organizations, also very much experts in law, had a very different response. They were very supportive of the agreement, firmly concluding that it could actually help break the cycle of impunity in the country.[17]

The question of sentencing includes both whether a prison sentence is required and how long a sentence must be. The legal requirement that there be "deprivation of liberty" might not mean time in prison per se; international law is not specific on this. Is "restricted liberty" and community service acceptable instead, or some form of modified detention such as house arrest? The Colombian accord relied on this broader understanding of penalties, referring to "effective restrictions on liberty" for those responsible for serious crimes. This would not include prison for those who fully cooperate with the system and confess to past crimes.

The ICC Prosecutor has stated that from the perspective of the Rome Statute,

> In sentencing, States have wide discretion . . . Effective penal sanctions may therefore take many different forms. They should, however, serve appropriate sentencing goals, such as public condemnation of the criminal conduct, recognition of victims' suffering, and deterrence of further criminal conduct.[18]

At a critical point in the Colombian talks, the ICC Deputy Prosecutor outlined specific guidance on sentencing requirements from the perspective of the ICC Prosecutor's office, in a public lecture in Bogota, which was very helpful to the Colombian process.[19]

ICTJ also argues that the policy objectives of punishment must be considered. In the abnormal circumstances of a negotiated transition from war, it argues, the objectives change. The goals of peaceful transition, disarmament and reintegration of the armed opposition, and "reinforcing society's values" might be better achieved through alternative punishment schemes, it says. These could include financial penalties or exclusion from public office, in addition to community service arrangements.[20]

These differences in legal interpretation, in all of these areas, played out forcefully in the context of Colombia. Some Colombian human rights leaders insisted that prosecution for all serious crimes was absolutely required, but not necessarily prison sentences for those convicted. Others argued that selective prosecution was acceptable, but that at least some prison time should be required for those convicted, especially those "most responsible."[21]

In the final renegotiation of the accord in Colombia, this was a critical point of discussion between the parties. The pressure for at least some minimal prison time for the FARC (Revolutionary Armed Forces of Colombia) was not ultimately addressed as a legal point, but as a political difference, leading ultimately to a political agreement. There would be "restriction of liberty" for those who complied with the system of confession and reparation, but not "deprivation of liberty" as demanded by those calling for more rigorous terms.

Most peace negotiations to date have not actually entered into detailed discussions of sentencing requirements or whether all or only the most responsible must be prosecuted, and these questions are not addressed in the text of most peace agreements. Rather, discussions usually center on the question on the other side of the issue, that of how far an amnesty can extend. Even on this issue, there is not full agreement from experts, as discussed in an earlier chapter.[22]

In areas of transitional justice that go beyond prosecutions, there is even less legal clarity on what is required. There is no legal document that spells out the "right to truth" in any specificity that would help in the design of a truth commission, or that would suggest what elements should be included in the text of a peace agreement on this issue. The general obligation to provide reparations for victims stipulates no guidance on what specifically should be provided, or how far the definition of "victim" should extend, or even whether reparations must include a financial component or whether it can instead focus on community-level needs or symbolic measures. "Guarantees of non-repetition," also considered an important pillar of transitional justice, is likewise relatively undefined in terms of specific legal obligations and its operational counterpart.[23] In many of these areas, the best results often arise from the demands of one or both parties in a negotiation, combined with guidance from the mediation team and general best practice gleaned from prior international experiences, as well as input from victims and civil society, rather than trying to follow any specific legal requirements.

In short, the letter of the law will not settle these issues. The spirit of the law in relation to each of these elements can help to define general parameters, but mediators and negotiating parties will have to be creative to work out an appropriate arrangement.

It's quite possible that further specificity in law would not be helpful in any case, depending on how this might develop. If international law made strict and universal requirements of aspirations that are neither politically feasible nor operationally realistic, it could have the effect of making negotiated peace incredibly difficult and theoretically even impossible. Those fighting to prevent atrocities imagine that such a development—ironclad requirements for serious prison terms for all involved in war crimes—would finally deter the barbarities of today's wars. But the evidence doesn't support this idea.

The Bottom Line

These issues will remain difficult. The inherent tensions cannot be easily resolved. But those working to stop wars and those working to protect rights and avoid impunity should be able to agree on this: obtaining justice and preventing further atrocities ultimately depends on peace, just as long-term peace will usually require a fair and realistic measure of justice. Handling each of these imperatives with sensitivity and with a strategic vision for the future is ultimately the only way to find a solution to these terrible dilemmas.

Notes

1 Jonathan Powell, who represented the British government in the Northern Ireland peace talks, recognized the weakness of the Good Friday Agreement in this respect. "[F]ailure to deal with the past can threaten to derail a peace

process, as demonstrated by the arrest of Gerry Adams in 2014 in connection with the [1972] murder of Jean McConville." Although neither negotiating party was interested in confronting the past, "disagreeable truths do not just disappear, and when the past comes back to haunt the present, there will be more arrests and further disruptions of the peace-building process unless a way of dealing with the past is agreed." Jonathan Powell, *Terrorists at the Table: Why Negotiating Is the Only Way to Peace* (New York: Palgrave MacMillan, 2015), 251.

2 Anthony Dworkin, *International Justice and the Prevention of Atrocity*, European Council on Foreign Relations, Oct 2014. Dworkin argued that the ICC and other courts are often burdened with a political role in contexts of conflict that extends far beyond their capacities.

3 Laura Davis, *Peace and Justice in EU Foreign Policy: From Principles to Practice*, Ulster University, Transitional Justice Institute Research Paper No. 16–13, June 2016, 18 and 42.

4 For more on U.S. government policy on transitional justice, see Annie R. Bird, *U.S. Foreign Policy on Transitional Justice* (New York: Oxford, 2015) and Zachary D. Kaufman, *United States Law and Policy on Transitional Justice: Principles, Politics, and Pragmatics* (New York: Oxford, 2016).

5 "Guidance on contacts with persons who are the subject of arrest warrants or summonses issued by the International Criminal Court," Annex to UN Doc. A/67/828—S/2013/210, "Identical letters dated 3 April 2013 from the Secretary-General addressed to the President of the General Assembly and the President of the Security Council," 8 Apr 2013, 2, peacemaker.un.org. There is no restriction on UN representatives meeting with persons who are the subject of an ICC summons to appear and who are cooperating. Some nonessential contact with Bashir by UN officials was criticized, and as a result this policy was clarified and tightened.

6 Erika Guevara-Rosas, Americas Director, Amnesty International, quoted in "Colombia: Agreement must guarantee justice for the millions of victims of the armed conflict," AI press release, 24 Sept 2015. Also based on interviews by author with several senior members of Amnesty International staff.

7 Ken Roth, Human Rights Watch Executive Director, interview by author, New York, 3 May 2016. See also "Human Rights Watch tacha de 'piñata de impunidad' pacto de justicia en Colombia," *El Universal*, 22 Dec 2015, and José Miguel Vivanco and Daniel Wilkinson, "Why Obama Should Press Colombia on Justice," *The Hill*, 4 Feb 2016.

8 Richard Dicker, director of international justice at Human Rights Watch, interview by author, New York, 10 May 2017.

9 Aryeh Neier, interview by author, New York, July 2015.

10 Interviews by author with Wilder Tayler, Secretary-General, International Commission of Jurists, Geneva, 14 Oct 2016; Philip Grant, director, TRIAL International, Geneva, 14 Oct 2016; and Antoine Bernard, director general, International Federation for Human Rights (FIDH), Paris, 17 Dec 2013.

11 There are many publications that spell out these obligations in detail. See, for example, the International Committee of the Red Cross, Customary IHL Database, "Rule 158: Prosecution of War Crimes", at ihl-databases.icrc.org, which concludes, "States must investigate war crimes allegedly committed by their nationals or armed forces, or on their territory, and, if appropriate, prosecute the suspects."

   Human rights advocates point to many different treaties and agreements that spell out a general obligation to prosecute international crimes. These include the Convention on the Prevention and Punishment of the Crime of Genocide (articles I, IV, and V); the Convention against Torture and Other Cruel, Inhuman or Degrading Treatment or Punishment (article 4); the

International Convention for the Protection of All Persons from Enforced Disappearance (article 7(1)); the International Convention against the Taking of Hostages (article 2); the Inter-American Convention to Prevent and Punish Torture (article 6); the Inter-American Convention on Forced Disappearance of Persons (article III); and the Basic Principles and Guidelines on the Right to a Remedy and Reparation for Victims of Gross Violations of International Human Rights Law and Serious Violations of International Humanitarian Law (Principles 18 and 22(f)).

12   Interviews with Tayler, ICG; Grant, TRIAL; and Bernard, FIDH.

13   The International Center for Transitional Justice sets out this argument in relation to Colombia. See Paul Seils, "Propuesta de criterios de selección y priorización para la ley de Justicia y Paz en Colombia," March 2012, and "Justice and Peace Process Should Lead to the Most Responsible" (article and podcast), 9 May 2012, www.ictj.org.

14   "Una Carta Bomba: La Fiscal de la Corte Penal Internacional se le atraviesa al Marco Jurídico para la Paz," *Semana.com*, 17 Aug 2013.

15   "Statement of ICC Prosecutor, Fatou Bensouda, on the conclusion of the peace negotiations between the Government of Colombia and the Revolutionary Armed Forces of Colombia—People's Army," 1 Sept 2016, www.icc-cpi.int.

16   Transitional Justice Institute, *The Belfast Guidelines on Amnesty and Account-ability* (Belfast: Transitional Justice Institute, University of Ulster, 2013).

17   See, for example, "Acuerdo sobre víctimas: necesario y oportuno," Comisión Colombiana de Juristas, press release, 21 Dec 2015; Gustavo Gallón, "Un acuerdo ponderado," *El Espectador*, 24 Dec 2015.

18   Fatou Bensouda, "The Peace-Justice Interface: Where are we now and what are the challenges ahead?" in Paul Dziatkowiec, Christina Buchhold, Jonathan Harlander, and Massimiliano Verri, *Peacemaking in the New World Disorder: Oslo Forum Meeting Report* (Geneva: Centre for Humanitarian Dialogue, 2015), 26, www.hdcentre.org.

19   James Stewart, "Transitional Justice in Colombia and the Role of the International Criminal Court," 13 May 2015, www.icc-cpi.int.

20   ICTJ notes that the policy objectives of punishment, in different situations, could include retribution, deterrence, reinforcing societal values, or rehabilitation of wrongdoers. Paul Seils, "Squaring Colombia's Circle: The Objectives of Punishment and the Pursuit of Peace," International Center for Transitional Justice, June 2015, www.itcj.org.

21   For example, two giants in the Colombian human rights community interpreted these legal requirements differently. Gustavo Gallon, the director of the Colombia Commission of Jurists, generally argued the first position; Rodrigo Uprimny, the founding director of Dejusticia (the Center for Law, Justice, and Society), took the second position.

22   In particular, see discussion in Chapter 3.

23   The legal foundation and potential reach of "guarantees of non-recurrence" is explored in "Report of the Special Rapporteur on the Promotion of Truth, Justice, Reparation and Guarantees of Non-recurrence, Pablo de Greiff," UN Report A/HRC/30/42, 7 Sept 2015.

Part II
Case Studies

10 Sierra Leone

Sierra Leone suffered a brutal civil war throughout the 1990s. Peace talks in 1999 led to a peace deal but confronted major hurdles that were only overcome with significant compromises.[1]

In many ways, questions of justice and impunity came to define both the talks and the difficult peace that followed. The International Criminal Court was not yet in operation and would hold no jurisdiction over events prior to 2002. But the talks concluded just weeks after the UN finalized a policy against amnesty for international crimes, and the UN made its views clear. The manner in which the amnesty question was handled in Sierra Leone thus became an important reference point, seen as the moment when the world's posture towards impunity for serious crimes suddenly changed.

The timing of the UN's engagement on the amnesty was awkward. The warring parties had accepted a broad immunity deal as central to the accord, but the UN representative added a reservation to the amnesty at the last minute—literally at the signing ceremony itself. This left many questions open, particularly for the warring parties who might now be vulnerable to prosecution. These questions played an important part in the difficult road to solidifying peace over the following years.

A Horrible War

Sierra Leone's civil war began in 1991, when rebels fighting for the Revolutionary United Front (RUF) entered Sierra Leone from Liberia, with the support of the Liberian rebel leader and later president, Charles Taylor. Profits from RUF-controlled diamond mines fueled the war. The RUF said it was fighting to end entrenched corruption and bad governance, but its political ideology and intentions were never very clear.

As the war broadened and intensified, it became particularly cruel. The RUF spread terror by amputating the limbs of civilians. Much of the country's population was displaced. Children were forced into fighting, and many women were raped and forced into marriage with rebel soldiers. A report by Sierra Leone's truth commission later showed that government forces were also responsible for serious atrocities, though in lesser numbers.

A first peace process, initiated in 1995, culminated in an agreement signed in Abidjan, Côte d'Ivoire, in late 1996. This accord contained a broad amnesty for the RUF; provisions for electoral, judicial, and police reform; protection of human rights; transformation of the RUF into a political party; withdrawal of regional forces; and expulsion of a foreign private security firm, Executive Outcomes, that backed the government. Implementation of this agreement was stalled from the start, partly because the leader of the RUF, Foday Sankoh, prevented the UN from deploying peacekeepers. Fighting resumed less than two months after the agreement was signed.[2]

Things got worse. In 1997, a military coup forced the government into exile in neighboring Guinea. The newly installed military authorities, called the Armed Forces Revolutionary Council (AFRC), promptly invited the RUF to join it in forming a government. This AFRC-RUF regime committed massive crimes, including executions, widespread looting, and rape. Within a year, forces of the Economic Community of West African States Monitoring Group (ECOMOG) were able to push them out of Sierra Leone's capital, Freetown, and restore the exiled government to power.[3]

The bulk of Sierra Leone's armed forces fled with the AFRC-RUF, leaving the government with little military force of its own. The government still tried to defeat the rebels militarily, in part relying on foreign mercenary forces, until a major rebel offensive on Freetown in January 1999. This again had to be repelled by ECOMOG. But the West African states made clear that their willingness to defend Sierra Leone was reaching its limits.[4] Sierra Leone came under intense pressure from the international community to negotiate an end to the war. Seeing no other options, the government finally agreed to talks.[5]

Peace Negotiations at Lomé

Lomé, Togo, was a natural venue for the peace talks partly because Togo was the chair of the Economic Community of West African States (ECOWAS) and was seen as a neutral party in the conflict; it had neither provided troops to ECOMOG nor supported the rebels. The government of Togo acted as the official mediator; the Togolese foreign minister, Joseph Koffigoh, led the talks on a day-to-day basis, and President Gnassingbe Eyadema sometimes stepped in. The UN's senior representative at the talks, Francis Okelo, served as deputy chair.[6] A facilitating committee emerged, composed of representatives of ECOWAS, the UN Mission to Sierra Leone, the Organization of African Unity, the Commonwealth of Independent States, the U.S., and the UK, with occasional participation by West African governments such as Nigeria, Liberia, and Ghana.[7]

The U.S. ambassador to Sierra Leone, Joseph Melrose, described the approach taken by many of the foreign diplomats:

> A large part of the logic under which the facilitating group operated was the need to not throw the situation in Sierra Leone into even a greater

state of chaos nor create an atmosphere in which it would be considerably more difficult to obtain the very necessary financial assistance from both institutional and bi-lateral donors that Sierra Leone desperately needed. It was pointed out to the RUF that the fact that the current Sierra Leonean government had been elected, even if under less than perfect circumstances, and enjoyed international recognition was important to remember in terms of the availability of future assistance.[8]

Civil society representatives were included as observers, and they were able to significantly influence the discussions.[9] They pressed the RUF to modify some of its positions and supported it on other issues, such as its demand for free public education. For example, after two months of talks, the RUF suddenly backtracked on several previously agreed points, insisting on such major changes that some participants thought the process would collapse. Civil society participants invited RUF leaders to dinner and pushed them hard to modify their position. The confrontation almost came to physical blows, but the next day the RUF did soften its position and the talks continued.

Delegates were grouped into three committees, covering military and security issues; humanitarian, human rights, and socioeconomic concerns; and political issues. The subject of amnesty was addressed in the political committee since it was considered primarily a political question. It was one of the first issues on the agenda.

The Immediate Question of Amnesty

All parties and participants quickly accepted that a proactive criminal justice approach was unrealistic, given the power wielded by those who might be prosecuted. The one explicit proposal for judicial accountability was in fact raised by the RUF. In one of the first formal sessions, the RUF demanded justice for the economic crimes and corruption of the government. But the RUF was told that its own war crimes would also have to be addressed, and it dropped the issue.[10] Ultimately, the issue of corruption—which remained a major problem—was left unaddressed in the final peace accord, other than by a passing reference in the preamble.[11] No one—neither the parties, international participants, nor civil society—seriously considered proposing a war crimes tribunal or other proactive measures to prosecute the war's crimes.[12] The issue of criminal responsibility for past crimes thus focused on amnesty.

In many respects, Sierra Leone presented a worst-case scenario for trying to preserve international standards of justice while negotiating peace. The government's military weakness gave them little leverage and few alternatives. There was huge public pressure to stop the war. The talks began just three months after Freetown had been overrun by the rebels, which left much of the city damaged and thousands of civilians dead, maimed, or raped. The rebels controlled two-thirds of the country, and the tenuous defense of the capital depended almost entirely on foreign troops.[13]

In addition, without an amnesty, the threat of punishment for the rebel leadership was very real. Five months earlier, twenty-four people had been executed for participating in the 1997 coup or the illegal regime that followed. Many others had been convicted of treason and sentenced to death and were in the midst of appeals.[14] RUF leader Foday Sankoh was among them: he had been detained while traveling abroad and transferred back to Sierra Leone for trial. The government allowed him to travel from his jail cell on death row to attend the peace talks in Togo.[15] He had no intention to return to jail.

The Sierra Leonean population was suffering intense violence in rebel-held areas, and they pressed for the war to end. Many saw the conflict as a result of decades of bad governance, just as the RUF claimed, which tempered somewhat the public's hatred for the rebels. The public readiness to forgive the rebels strengthened in the face of continued atrocities, which the government could not stop. "Give them what they want as long as they agree to stop killing us" was a common refrain.

Consultations in the months before the Lomé talks reflected a practical view from the Sierra Leonean public, but not without limits. The National Commission for Democracy and Human Rights, a government body, consulted widely and held a national conference on these questions.[16] The conference concluded that "in the interest of peace, national reconciliation and unity there should be an amnesty for all combatants, but cases of serious human rights violations should go through the proposed Truth and Reconciliation Commission."[17] Foday Sankoh could be pardoned if he fully supported the peace process, the conference concluded, but it opposed giving political positions to the RUF.[18] Many of these recommendations were not ultimately followed.

Specifics of the Amnesty Discussion

In these circumstances, virtually everyone close to the Lomé talks agreed that an amnesty was necessary for a peace agreement. The question was whether an amnesty could be limited in some way.

The subject of amnesty was the first item to be addressed by the political committee, in its first meeting. Participants understood it to be "a prerequisite for any meaningful negotiation." It was a short discussion: one participant recalled the government beginning the meeting by offering a blanket amnesty to the RUF.

Then Attorney-General Solomon Berewa, who headed the government delegation, generally agreed with this account. He told me that the government offered the RUF an amnesty as an incentive, to move things forward. "They didn't ask for an amnesty; we suggested it," he said. Berewa knew that the government would only offer limited power sharing, and thus the RUF would want legal protection. "There would not have been a peace agreement without an amnesty," he said.

Many of those at Lomé had also taken part in the peace process three years earlier, and this was their point of reference. The 1996 agreement had also included a blanket amnesty, but this received very little attention from the international community at the time. Indeed, the U.S. ambassador to Sierra Leone who took part in the earlier talks described the amnesty as the "least controversial" of all issues discussed in 1996.[19]

The 1996 accord was also the departure point for Sierra Leone President Ahmad Tejan Kabbah. An international diplomat who met him before traveling to Lomé recalled Kabbah's one comment on the impending negotiations. "I was looking over the Abidjan agreement." Kabbah told him. "I realize that the date on the amnesty will have to be changed."

If all parties took for granted that some form of amnesty was inevitable, side discussions did take place on whether it should be limited or conditional. Michael O'Flaherty, a UN human rights official, wrote that local and UN human rights actors

> were of the view that a range of options could be considered side by side with some form of amnesty—such as for the amnesty to exclude war crimes and crimes against humanity, for amnesty to be conditional on cooperation with a truth commission, for such a commission to have the power to recommend prosecutions, and for establishment of an international commission of inquiry. That none of these options was explored at the time may reflect a failure of imagination the part of negotiators rather than any validity in the claim that the proposals would undermine the peace process.[20]

The Sierra Leone Bar Association thought that a blanket amnesty would violate the constitution, but they found no opportunity to raise these concerns in the initial rush of the first meetings.[21] Some observers remember brainstorming about alternatives towards the end of the talks three months later, and a few days before the final accord was signed an international advisor prepared a memo that set out options for constraining, limiting, or conditioning amnesty. This was apparently the only document produced at Lomé that offered specific alternatives and options on the question. The options it presented implied an approach based on individual rather than blanket amnesty. It suggested that the text state that the amnesty would have no bearing on crimes of universal jurisdiction; that nothing in the agreement would prejudice the international legal obligations of Sierra Leone or the application of international law; and that the amnesty would be dependent on full cooperation with the Truth and Reconciliation Commission (TRC). In addition, the memo proposed elements that it said were desirable but not necessary under international law: that amnesty applicants should make a public apology for their acts; that the amnesty would be subject to review based on recommendations by the TRC; and that those seeking amnesty must compensate victims.

But ultimately, the parties did not consider such conditions or limitations. Civil society and UN human rights officials argued against a general amnesty, on the basis of international human rights standards and the need to combat impunity, but these conversations were limited to informal meetings on the periphery of the talks. The final language on amnesty echoed the 1996 agreement, though it added a reference to pardon, to respond to the needs of Foday Sankoh and others already convicted. The final agreement read:

Article IX: Pardon and Amnesty
1. In order to bring lasting peace to Sierra Leone, the Government of Sierra Leone shall take appropriate legal steps to grant Corporal Foday Sankoh absolute and free pardon.
2. After the signing of the present Agreement, the Government of Sierra Leone shall also grant absolute and free pardon and reprieve to all combatants and collaborators in respect of anything done by them in pursuit of their objectives, up to the time of the signing of the present Agreement.
3. To consolidate the peace and promote the cause of national reconciliation, the Government of Sierra Leone shall ensure that no official or judicial action is taken against any member of the RUF/SL, ex-AFRC, ex-SLA [Sierra Leone Army] or CDF [Civil Defence Force] in respect of anything done by them in pursuit of their objectives as members of those organisations, since March 1991, up to the time of the signing of the present Agreement. In addition, legislative and other measures necessary to guarantee immunity to former combatants, exiles and other persons, currently outside the country for reasons related to the armed conflict shall be adopted ensuring the full exercise of their civil and political rights, with a view to their reintegration within a framework of full legality.[22]

UN Disclaimer

While the Lomé talks were under way, but quite separately, staff at UN headquarters in New York were formalizing the UN's position on amnesty for serious international crimes. In June 1999, the office of the UN secretary-general sent a cable to all UN representatives, attaching "Guidelines for United Nations Representatives on Certain Aspects of Negotiations for Conflict Resolution." These Guidelines indicated that the UN could not give its support for any amnesty for war crimes, crimes against humanity, or genocide.

It is not clear when the Guidelines were first brought to the attention of the head of the UN delegation in Lomé, Francis Okelo; one UN participant remembers first seeing the Guidelines just two days before the signing ceremony. Other senior UN personnel working with Okelo were not aware of the Guidelines or learned of them very late. One senior UN official at Lomé recalled that the UN's options were limited. "Were we going to say that because of that amnesty, the whole document was to be scrapped? If we didn't sign, then the agreement couldn't be implemented. We wouldn't have a mandate for a UN mission, for example. It was a big dilemma." Ending the war was their most urgent objective. "It was about strategy and tactics. The strategy was to pursue peace. The tactics included: don't let justice get in the way. It was the price to pay for peace."

This presented a problem for UN representative Okelo. The day before the scheduled signing ceremony, he received a phone call from Secretary-General Kofi Annan, who made clear that the UN could not give its support to the amnesty provision. Okelo spoke with Attorney General Berewa, but Berewa refused to change the amnesty provision.

Okelo resolved this dilemma by deciding to sign the agreement with a disclaimer in relation to the specific element pertaining to amnesty. When the copies of the agreement were passed around at the signing ceremony the following day, he wrote in next to his signature:

> The United Nations holds the understanding that the amnesty and pardon in Article IX of the agreement shall not apply to international crimes of genocide, crimes against humanity, war crimes and other serious violations of international humanitarian law.[23]

The other signatories were surprised by this unexpected amendment. Sankoh was taken aback when he saw it. "What does this mean?" he said to no one in particular. "Are you going to try us?" No one answered, and the signing ceremony continued.

The implications of the UN disclaimer were left open. It gave hope to those fighting the country's entrenched culture of impunity. And it left the rebels suspicious of the international community and the government's intentions. The possibility that former rebels might in the end be held to account hung in the air through the first difficult, slow-moving months after the peace agreement was signed.

National and International Reaction

News of the amnesty was received differently inside and outside Sierra Leone. The abuses of the war had been so atrocious that many in the international community saw an amnesty as profoundly unacceptable. The international human rights community, in particular Human Rights Watch and Amnesty International, condemned the idea of a blanket amnesty for egregious crimes.

The Sierra Leone public remained focused above all on the need to end the violence. The amnesty agreement, "came as no surprise and there was no Sierra Leonean public outcry opposing it," according to UN human rights official O'Flaherty.[24] The public responded with irritation and anger when the details of the final accord became clear—but not because of the amnesty. Rather, they were upset that Sankoh and others in the RUF and former AFRC were to be rewarded with plum positions in the transitional government.

The government was unfazed by the international reaction. As Berewa explained,

> The government's position was clear. What we wanted most, above everything else, was peace, for the war to come to an end. Whatever the view

of the international community, this was not our business. Whatever we could do to produce that result, we would do.[25]

Berewa saw the accord as a political document; he was less concerned with the "fine niceties of the law." However, he insisted that the agreement should fall within the parameters of the Constitution and should require no constitutional amendment for implementation.[26] Berewa saw this as providing a natural constraint, in particular limiting possible power-sharing arrangements, as addressed further below.

There were some missed opportunities. Significant misunderstandings in relation to legal obligations of the state and acceptable parameters of an amnesty—including by foreign diplomats helping to guide the talks—could have been addressed through input from legal experts. This has since become common in other peace processes. Expertise was available, such as from UN human rights experts already present at Lomé, but these connections were apparently not made.

One basic condition that might have been added to the text could have strengthened implementation. If the pardon and amnesty were contingent on each person's compliance with the full peace agreement, this might have offered a powerful point of leverage. In the end, while not spelled out in the agreement, at least some signatories to the Lomé Accord understood this condition to be implied. But including this explicitly could have given important leverage to those who were later trying to push the recalcitrant RUF leadership to comply with demobilization and post-conflict normalization.

Other Justice Issues in the Peace Talks

Once the amnesty was essentially settled, early in the talks, the question of justice turned to truth, victim reparations, and reforms.

Truth and Reconciliation Commission

Civil society first pushed for a Truth, Justice, and Reconciliation Commission that would have the power to recommend prosecutions for past crimes.[27] The government instead suggested a Truth and Reconciliation Commission, which was silent on criminal justice. But the RUF representatives resisted the proposal; the initial draft was one-sided, focused only on RUF actions, and they thought the Commission would look too much like a court. The language was finally broadened to cover everyone, by implication government as well as international troops, and other delegates assured the RUF that the amnesty would protect them. The RUF then came around to supporting the proposal.

The final text agreed to a TRC "to address impunity, break the cycle of violence, provide a forum for both the victims and perpetrators of human rights violations to tell their story, [and] get a clear picture of the past in order to facilitate genuine healing and reconciliation." Membership of the Commission would "be drawn from a cross-section of Sierra Leonean society with the participation and some technical support of the International Community."[28]

The senior RUF legal advisor at the talks later insisted, when I interviewed him, that both the TRC and the amnesty could have been implemented in the style of South Africa's TRC, which required perpetrators to tell the full truth about their crimes in order to receive amnesty. He had understood this to be the intention at the time, he said, and he saw it as a feasible approach.

Some international participants also remembered discussing the South African TRC as a model. "Certainly I, and I believe others, had the impression that the South Africa model would be followed at least in large part," one foreign diplomat recalled. But the fairly complex idea of linking amnesty to truth telling was never spelled out in any draft of the agreement.

Reparations

The Lomé Accord also committed to a fund for the rehabilitation of victims of the war, a proposal from civil society that was agreed without controversy. Both sides of course had an interest in such a fund, since there were victims on all sides of the war. But the question of who precisely would finance this was not discussed. The final agreement indicated only that:

> The Government, with the support of the International Community, shall design and implement a programme for the rehabilitation of war victims. For this purpose, a special fund shall be set up.[29]

U.S. Ambassador Joseph Melrose noted the difficulties of this vague language. He writes that the provisions in the accord,

> such as that of creating a fund to assist war victims were vague in terms of specific objectives, lacked specificity of purpose and [made] no mention of the source of the funding other than the frequently used phrase 'with the help of the international community.' Efforts by members of the facilitating committee to convince the sides that more specificity was needed and would be helpful in securing international assistance were unsuccessful. This lack of specificity and lack of evidence of a commitment on the part of the Sierra Leoneans to show their own willingness to provide at least token resources proved to be detrimental in implementing many of the social and economic reforms, despite their laudable objectives.[30]

Reform of the Security Forces and Demobilization

The accord agrees to the demobilization of rebel forces and the incorporation of some of these forces into the army, but set out no specific conditions in relation to individuals' past record on human rights. It only stated: "Those ex-combatants of the RUF/SL, CDF and SLA who wish to be integrated into the new restructured national armed forces may do so provided they meet established criteria."[31] The criteria were left unspecified.

The possibility of vetting on human rights grounds was apparently never discussed. A member of the government delegation who served on the security and military committee saw this idea as violating the agreed amnesty.[32] Others said that vetting would have "created a difficulty," and that it was important instead to make the security forces accessible to all combatants, and then retrain them as necessary.

There were many problems in the subsequent demobilization and integration of ex-combatants. Many former RUF fighters were unable to return to their home communities, since their association with the widely abhorred rebel forces was known. Many remained in Freetown, unemployed. These problems could have been foreseen, and in the interests of long-term stability a more robust approach to reintegration might have been included in the peace agreement. Creative approaches to community service or symbolic individual reparations and apologies might have advanced reconciliation at the community level and helped moderate what became an entrenched problem of displacement of former rebels. While the TRC included some public sessions in its work that effectively played this role—opening space for apologies and forgiveness—these were few in number and not strategically designed for purposes of broader reintegration.

Protecting Rights in the Future

The accord committed to a new Human Rights Commission and to human rights education in schools and in the armed forces. But it included no provisions for judicial reform, despite clear needs. Prolonged pre-trial detention was rampant, prison conditions poor, and access to the courts scarce, especially outside Freetown. This would only be slowly taken up, with a push from the international community, over the next years.

Power Sharing

The decision to offer rebels senior positions in a transitional government was the most difficult concession of the government negotiating team, and was far more controversial than the issue of amnesty. Years of brutal violence had left the RUF with very little public support,[33] but nevertheless the RUF demanded a prominent role in a government of national unity and insisted that the AFRC and RUF should together be allocated half the ministerial posts. The government was initially unwilling to concede more than two ministries. Both parties remained steadfast, reaching an unresolvable breaking point.

At a moment when the talks were at risk of collapse over this issue, a senior government negotiator received a visit from a Nigerian official. The official made clear that Nigeria's continued commitment to maintaining troops in

Sierra Leone was doubtful. He then proposed that the RUF/AFRC be offered a minimum of four positions.

The government finally conceded four ministerial posts.[34] The RUF requested foreign affairs and finance, but was refused. The government insisted that the authority to appoint ministers lay with the president and could not be usurped by the negotiations. The final text of the accord stated that the RUF/AFRC would be given "one of the senior cabinet appointments such as finance, foreign affairs and justice, and three other cabinet positions." The accord also granted them four deputy ministerial posts, to be appointed "bearing in mind that the interests of other political parties and civil society organizations should also be taken into account."[35] After the signing, the RUF/AFRC was eventually appointed to head the ministries of trade and industry; energy and power; lands, housing, country planning, and the environment; and tourism and culture. The RUF protested, saying that none of these was a senior cabinet position and that the spirit of the accord has been violated, but the president held firm.

One of the last issues to be resolved was the position that RUF leader Foday Sankoh would hold in the transitional government. He had rarely attended the talks themselves, although he was on the premises; he remained in his hotel room and received briefings from RUF delegates. Just days before the scheduled signing ceremony, he suddenly announced that he was unwilling to sign. The talks were again in crisis. Several international delegates met with him and hatched an idea that clinched the agreement: Sankoh became chair of a new Commission for the Management of Strategic Resources, National Reconstruction and Development. Furthermore, the accord stated, "he shall enjoy the status of Vice President and shall therefore be answerable only to the President of Sierra Leone."[36]

For many Sierra Leoneans, the award of lucrative ministerial posts to rebels, and to Sankoh in particular, was hard to accept. Even members of the government delegation left Lomé feeling dispirited and cynical; they saw the accord as a pragmatic step to stop the carnage, they told me, but they were well aware it was imperfect. Public anger and frustration was palpable throughout the implementation period, especially as the former rebels flaunted the perks and power of their high offices, but never seemed to take their responsibilities seriously. This foreshadowed problems to come.

A Difficult Peace

In the months after the Lomé accord was signed, frustration mounted. International peacekeeping forces were slow to arrive, while the RUF violated several aspects of the agreement, resisted disarmament, and even took several hundred UN soldiers hostage for a short period.

Just ten months after the signing, there were rumors that RUF soldiers were on the outskirts of Freetown, threatening to storm the capital as they had the previous year. A large group of protesters approached Foday Sankoh's residence demanding that the RUF stop the advance of its troops. Sankoh's jittery security guards fired on the group, killing over twenty. Sankoh fled, and only after several days was found and arrested. This changed the course of events.

The quick deployment of a thousand British troops prevented the crisis from worsening. The UN also strengthened its forces. But the peace was very fragile. Several months later, now fifteen months after the Lomé signing, a report from the UN Secretary-General still described the security situation as "precarious and unpredictable."[37]

An expert analysis by the London-based NGO Conciliation Resources argued that the RUF's behavior reflected "their fear of being brought to justice," and that "their hesitations, misgivings, reluctance to disarm, and arrogant behavior betrayed a deep sense of guilt and an unwillingness to face their victims."[38]

International human rights advocates have argued that the amnesty, as well as awarding the RUF senior posts, was the cause of the crises in peace implementation. As Corinne Dufka of Human Rights Watch said, "if you put persons known for having committed violations in positions of power, then you can expect them to continue to violate the rule of law—like criminals guarding the chicken coop."[39] Human Rights Watch concluded that the amnesty "failed to bring 'lasting peace' to Sierra Leone," and indeed "emboldened potential rights abusers" by showing that combatants would pay no price for their crimes.[40] In interviews and public statements, Human Rights Watch has repeatedly blamed the resurgence of violence on the fact of the blanket amnesty. But this is too narrow of an understanding of the dynamics that were playing out in the post-accord environment.

Sierra Leonean civil society and other close participants generally gave a number of more direct causes for these crises. In particular, the delay in the arrival of international peacekeeping troops led the RUF to believe the international community had lost interest. Echoing others, former U.S. Ambassador Melrose wrote,

> One is left to wonder if the May 2000 events could have been avoided if the [UN] peacekeepers could have been deployed in a timely manner. The first peacekeepers arrived more than four months after the agreement had been signed and had not reached operational effectiveness before the May 2000 events, nine plus months after the signing.[41]

In retrospect, it seems Sankoh should not have been trusted. But there was a desperate desire to believe he would abide by the peace deal, especially in view of the handsome rewards he would enjoy. Sankoh was a difficult partner, for sure, but at the moment of the Lomé peace conference he was the only person in a position to deliver peace, and thus had to be included and reckoned with.

In November 2000 and in May 2001, the government and the RUF signed two additional agreements, in Abuja, Nigeria. The first recommitted the parties to the Lomé Accord and declared a new ceasefire. The second set out a vigorous program of disarmament, demobilization, and reintegration, leading to a significant easing of hostilities.[42] With these agreements, and with a disruptive Sankoh out of the way, peace implementation finally began to take hold.

The Special Court for Sierra Leone

After the arrest of Sankoh in the May 2000 crisis, the Sierra Leone government formally requested the UN to establish a special court in order to take him to trial. This was entirely unforeseen and certainly nowhere in the conversations or considerations during the Lomé talks just a year earlier.

Many observers of the Sierra Leone peace process have assumed that a special court was necessary because the amnesty in the Lomé agreement prevented prosecutions in national courts. But those closest to these initial decisions for a special court did not see it this way. The foreign diplomat who first discussed the idea of an international court with President Kabbah, shortly after Foday Sankoh was arrested, remembers Kabbah outlining two reasons why it would be difficult to prosecute Sankoh in a national court: the inherent weaknesses in Sierra Leone's judiciary and the fact that the country had not signed the Convention on the Safety of United Nations and Associated Personnel, which would have facilitated prosecution for the RUF's kidnapping of UN peacekeepers.[43] This diplomat remembers saying to Kabbah that the amnesty was no longer applicable because Sankoh had violated the terms of the accord, and Kabbah agreed.

A Special Court for Sierra Leone was ultimately created in 2002 through an agreement between the Government of Sierra Leone and the United Nations. Over the next years, it indicted thirteen people for crimes against humanity and war crimes by the RUF, the AFRC, and the government-aligned Civil Defense Forces. Foday Sankoh died in jail before his trial took place. At the national level, the amnesty set out in the Lomé accord was still in force, and no national trials took place.

Conclusion

The Sierra Leone experience demonstrates how issues of justice and amnesty are unlikely to be resolved with the signing of a peace agreement. The idea of a special court was not even considered during the negotiations in Sierra Leone, but turned out to be a major element of the post-war transition over the next years.

For many international observers, the blanket amnesty and the disclaimer added by the UN were by far the most prominent elements of Sierra Leone's peace agreement. But many assumptions about the amnesty and its impact on the transition have been misunderstood or overstated.

Sierra Leone's political class could not imagine that a peace agreement was feasible without a broad amnesty for war crimes. The relative military strength of the warring parties helped determine these calculations. On the other hand, the government was able to repel some of the RUF demands for robust power sharing. The government simply never placed as much importance on the idea of accountability for the war's crimes and felt no need to dwell on the issue.

In this respect, we can see a clear change in the international context and the expectations placed on peace negotiations in the years after the Lomé agreement was concluded. If these talks took place ten or fifteen years later, much more attention would have been placed on accountability for serious crimes, and it seems unlikely that an unconditional, blanket amnesty would have emerged. The talks would have been more difficult, without a doubt, and may have taken longer than the four months to arrive at the Lomé accord. But maybe the result would have been more sustainable, the implementation less rocky, and the impact deeper on the Sierra Leonean institutions and culture of impunity that was much in need of reform.

Notes

1 This case study is based in part on a series of interviews in 2006 with many of those who had been directly involved in the 1999 peace negotiations. A longer version of this study was published as Priscilla Hayner, "Negotiating Peace in Sierra Leone: Confronting the Justice Challenge," Centre for Humanitarian Dialogue and International Center for Transitional Justice, Dec 2007. Adapted with permission.

2 See Lansana Gberie, "First Stages on the Road to Peace: The Abidjan Process (1995–96)," in David Lord, ed., *Paying the Price: The Sierra Leone Peace Process*, Accord 9 (London: Conciliation Resources, Sept 2000).

3 The Economic Community of West African States (ECOWAS) was centrally involved in trying to end or alleviate the Sierra Leone war throughout the 1990s. It formed ECOMOG in 1990 to provide a structure for joint military defense efforts in the region, first in Liberia and later in Sierra Leone and elsewhere.

4 Nigeria provided the largest contingent and had already warned that it planned to withdraw its troops from Sierra Leone after its forthcoming presidential elections.

5 The UK, for example, conditioned its military aid on a commitment from the government to pursue a "twin-track" military and diplomatic policy. See remarks by the British high commissioner, Peter Penfold, to the National Consultative Conference on the Peace Process in Sierra Leone, in National Commission for Democracy and Human Rights, *The Road to Peace: Report of National Consultative Conference on the Peace Process in Sierra Leone*, Volume 1 (Freetown: National Commission for Democracy and Human Rights, Apr 1999), 50–51, www.democracy.gov.sl. See also Michael O'Flaherty, "Sierra Leone's Peace Process: The Role of the Human Rights Community," *Human Rights Quarterly* 26:1 (Feb 2004): 32–33.

6 Francis Okelo served as UN special representative of the secretary-general for Sierra Leone from June 1998 to November 1999.

7 Joseph H. Melrose, Jr., "The Sierra Leone Peace Process," in Eileen F. Babbitt and Ellen Lutz, eds., *Human Rights and Conflict Resolution in Context* (Syracuse, NY: Syracuse University Press, 2009), 129.

8 Ibid., 129–130.

9 Civil society and the private sector was represented by a range of organizations, including the Inter-Religious Council of Sierra Leone, the National Forum for

Human Rights, the association of war victims and amputees, Women's Forum, Labour Congress, Chamber of Commerce, Sierra Leone Indigenous Business Association, and the Sierra Leone Association of Journalists.

10 This chain of events—the rebels demanding accountability for economic crimes and other abuses by the government, and then dropping the issue when informed that their own war crimes would also be covered—was echoed in the Liberia peace talks a few years later.

11 The Preamble to the Lomé Accord calls for a democratic system "in a socio-political framework free of inequality, nepotism and corruption."

12 According to Michael O'Flaherty, "neither the local nor the UN human rights actors ever called for comprehensive and immediate judicial accountability. They were not blind to the argument that the rebels need to be attracted to the negotiation table." Michael G. O'Flaherty, "Human Rights in Negotiating Peace Agreements: Sierra Leone," para. 123, presented at "Peace Agreements: The Role of Human Rights in Peace Agreements," a review meeting of the International Council on Human Rights Policy, 7–8 March 2005, Belfast. Available at www.ichrp.org.

13 Civil defense militias provided some additional defense against the rebels, especially in the south and part of the eastern region, where the government party was strong.

14 Those convicted of treason in civilian courts were appealing their sentence when they were freed from prison during the rebel assault on Freetown in January, with about one thousand other prisoners. The authorities had removed Sankoh from the prison just before the attack. Some reportedly turned themselves back in, to be cared for in prison by the International Committee of the Red Cross and await their formal release with the signing of the peace agreement.

15 No other leader was in a position to replace Sankoh at the talks. Extraordinary efforts were thus made to win his support. When he arrived at the talks, international participants provided him with satellite phones to communicate with his forces. When further massacres took place, he was directly confronted with photographic evidence, and he acknowledged for the first time that perhaps the RUF was responsible. U.S. Ambassador Joseph Melrose reported that Sankoh's demands for an unconditional pardon and the removal of any restrictions on his movement "almost caused the talks to end before they had begun . . . The position that the clemency was related to a peace agreement was not satisfactory to him and he often resorted to describing himself as a 'prisoner of peace.'" Melrose, "The Sierra Leone Peace Process," 131.

16 Some rights advocates whom I interviewed pointed out that several key human rights activists had not been invited to the conference. They wondered whether this was an intentional strategy to weaken the voice of those most strongly opposed to amnesty and impunity.

17 *The Road to Peace*, 36.

18 Ibid., 37. The statement read: "The President can use his Prerogative of Mercy to pardon [Sankoh] in the interest of peace and reconciliation, on condition that he renounces violence, unconditionally releases all abductees and allows his combatants to go through the DDR programme."

19 John L. Hirsch, *Sierra Leone: Diamonds and the Struggle for Democracy* (Boulder and London: Lynne Reinner, 2001), 52.

20 O'Flaherty, "Human Rights in Negotiating Peace Agreements," para. 123.

21 A previous consultative report had also questioned the constitutionality of a broad amnesty. This report asserted that a blanket amnesty would violate Chapter III of the Sierra Leone Constitution. *The Road to Peace*, 41–43.

22 Lomé accord, Article IX.

23 See UN Document S/1999/836, para. 7. This wording is often cited, but must be considered an approximation because neither the UN nor others have a copy of the marked-up document. There were twelve physical copies of the agreement signed by the parties. Okelo reportedly added this disclaimer to only one of his twelve signatures.

24 O'Flaherty, "Human Rights in Negotiating Peace Agreements," para. 92.

25 Solomon Berewa, interview by author.

26 The accord does agree to a constitutional review, however, to allow for a separate process of considering any necessary constitutional changes. The government did not oppose this.

27 The idea for a truth commission first emerged in early 1999 when a coalition of NGO and UN human rights advocates proposed a Truth, Justice, and Reconciliation Commission with powers to "recommend judicial prosecutions for some of the worst perpetrators." To the disappointment of human rights advocates, "justice" was dropped from the title at the consultative conference. See O'Flaherty, "Sierra Leone's Peace Process," 49–50.

28 Lomé accord, Article XXVI, "Human Rights Violations."

29 Lomé accord, Article XXIX, "Special Fund for War Victims."

30 Melrose, "The Sierra Leone Peace Process," 134–135.

31 Lomé Accord, Article XVII.

32 Senior official in the Office of the President, interview by author.

33 This was seen in the next elections, the 2002 legislative contest, when the RUF Party received only 2% of the vote.

34 One international participant remembers working out the specifics of these arrangements with the government; they concluded that, given current vacancies and other changes, four ministries could be awarded to the RUF without any current ministers having to be removed.

35 Lomé Accord, Article V.

36 Ibid.

37 "Seventh Report of the Secretary-General on the United Nations Mission in Sierra Leone," UN Doc. S/2000/1055, 31 Oct 2000.

38 Dennis Bright, "Implementing the Lomé Peace Agreement," in David Lord, ed., *Paying the Price: The Sierra Leone Peace Process*, Accord 9 (London: Conciliation Resources, 2000).

39 Corinne Dufka, interview by author.

40 Human Rights Watch, *Selling Justice Short: Why Accountability Matters for Peace* (New York: Human Rights Watch, July 2009), 57–61.

41 Melrose, "The Sierra Leone Peace Process," 137.

42 See "Agreement Between the Government of Sierra Leone and the RUF," Abuja, 10 November 2000, and "Communique," released after a meeting of the Joint Committee on Disarmament, Demobilisation and Reintegration by the Government of Sierra Leone, the RUF, and UNAMSIL, 15 May 2001.

43 The Convention on the Safety of United Nations and Associated Personnel was adopted by the UN General Assembly and opened for signature in December 1994. It creates a system for prosecution or extradition of those accused of attacking UN personnel.

11 Liberia

The Comprehensive Peace Agreement (CPA), signed in Accra, Ghana, in 2003, was the fifteenth peace agreement for Liberia since war began in 1989.[1] Most peace pacts held for only a few weeks. The 2003 agreement covered a broader range of issues and was more detailed than previous accords. Questions of justice were prominent in the negotiations, but left fundamentally unresolved in the final text. Investigation into the truth of the war's crimes, and any threat of possible prosecutions, remained highly contentious for many years following the peace agreement.[2]

The fifteen-year Liberian civil war was marked by brutal and wide-scale atrocities that fueled and were fueled by interethnic tensions. The war was started by Charles Taylor, then a rebel leader. Taylor was elected president in 1997 following a peace agreement signed in Abuja in 1995. His repressive policies at home and continued support for rebels in neighboring countries led opponents in 1999 to found LURD (Liberians United for Reconciliation and Democracy) and then, shortly before the final peace talks, MODEL (the Movement for Democracy in Liberia).

The peace negotiations were led by the Economic Community of West African States (ECOWAS). While civil society and ECOWAS had been pushing for a negotiated settlement for years, it was ultimately the escalation of the war that drove the fighting parties to more serious talks. By 2003, the rebels had closed in on Monrovia, Liberia's capital; many feared they could take government by force. This outcome would have suited almost no one; even rebel leaders later acknowledged that they did not have the leadership in place to run the country, it could have triggered a new cycle of war, and they had been firmly warned (by the U.S. and others) that a government taken by force would receive no international support.

Ghana offered to host peace talks, and the former President of Nigeria, General Abdulsalami Abubakar, was agreed as mediator.

The Indictment of Charles Taylor

The formal opening of the peace conference in Accra, Ghana, was met with an unexpected announcement: President Charles Taylor was under indictment for war crimes and crimes against humanity. The indictment came from the Special Court for Sierra Leone in relation to his support for rebels there. Taylor learned of the indictment at the moment it became public, just before the ceremony to open the peace conference began. According to a close advisor, Taylor was shocked at the news. "What do you mean, indictment? It's not possible to indict a head of state," he said.[3] He chose to attend the opening, and took the microphone to offer to step down from the presidency "for the sake of peace." He then promptly departed and flew back to Liberia to avoid arrest. While Ghana was technically obliged to detain him, the government insisted that it had not formally received the legal papers from the Special Court before Taylor left the country.

With the indictment of Taylor, the prospects for the peace conference suddenly changed. Few had held high hopes for the meeting, and most expected it to last less than two weeks. Taylor's offer to vacate the presidency fundamentally shifted the outlook for the talks and opened up possibilities for a serious peace process. In previous attempts at negotiations, Taylor was always able to manipulate the process to retain control in order to prevent any fundamental change.

The chief prosecutor of the Special Court, David Crane, had intentionally taken the decision to unseal Taylor's indictment at this moment. He told few people in advance: he worried that informing African governments would have leaked and Taylor would have avoided travel, thus making an arrest near impossible. He had informed U.S. policymakers of his intentions, and received contradictory reactions from different officials in Washington, ranging from support to worry and a strong urging to defer his plans. But the Prosecutor's office had not considered nor tried to assess the risks of a backlash in Monrovia, believing this to be outside of their mandate and their own concerns, according to Crane.[4]

But this action carried many risks, and there were strong critics of the Special Court's timing and manner of unsealing the indictment. At the time, many observers feared that the indictment would damage the peace talks and make it harder to extract Taylor from the presidency. They said that the prosecutor was acting rashly, indelicately, and with insufficient political knowledge and preparation, and that the prosecutor should have known that Ghana was unlikely to send Taylor to the Court just as he was opening major peace talks.

Crane described his decision to unseal the indictment as a calculated move, to "embarrass Taylor in front of his West African colleagues," to humble Taylor and make it impossible for him to continue to play a role in the peace talks. He thought it was important to do this at the beginning of the talks, so that everyone would know that Taylor was not a suitable guarantor for any peace deal. Given Taylor's record of violating previous peace accords and new evidence that a shipment of arms was soon to arrive to reinforce Taylor's forces in Monrovia, Crane was also convinced that unsealing the indictment would actually support the peace process. If he thought otherwise, he would have delayed, he said.[5]

Most African states involved in the peace talks reacted badly, and Ghana, as host, was particularly angry. The Ghanaian government insisted that arresting Taylor would violate their commitment to guarantee the security and freedom of all parties while attending the peace conference.

Apparently, none of the African participants or observers had any expectation that Ghana would turn Taylor over to the Court. He was in Ghana as a guest of the government, and his removal would have been a violation of African hospitality, many say. West Africans saw the indictment largely in political and regional terms, a dynamic that was underappreciated by many of the Court's backers. "Africans would never have allowed Europeans and Americans to come to Africa and arrest a sitting president," noted one Liberian rebel faction leader, in a typical reaction. A senior Taylor aide later said, "ECOWAS was opposed to anything that would have disgraced a sitting head of state. Could African leaders go to Europe and insist that a European head of state be arrested?"[6]

The mediator, former President Abubakar, believed that the indictment may have had the effect of "undermining the role of African heads of state" in relation to other mediated conflicts.[7] There were, however, reports of one or two West African leaders trying to work behind the scenes to support the Court and its indictment of Taylor, and the Court says it received private messages of support.

The perception of the Court's general posture towards the region continued to influence its work over the following years. The foreign minister of the transitional government of Liberia refused to meet with the Prosecutor during the entire two years of the transitional period, despite being a firm opponent of Taylor, because of how he saw the Court's manner of engagement.

Nevertheless, the indictment of Taylor ultimately had a deep effect on the peace process itself. Many Liberians involved in the talks look back on the indictment as the single most important element in changing the Accra peace talks from an effort with little chance of success to a serious meeting where the parties could in fact debate the future of the country—and without the ever-present control and manipulation of the seemingly unmovable Taylor.

Regardless of their view at the time, there seemed to be almost universal agreement later that the unsealing of the indictment had an overall positive effect on the actual negotiations. "The indictment was the single most important factor that influenced how the peace talks would turn out," argued a political party representative who played a central role in the talks. "Had the indictment not been unsealed we probably wouldn't be enjoying the peace we have now," noted a leading advocate of human rights. A religious leader who was active in preparing for the talks agreed: "Charles Taylor saying he wouldn't take part in the elections was a major contribution to resolution of the conflict. No one had that thought in mind." Many others make the same point: Taylor's departure immediately changed the dynamics and presumptions behind the negotiations.

The indictment delegitimized Taylor, both domestically and internationally. It effectively removed any last support for him from international partners. Once it was evident that he could not rely on international support, and especially that the U.S. had publicly turned against him, it became clear that he would have to leave the presidency. Equally important, it affected the morale of his own troops, which was already low because the soldiers had not been paid in months.

During the first two weeks of negotiations, the warring parties worked out the terms of a ceasefire. While this truce did not hold on the ground, this framework agreement did include the key clause that Taylor would not be included in the transitional government. "That was the sticking point: it took 14 days to negotiate that one clause," commented one LURD representative. It was clear to all that the Special Court's indictment was the single most important factor that led to this agreement.

However, when the indictment was first announced on that fateful opening day, many in Liberia feared it might lead to much more violence. Threats against Ghanaians living in Liberia were reported almost immediately. At exactly the same time, LURD began shelling the capital, striking the heart of downtown Monrovia. These two developments were unconnected to each other, but they were both certainly connected to the fact of the indictment. However, a closer look suggests a more benign effect than might first be assumed.

Many worried that if Ghana detained Taylor and then extradited him to the Special Court, his militant followers back home would take revenge against the large Ghanaian community in Liberia.[8] The streets in Monrovia were tense, and many who were in Monrovia as well as those at the talks in Accra say they expected a mass slaughter if Taylor was not returned home. The Ghanaian ambassador to Liberia reportedly received a message from Taylor's militia threatening to target and kill Ghanaians if Taylor was arrested. The ambassador sent the message to Accra, urging his government to ensure Taylor returned.

The U.S. ambassador in Monrovia, John Blaney, was working intensively to stop the fighting in Monrovia, and his role in keeping the embassy open throughout this period and actively pushing to stop the fighting was praised by all sides. He strongly opposed the timing of the indictment, and believes that "hundreds if not thousands of people would have died" in retribution if Taylor had been arrested in Ghana. "It would have ended the peace process and the war would have continued. How can you morally put at risk three-and-a-half million people?" he asked.[9]

U.S. citizens and the U.S. embassy were also directly threatened, given the belief widely held in Liberia that the U.S. was the real power behind the Special Court. As tensions increased in the hours after the indictment was announced, the U.S. embassy in Monrovia contacted senior Liberian government and military officials and made it clear that they would be held responsible for any breakdown in law and order.[10] A key General went on the radio and urged calm.[11]

While many insist that massive revenge attacks were imminent, some well-placed observers strongly dispute that this was likely. Even on the very day of the indictment, some civil society activists in Monrovia argued about whether the Taylor forces would react with customary violence. Some recount an air of calm within the senior Taylor leadership in Monrovia and a readiness for a smooth transition to the vice president. Playing up the threat of violence was in the interests of Taylor's allies, they note. Taylor returned home later that same day and the militia immediately calmed down; whether there was a real threat of violence as a result of the indictment remains a question.

Meanwhile, as tensions increased within Monrovia over concerns for how the Taylor forces would react, the rebel forces of LURD were quickly approaching the outskirts of Monrovia and preparing their first attack on the capital city. They had been planning for this attack on Monrovia at this time, in early June, and thus LURD troops were poised nearby. As long as Taylor was in power, they saw no reason to change that plan. Pushing Taylor to resign was their first priority. The LURD chairman, Sekou Conneh, was just beginning a BBC radio interview when he heard that Taylor was flying home to avoid the arrest warrant. He used the interview to order his forces, through the BBC, to move on Monrovia.[12]

LURD Chairman Conneh made clear that it was not because of the indictment that they attacked, but because of Taylor's return to Monrovia. Taylor was scheduled to return to Monrovia a few days after the opening ceremony in any case. If he had been arrested in Ghana, LURD would have held their attack, they say. "It wasn't because of the indictment. Whether indicted or not indicted, we were going to fight until he would leave. That was our goal," he told me. From this perspective, the indictment came close to halting the planned attack and perhaps could have ended the fighting two months earlier, saving countless lives.

The rebels' shelling of Monrovia continued throughout the three months of talks. LURD never invaded the city with troops, but it wreaked constant terror and death on the capital.

The Dynamics of the Peace Talks

The three "armed factions"—the government, LURD, and MODEL—were the central actors at the talks. During the ceasefire negotiations in the first weeks, they negotiated directly with each other without the involvement of civil society or other parties. For the remainder of the negotiations, representatives of the international community and national civil society also played an important role.

The primary international actors, in addition to ECOWAS, were the U.S., represented by persons who rotated in from the State Department's Bureau of West African Affairs in Washington, and the European Union/European Commission (EC), represented by the head of its Monrovia office.

Eighteen Liberian political parties were represented at the talks. The majority of these were recent creations of Charles Taylor, according to participants; he diluted the process by registering new parties just before the talks began. These eighteen parties were organized into a "group of eight," considered independent parties, and a "group of nine," the parties aligned with Taylor, in addition to Taylor's own party, the National Patriotic Party.

The drafting was done by a number of international participants, including the EC and, on at least one occasion, the U.S. representative. ECOWAS was in control, however, and sometimes removed any sections it considered controversial before distributing drafts for discussion.[13] Suggested language pertaining to accountability was among those issues removed from early drafts, according to one participant. The LURD also put forward its own alternative text very early in the process.

Plenary discussions addressed general points for the accord, rather than details or specific language. There were no subcommittees for more in-depth discussion, although much debate and lobbying took place outside the formal meetings. The final language of the agreement was seen by delegates only a day or two before the signing, with little opportunity for further input on specifics at that late stage.

Civil society was strongly committed to supporting the talks; some had worked for a negotiated end to the war since the early 1990s. A few representatives of interreligious, human rights, pro-democracy, women's rights, and legal organizations were included as official delegates, and many others attended unofficially as observers. They did not always work in close coordination, however, reducing their potential impact.

Liberian women played an important role. A number of representatives of women's organizations from Monrovia were official delegates at the talks, and some 150 refugee women traveled from a nearby Liberian refugee camp each morning to demonstrate for peace.[14] The refugee women sat outside the hall holding placards urging an end to the violence and confronted some faction leaders directly. Women activists in Monrovia sought out family members of rebel leaders, including the mother of one, and facilitated their traveling to Accra to make a personal plea that the shelling of Monrovia stop.

The civil society and refugee women pushed first and foremost for an end to the fighting. They were in regular touch with contacts in Monrovia. "We would make calls to frantic relatives and friends, which would make us even more alarmed," one recounted. "You called someone and could hear shooting, missiles, screams. 'They're shooting, we're on the floor, they're all around us!' they would say." One of the women who had traveled from Liberia to the talks returned home for a few days. While driving in downtown Monrovia, she watched as a man walking in front of her had his head cut clear off by an incoming shell. She returned to Accra incensed and insisting on change.

These civil society actors provided a direct link to the horrors of the fighting and put pressure on the participants to come to an agreement. On one occasion, when one woman received news of a relative killed in Monrovia, the group of women responded by physically blockading the door to the delegates' meeting room for several hours, refusing to let them leave (or even, as many remember, to use the toilet) until they came to agreement on the specific order of business before them. On another occasion, the women threatened to take their clothes off in protest that the talks were moving too slowly. "For a son to see his mother's nakedness—it's considered a curse. And to do it in public! So the men were saying, 'we better do something because they're threatening to take their clothes off,'" remembered one of the women.

The choice of the two-year transitional head of state—to be given the title of chairman—took place in the very last days at Accra. Civil society and political party delegates first voted on a slate of declared candidates, narrowing the choice to three. The final selection was then made by the three warring factions. Worries that war criminals might be held to account influenced the factions' calculations. Ellen Johnson Sirleaf, who two years later would be elected president, was one of the three finalists and received the most votes in the civil society and political party tally. But the factions were worried that she might push justice, which "would lead to further fighting," several faction representatives told me. This was a key reason why she was not chosen as interim head of state.

Using the Fighting as Leverage in the Negotiations

The continuing violence in Monrovia was primarily of two types: indiscriminate shelling of the city, mostly by the rebels on the outskirts of the city, and both targeted and random violence by gangs and militia within the city. The targeted attacks were particularly severe in the government-controlled areas, by government-aligned militia, although extensive looting also took place where LURD was in control. Human rights organizations reported fifteen to twenty people dying in Monrovia each day during the worst of the shelling.[15]

The delegates at the talks maintained close contact by cell phone with their forces on the frontlines, either directly (in the case of MODEL and the government) or indirectly (in the case of LURD, which usually communicated through its commanders in Guinea).[16] Those at the peace talks could also watch live coverage of the war on CNN. The shelling of the city was covered extensively, with mixed effect on the talks. What the parties saw on TV one day might further strengthen their resolve to stop the war. But sometimes the shelling was so intense that it stopped the talks altogether.

The warring parties also used their influence in the field of battle to improve their lot at the peace table. On at least one or two occasions, according to a number of participants, a faction representative who insisted on obtaining certain ministries in the transitional government, but found himself blocked, used the shelling for leverage. He made a call to the frontlines and ordered more shelling of Monrovia. All watched live on TV as mortar rounds landed in Monrovia. The opposing parties at the talks then granted that faction what it demanded.

Civil society delegates also felt the pressure. "One or two rockets would fall in Monrovia, and people would call us from home, pleading. 'You have to give them anything they want, to get it to stop,' they would say," recalled one participant. "When the faction leaders felt they were getting what they wanted, the fighting would simmer down." It felt like blackmail, they said.

The first draft of an agreement was distributed in mid-July. The draft reflected the firm position of the U.S. at that time: no faction representatives should hold a position in the transitional government. Civil society participants gave a round of applause. The rebel factions, however, were furious and, according to one observer, threatened to take action to obtain their desired ends. The next day, the most serious assault on Monrovia began, with intense shelling of the city. It was the beginning of a two-to-three week period that Liberians refer to as "World War Three."[17] The fighting was so intense on July 19, the first day of renewed shelling, that the peace talks stopped altogether. The delegates watched the war on their hotel television sets.

The heavy shelling increased the pressure for them to reach a deal. The mediator quietly brokered an arrangement that some felt swung too far in the opposite direction, awarding the great majority of ministries to the three warring factions. The idea of vetting persons nominated as ministers was also dropped. Civil society had pushed for a review on the grounds of competence, at least; this was left out. At least in the short term, the spoils of peace would reward those who had also benefited from the spoils of war.

Issues of Justice

War Crimes Tribunal, Amnesty, or Truth Commission?

Issues of accountability emerged early in the negotiations, shortly after the ceasefire agreement was signed. It first arose as a proposal for a war crimes tribunal, pushed by civil society representatives. The rebel factions were also demanding justice for the Taylor government. The mediator, General Abubakar, quietly told the rebels that they could also be accused of war crimes, "and then they were much more careful about their call for justice," Abubakar noted.[18] Some remember the factions proposing an amnesty, but this was not pushed hard. Abubakar, for example, remembered no discussion of an amnesty, and told me that some atrocities were so severe that they could simply never be amnestied. Instead of further debating either a war crimes tribunal or an amnesty, a truth and reconciliation commission was proposed and fairly quickly accepted.[19] The whole discussion took less than a week, perhaps three or four days, in plenary session.

The trade-off between a tribunal and a TRC seems to have been explicit in everyone's minds. "We chose a TRC because we didn't want a war crimes tribunal. A war crimes tribunal would be seen as witch-hunting," was a typical comment—in this case, from the military leader of one of the rebel factions. A leading civil society delegate remembers this dynamic clearly,

> The TRC became a very attractive option, because the dominant view of participants from civil society and political parties was for a war crimes court. You didn't need a general amnesty, because the TRC would give you an amnesty, it was thought. There was a sense that it was clear: a tribunal means you'd be put away, but the TRC wouldn't put you in jail. No one paid any attention to explaining what this meant.

The agreement on a TRC effectively ended the discussion about criminal justice.

In the course of these trade-offs, any suggestion of a general amnesty was short-lived. Many participants say that this was never seriously proposed or considered. Indeed, draft text presented by LURD early in the talks called for amnesty in the context of demobilization and disarmament of troops, but in a qualified manner that explicitly excluded serious human rights crimes.[20] One LURD legal advisor had been an independent human rights advocate in the 1980s, and another was generally knowledgeable of international human rights and humanitarian law. They also relied on Liberia's previous peace agreements, all of which excluded amnesty for serious crimes.[21]

Because the war was playing out in Monrovia and killing many civilians daily, many delegates, even among the armed factions, considered it "bad taste" to speak of an amnesty. There was also a sense that anyone calling for an amnesty would be perceived as guilty. Informally, assurances were given that neither the parties nor the international community wanted to see "witch-hunting," such that the factions didn't fear prosecutions.

They were also operating in a historical context where no one had been held accountable for human rights crimes since war began in 1989. Even the most notorious perpetrators, whose crimes were well-known, had never been prosecuted.

Thus, a level of comfort developed such that no one feared prosecution and many even assumed that an amnesty was guaranteed in the text, even though it was never spelled out in the agreement. In the end, the final text only suggested that an amnesty would be considered in the future:

> The NTGL (National Transitional Government of Liberia) shall give consideration to a recommendation for general amnesty to all persons and parties engaged or involved in military activities during the Liberian civil conflict that is the subject of this Agreement.[22]

The intention was to leave the issue open. Among those who were watching this issue closely, this was based on clear logic. One senior advisor with the Taylor government said they wanted to avoid an amnesty for rebels because they feared it would encourage war in the future. But if they threatened pros-ecution, they knew it would make it difficult to end this war. So it was inten-tional not to spell it out. They had the same reason for wanting to bar rebel leaders from senior positions in the transitional government—so as not to encourage future rebellions—but on this point they ultimately lost.

Civil society participants, such as those from the Association of Female Law-yers of Liberia (AFELL), also watched the discussion around accountability closely. While their main interest was to ensure that faction leaders did not get senior positions in government, they also kept an eye on any discussion around amnesty. If there had been a blanket amnesty on the table, they would have insisted that it should exclude crimes against humanity, war crimes, and other serious abuses, AFELL said. They also noted that the final accord refers to future consideration of an amnesty for "military activities," which in their view would exclude acts such as rape and maiming.

Meanwhile, several international delegates insisted that an amnesty for serious crimes was not allowed under international law. They cited the "war crimes convention" as prohibiting such amnesties. In fact, no such war crimes convention exists, as such—although it is true that customary and treaty-based international law generally frowns on, and in some cases prohibits, amnesty for certain crimes. One international delegate was also worried that granting an amnesty would establish an unacceptable precedent, which he was intent on avoiding—unaware that other recent peace agreements, even recently in neighboring Sierra Leone, had in fact granted such an amnesty (even if in Sierra Leone the UN tried to limit the amnesty's reach).

In any event, it is not clear how important these international voices were in the decision-making. The dynamic of the talks already moved against any idea of a blanket amnesty, and Liberians rarely cite the role of foreigners when explaining the outcome.

Informal discussions also led to other unfounded assumptions about the justice arrangement. One was that the truth commission would grant indi-vidual amnesties for past crimes. The legal advisors for two of the factions both told me they had understood this, although they had only a skeletal idea of how it might work. A senior religious leader who represented the Inter-Religious Council at the talks said he discussed the idea of individualized amnesty with many participants:

> It was understood that a list will be prepared by warring factions, and sub-mitted for consideration. But first, it will pass through the TRC. The TRC will examine the case of any person and ascertain whether he deserves amnesty. The idea was to include a provision for amnesty, but you need a methodology for how it is to be done. But then the TRC didn't come into being during the transitional government, so we couldn't do it.

The idea of amnesty-for-truth isn't surprising, given that most of the delegates knew only of the prior existence of the South African Truth and

Reconciliation Commission and were unaware of any other examples. Even the transitional head of state, Gyude Bryant, said, three years after the talks and well after the Liberian TRC had started work, that he didn't know of any truth commission other than the South African TRC.[23] Surprisingly, participants seem to have been unaware that the country next door, Sierra Leone, had included a truth commission in its peace accord of 1999. At the time of the Liberia peace discussions in 2003, the Sierra Leone TRC was entering into full operation. There had been at least thirty other truth commissions around the world, each quite different from the South African model. During the talks, several faction representatives were actively seeking further information about how truth commissions work. The protocol officer at the South African embassy in Accra brought them some background materials on the South African TRC, which became their main reference source.

In the end, the TRC Act that was later enacted by the Liberian legislature gave the Commission the power to recommend individual amnesties, but it explicitly prohibits amnesty for violations of international humanitarian law and crimes against humanity.[24] It also indicated that the Commission could recommend prosecutions. When the TRC completed its work several years later, the Commission indeed recommended numerous prosecutions at high levels.

The confusion in the minds of many signatories about what the final agreement said on many key points may have stemmed in part from the tight deadline for its signing. After three months of slow-moving negotiations and mounting frustration on the part of observers, there was considerable pressure to sign, and limited opportunity to go over specific language of the final draft. Donor states forced a conclusion by setting a firm deadline, allowing a few days for final matters to be agreed. They made clear that they wouldn't cover costs beyond this date.

Meanwhile, unknown to most delegates in Accra, Charles Taylor was trying to short-circuit the accountability issue by having an amnesty passed by the Liberian legislature just days before he left office in early August.[25] The "Act to Grant Immunity From Both Civil and Criminal Proceedings Against All Persons With In the Jurisdiction of Republic of Liberia From Acts or Crimes Committed During the Civil War From December 1989 to August 2003" was published in the official handbill, dated 8 August 2003. Taylor government officials and then-legislators insist it was legitimately passed, but many others question whether Parliament was even meeting at that time and had quorum, given the chaos in the city.[26] This supposed amnesty law was never applied, nor its validity clarified.

News of the Taylor amnesty reached some (but not all) of the delegates in Accra. A legal advisor to LURD said that he had heard of it and immediately wondered whether it complied with international law. The mediator, General Abubakar, was not aware of it and thought such a unilateral act could have created difficulty in the talks if it was more widely known.

Reform of the Security Forces

The final agreement included strong language on the reform of the security forces, including vetting on human rights grounds. It calls for restructuring of the army, and states that:

> Incoming service personnel shall be screened with respect to educational, professional, medical and fitness qualifications as well as prior history with regard to human rights abuses.[27]

This does not seem to have been controversial in the negotiations, although LURD was disappointed that its proposal that an American should lead the army and police, argued on the grounds of competence and to avoid corruption, was not accepted. When the transitional government interpreted "restructuring" to mean disbanding the army entirely, the military was surprised, and displeased. The U.S., through an agreement with the government, subcontracted the private contractor Dyncorp International to oversee a process of retiring all existing military forces and recruiting and training a new army. This process was intended to include extensive vetting and background checks on each new recruit. However, the Dyncorp process was criticized by civil society and other independent observers for limited consultations and for lacking transparency.

The language in the agreement pertaining to the police, on the other hand, does not specifically call for vetting on human rights grounds, but it does indicate that a restructured police force shall emphasize "a respect for human rights." The UN Mission in Liberia was given the lead role in police reform, and it decided to include procedures to screen for past human rights abuse.

Judicial and Legal Reform

Also uncontroversial and little discussed during the negotiations was a means to strengthen the judiciary through the appointment of temporary Supreme Court judges. The agreement simply states that all members of the Supreme Court shall be deemed to have resigned with the signing of the accord. Many participants saw this as necessary since the serving judges had been appointed by Taylor and were not considered impartial. Thereafter, new judicial appointments were to be made from a shortlist provided by the National Bar Association. The agreement also stated that these interim justices would be prohibited from contesting elective office during the next elections.[28]

However, the final text did not otherwise grapple with the massive needs of the justice sector. There could be no reasonable expectation for a serious national prosecutions program for war crimes without deep reforms. This was not discussed at Accra; serious proposals for reform did not emerge until several years later. The silence on this issue at Accra was a lost opportunity to focus more forceful attention to this sector much earlier.

The LURD proposed that a commission be established to review the Constitution, especially in relation to presidential powers, and to undertake other law-reform measures, both areas where they saw an urgent need. There was apparently no objection to this from the other factions, but international participants opposed the idea, and it was ultimately taken out of the draft. One foreign delegate remembered that he responded negatively to the idea; his main concern was that proposals for a parliamentary system, then quietly being discussed, would be given life in any constitutional review. This participant was sure that a parliamentary system wouldn't work, as Liberians were unfamiliar with it, and that this could cause havoc in a transitional government.

The LURD was disappointed, and several years later its representatives still spoke at length about the need for legal and constitutional reform. "The moment they got our proposal, they said we can't do it," said one LURD representative.

> I was devastated, to be honest. It took the breath out of me. You then realise you have people around the table with very little understanding of our problems, yet they were the brokers—and they threaten you with being 'obstacles to the peace process' if you hold out for too long.

Other Forward-Looking Commitments on Human Rights

The accord states a commitment to guarantees of "civil and political rights" as set out in a number of international instruments. An Independent National Human Rights Commission would monitor compliance and promote human rights education. In addition, the accord states a commitment to international humanitarian law, humanitarian relief, attention to vulnerable groups, the physical rehabilitation of war victims, the return of refugees and displaced persons, and governance and electoral reform. These elements met with little resistance or debate.

Left Unaddressed: Reparations and Other Questions

The subject of reparations for victims was never seriously addressed at the talks. Some international participants considered it briefly, but decided it would be too costly. The starting assumption was that virtually everyone in Liberia is a victim, and therefore reparations could not realistically be undertaken. But leaving the subject in silence missed an opportunity to explore creative approaches from other countries and to consider less costly forms of reparation (memorials, apologies, days of remembrance, or services such as schooling or health care). To make up for this gap, when the TRC Act was passed two years later, it mandated the Commission to make recommendations for victim reparations.

Second, while vetting the security forces was accepted easily, the idea that candidates for public office should be vetted on human rights grounds (and might be barred from office if there was evidence against them) was apparently never discussed. When I raised the question with former faction leaders several years later, it met with strong opposition, perhaps unsurprisingly. "If someone committed atrocities, you have laws to prosecute them," said a senior member of LURD. "Our view was: if you don't want a murderer in power, vote against him," said a senior member of the Taylor government. This soon became an issue, as the 2005 elections put several people into Congress who were well-known for serious human rights violations, some of them elected as senior senators with nine-year terms.

Conclusion

The challenge of justice for massive crimes of the war remained controversial in peacetime just as it was during the negotiations. The peace agreement did not finally settle how the country would handle the central question of accountability for these crimes. While it managed to end the war without violating any principles of international law, such as a blanket amnesty, it essentially left open some of the most difficult and controversial questions. Known war criminals took up positions in the transitional government and later in the elected Congress, and former leaders of the armed factions were appointed to the Supreme Court and government commissions. When the truth commission concluded its report several years later with recommendations for far-reaching prosecutions and exclusions from political office, the former warlords joined together to threaten to take up arms again if any one of them was prosecuted.

The truth commission report also recommended the creation of a new hybrid court, with national and international judges, to take on the highest-level cases. But there was no action on this recommendation, or other progress on national prosecutions, for many years after the Accra agreement. Independent organizations worked to implement community-based reconciliation programs, some of which had been put forward in the truth commission's sweeping conclusions and recommendations.

The biggest post-war event in the justice arena was the arrest of Charles Taylor and his transfer to the Special Court for Sierra Leone, from his comfortable exile in Nigeria, two-and-a-half years after his indictment was unsealed at Accra. Liberia's newly elected president, Ellen Johnson Sirleaf, made the request to Nigeria not long after she came to power. The Liberian public response to his arrest was generally positive: people described a "calming" effect; he still had many supporters, and many worried about his ability to destabilize the country through covert means. Taylor was tried by the Special Court in The Hague, convicted, and sentenced to fifty years in jail. But these charges related to events in Sierra Leone, and many Liberians were frustrated that his crimes at home were still unaddressed.

Major challenges confronted Liberia at the end of its civil war: massive economic needs; a crippled judicial system; high unemployment, including of demobilized combatants; and unsteady bordering states that threatened renewed conflicts. Many of these problems continued, with accusations of corruption and political polarization worsening. National elections since the peace agreement have shown deep fault lines on ethnic, political, and regional grounds. Many years after the war, democracy remained fragile, analysts said.[29] The truth commission's recommendations for national reconciliation programs remained an important reference point, but a political commitment to deep change was not evident. The dynamics that played out so clearly in the 2003 peace negotiations, with powerful interests resisting fundamental change or any challenge to the culture of impunity, continued largely unabated.

Notes

1 For an analysis of peace agreements between 1990 and 1996, see Adekeye Adebajo, "Liberia: A Warlord's Peace," in Stephen John Stedman, Donald Rothchild, and Elizabeth M. Cousens, eds., *Ending Civil Wars: The Implementation of Peace Agreements* (Boulder and London: Lynne Rienner, 2002), 599–630. Some analysts have concluded that the CPA was the fourteenth, not the fifteenth, official peace agreement.

2 This case study is based on extensive interviews with many persons directly involved in the 2003 Accra talks, including the mediator and representatives of the warring factions, civil society, political parties, and the international community, as well those involved in the implementation of the accord. In-country interviews were undertaken in July and September 2006. A longer version of this study was published as Priscilla Hayner, "Negotiating Peace in Liberia: Preserving the Possibility for Justice," Centre for Humanitarian Dialogue and International Center for Transitional Justice, Nov. 2007. Adapted with permission.

3 Those watching the Special Court closely should have understood that a sealed indictment awaited Taylor, say observers. The Special Court prosecutor had offered many hints in the previous months and had privately told a number of governments that he did intend to indict Taylor. This was Taylor's first confirmed trip outside Liberia in many months. Officials at the Court thought it odd that so many people were surprised by the indictment when it was finally unsealed. (Interviews by author.)

4 David Crane, interview by author, August 2006.

5 Ibid.

6 These reactions reflected the perception that so many of the senior officials of the Court were American, Canadian, or European.

7 General Abdulsalami Abubakar, interview by author.

8 Hundreds of thousands of Ghanaians lived in Monrovia. Many of them have lived there for generations but are still considered Ghanaian and retain their native language. They mostly live together in coastal fishing communities.

9 Ambassador John Blaney, interview by author.

10 For a detailed account of these events from a participant inside the U.S. embassy see Dante Paradiso, *The Embassy: Frontline Diplomacy in Liberia* (New York: Beaufort Books, 2016).

11 This general threatened military action against any subversive activities to unseat Taylor. Vice President Moses Blah and another general were arrested under accusation of usurping power; the arrested general was assassinated shortly after Taylor returned.

12 Sekou Conneh, interview by author.

13 Drafters provided suggested language to ECOWAS, often reaching ECOWAS representatives late at night. The drafts were distributed for discussion in the morning, but the complete suggested text was not always distributed, participants recount, allowing ECOWAS to reserve some issues for final discussion or agreement until later in the process.

14 This effort to engage refugee women in the talks was organized by Women of Liberia Mass Action for Peace.

15 There was also continued fighting in the southeast of the country, where MODEL was making advances, especially towards the end of the peace talks.

16 As a result of the peace conference, contact with the front lines sometimes crossed warring lines. Charles Taylor's minister of defense attended the first weeks of the Accra talks and became well acquainted with the rebel leadership. When the shelling of Monrovia worsened, he returned home to lead the defense of the city. On two occasions, when the shelling was particularly intense, he made a phone call to the LURD delegation in Accra and asked them to "cool it down." (Interviews by author.)

17 Liberians refer to the three periods of shelling that took place from June to August 2003 as World War One, World War Two, and—the most intense—World War Three.

18 The rebels did not at first see themselves as committing crimes, but rather acting justifiably in response to the crimes of the government. As reported by General Abdulsalami Abubakar, who discussed this with them at the time (interview with Abubakar by author).

19 A proposal for a truth and reconciliation commission was first put forward in a document prepared by representatives of civil society and political parties in 2002, calling for the creation of such a commission as a "critical path to security" and a means to address impunity. See *Position Statement on Security, Reconciliation and Peace in Liberia* (presented to the Authority of ECOWAS and the Government of the Federal Republic of Nigeria), 15 March 2002, 3.

20 The LURD's proposal suggested that demobilization "may include the granting of amnesty and political asylum, except for genocidal [sic]," and that disarming armed groups "may include the granting of amnesty. It shall, however, not apply in the case of suspects of crimes against humanity." In "LURD Draft Proposal," Articles 7.2 and 6(q) respectively (on file with author).

21 Of the 14 prior (failed) Liberian peace agreements since 1990, only one contained an amnesty: the Cotonou Agreement of 1993. But this amnesty clause refers repeatedly to acts committed "while in actual combat," and was clearly understood not to cover war crimes, according to a key delegate who took part in these talks. The Cotonou Agreement states that "there shall be a general amnesty granted to all persons and parties involved in the Liberian civil conflict in the course of actual military engagements. Accordingly, acts committed by the Parties or by their forces while in actual combat or on authority of any of the Parties in the course of actual combat are hereby granted amnesty." (Article 19, "General Amnesty," Agreement signed at Cotonou, Benin, 25 July 1993.) In any event, that Cotonou amnesty was contingent on a successful ceasefire and disarmament process, neither of which took place. In addition, Article 97 of the Liberian Constitution provided a broad amnesty for events during and after the 1980 coup by the People's Redemption Council, but this was not a point of reference for the parties to the Accra peace talks.

22 Accra Comprehensive Peace Agreement (CPA), Article XXXIV.

23 Gyude Bryant, interview by author.

24 The TRC Act states that the commission may recommend amnesty "under terms and conditions established by the TRC upon application of individual persons making full disclosures of their wrongs and thereby expressing

remorse for their acts and/or omissions, whether as an accomplice or a perpetrator, provided that amnesty or exoneration shall not apply to violations of international humanitarian law and crimes against humanity in conformity with international laws and standards." (Article VII(g))

25 Charles Taylor resigned from the presidency on August 11, 2003, and was granted asylum in Nigeria. He turned over the presidency to his vice president, Moses Blah, until a transitional government was installed in October of that year.

26 The Act states that "from and immediately after the passage of this act, immunity is hereby granted from both civil and criminal proceedings against all persons, Officials of Government, Representatives of Warring Factions and combatants within the jurisdiction of the Republic of Liberia from all acts, and or crimes committed by them during the 13 (thirteen) years and 8 (eight) months of the civil wars covering from December 1989 to August 2003" (Section 1, Published by Authority of the Ministry of Foreign Affairs, Monrovia, Liberia, 8 August 2003).

27 CPA, Article VII(2)(a).

28 CPA, Article XXVII, "The Judiciary."

29 International Crisis Group, "Liberia: Time for Much-Delayed Reconciliation and Reform," Africa Briefing #88, 12 June 2012.

12 Uganda

Peace talks between the Ugandan government and the Lord's Resistance Army (LRA), a brutal rebel group, began shortly after the International Criminal Court released arrest warrants for the LRA leadership. The talks would be greatly affected by the ICC's engagement, which was often misunderstood in Uganda and especially by the LRA.[1]

The nature of the ICC impact on the negotiations remains controversial. It is a sensitive issue for those who care deeply about Uganda and for those who believe in international justice as a means to limit atrocities. The differences of opinion partly reflect one's viewpoint, understandably. This chapter shows that the views of Ugandans, and especially those most directly affected by the war, were often different from those of international justice advocates and of the ICC itself.

In the end, the 2006–2008 negotiations were unsuccessful in demobilizing the LRA. After the talks collapsed, the LRA became a splintered rebel group, inflicting violence on a wide area across several neighboring countries. While the LRA did not return to northern Uganda, there were many Ugandan fighters—many of them forcibly conscripted—who remained trapped within its forces.

Advocates for peace and those pushing for international justice both wanted accountability and an end to the conflict, but in different ways or in different measures. The Ugandan experience is important in part because questions linger about the manner and timing of the ICC's engagement and whether it played any role in the ultimate failure of the peace process. As we shall see, the answer to this question is not simple.

The Lord's Resistance Army

The LRA was founded in northern Uganda under the leadership of Joseph Kony in 1986, ostensibly to fight for the rights of the Acholi people. It soon began to target civilians throughout northern Uganda, and the conflict took on an increasingly gruesome character. As the security situation worsened, the Ugandan army (Ugandan Peoples Defence Force, UPDF) relocated most of the civilian population into camps, where conditions were horrendous, causing many deaths.[2]

A high proportion of northern Ugandans were direct victims of the conflict. Population-based surveys in 2005 and 2007 showed that 40% of civilians in northern Uganda had been abducted by the LRA for at least a brief period, 76% lost a family member to the conflict, and 45% directly witnessed the killing of a family member. Eighty-six percent had been displaced from their homes. Though the LRA committed most abuses, the UPDF was also a major perpetrator: 6% of respondents said that Ugandan soldiers had physically beaten them and 4% reported that a family member had been killed by the army.[3]

There were many attempts to resolve the conflict through negotiation, beginning in the early 1990s. Local community and religious leaders were able to make contact with the LRA leadership at various times. A Ugandan government official, Betty Bigombe, reached out to the LRA in 1994 and again in 2004. Her second initiative went further than any previous official process, but because Bigombe represented the government, the LRA understood that she could not act as an independent mediator as such.[4] Ultimately, she was unable to meet with Kony, and her peace efforts ended in 2005.[5]

At about this time, Southern Sudan, which borders northern Uganda, offered to facilitate a new line of peace talks between the LRA and the government of Uganda. The LRA had been causing increasing havoc in Southern Sudan, where it was based to avoid the Ugandan army, and large parts of the territory were inaccessible due to LRA presence or threat. Southern Sudan had just reached an agreement with the government of Sudan in January 2005, bringing their own long civil war to an end. Resolving the LRA issue became a priority, and the newly autonomous Southern Sudan pushed Uganda to engage in talks with its hated enemy. These talks were agreed to take place in the Southern Sudanese capital, Juba.

The ICC and the Start of the Juba Talks

Uganda was among the first countries to ratify the ICC Rome Statute, in mid-2002. The ICC Prosecutor soon met with the Ugandan president, and in January 2004 Uganda referred the situation of northern Uganda to the ICC, under the presumption that the LRA was out of reach of the national authorities. But the manner in which the Prosecutor announced this new engagement raised questions about his impartiality; he called a press conference together with the Ugandan president, implying that the only interest of the Court would be the LRA's crimes and not any of the accusations against government forces. ICC investigations led to arrest warrants for five members of the LRA leadership, first kept sealed but then released to the public in late 2005, just as the new peace talks were being planned.

The announcement of the Southern Sudan initiative for peace talks in early 2006 was met with criticism from international rights advocates, who argued that it was somehow illegal to negotiate with persons under ICC indictment. As Ugandan lawyer Barney Afako wrote at the time,

> Juba's simple idea that the two parties should talk rather than wage war on Southern Sudanese territory has raised a chorus of protest from various international actors, especially human rights organisations and other States Parties to the Rome Statute of the International Criminal Court (ICC).

In the light of the ICC's interest in leaders of the LRA, legal obstacles to talks have widely been cited as precluding dialogue with the LRA.[6]

Afako penned a nine-page note titled "Not a Crime to Talk," making the case that it was not only legally permissible, but indeed was a duty of the Ugandan state to seek peace and try to end the violence, regardless of the arrest warrants.[7] This paper circulated widely and quickly ended the argument from those who had opposed negotiations on legal grounds.

A number of international commentators have since concluded that the Juba talks were made possible, or became much more serious, as a result of the ICC's engagement. They argue that LRA leaders were motivated to participate because they wanted to evade ICC arrest warrants. The ICC Prosecutor and his staff took this view, as have others.

But many of those closest to the talks, and those deeply involved in parallel efforts before the Juba process began, strongly disagree. In separate interviews, they expressed similar views on this. "No, the ICC had nothing to do with it," said Bishop Macleord Baker Ochola, a well-respected leader in northern Uganda. "I don't agree with that at all. There were other factors," said Sheikh Al-Hadji Mousa Karim, also highly regarded. "It is wrong to suggest that the ICC instigated the talks: they were already meeting in 2005," said a prominent NGO representative who closely tracked the peace process. "I've heard that, but that's not true," says the first head of the LRA delegation, Martin Ojul, who spent a lot of time with Kony at the start of the talks. Ojul continued, "This discounts how much persuasion there was to get them involved and serious about the talks. Kony came because they hadn't been able to win after twenty years of war."

An international advisor to the mediator also disagreed. In his conversations with many LRA commanders in the first months of the talks, he found that their concerns around justice were much less than many other issues. His impression was that Kony was initially worried about the ICC mostly because he didn't understand it, and that it became a more prominent issue for him later.

These Ugandans and other participants point to a number of other factors that brought the LRA to the peace table. LRA forces were in decline, increasingly under attack and on the defensive. Some LRA fighters who escaped or were captured joined the army and provided inside information, making the LRA's military tactics less effective. Kony was tired from two decades fighting in the bush, and he suffered serious and debilitating medical problems that needed treatment.[8] Former combatants remember his talking about ending the war long before the warrants were released in 2005, often telling them that it would soon be time for peace.

One of Kony's wives, who had managed to escape, described an unexpectedly human factor: he worried about his children. "He loved his children so much," she said.

> He talked about them a lot. He cared for them. Fighting in the bush, he wasn't sure of their future, how long they would live. He could see for

himself that his children were dying—drowning crossing the waters, or by other means, and there were guns following everywhere.[9]

Meanwhile, the political changes in Southern Sudan put Kony at risk and gave the Southern Sudanese every incentive to find a solution to the LRA problem. Southern Sudan President Salva Kiir met with Ugandan President Yoweri Museveni, urging him to support a peace process in Juba and to send a high-level government representative. The vice president of Southern Sudan, Riek Machar, met with Kony and insisted that now was the time for peace.

Other means were also used to persuade Kony that peace might be possible. Family members were flown up to meet him, bringing a videotaped message from his mother. Northern Ugandan religious and community leaders, whom Kony continued to trust, visited him on several occasions to push for peace. Community representatives in northern Uganda tried to assure him that he was welcome to return and would not be at risk of reprisal. Indeed, a number of former high-level LRA commanders, known for their brutality in the LRA, had resettled in towns and cities and lived quietly, without being bothered, although their presence was well-known and some of their direct victims lived nearby. Many participants in the early stages of the talks reported that these were among Kony's biggest concerns, and that these assurances were important.

While close participants did not believe the ICC warrants were the first or main reason for the LRA to agree to talks, they saw that the warrants soon became one of the LRA's primary concerns, and perhaps the most critical substantive issue that the talks would need to resolve.

The Justice Conundrum: A Barrier to Peace?

The ICC warrants shaped both the substance and agenda of the talks. As analyst Mark Kersten noted after close research on this subject, "The ICC's investigations and arrest warrants affected every stage and element of the peace process in Northern Uganda," though he concludes that ultimately the quality of this effect was mixed.[10]

A major item on the agenda of the talks was "accountability and reconciliation," and the fact of the warrants was a major reason these issues received such prominent attention. Some close participants and observers thought that the ICC's primary impact on the peace process was the fact that it fundamentally shaped the agenda for the talks.[11]

Just as the parties were to begin formal discussion on this agenda item, the UN High Commissioner for Human Rights, Louise Arbour, released a statement saying that the discussions should focus only on "the terms and circumstances of surrender" of those indicted, so that they could face the ICC charges.[12] As noted by Warner ten Kate and Sarah M. H. Nouwen, this statement reverberated through the peace talks, causing "considerable confusion and apprehension on the side of the LRA," and "undermined the lawyers at the peace process who had been trying to explain the principle of complementarity to the LRA delegation." This statement from the High Commissioner only further decreased the LRA's trust in the process.[13]

The ICC and its warrants became the major substantive hurdle as Kony made clear he would not submit to the ICC warrants. As one UN official who was present at Juba recalled, the warrants were "the main stumbling block. Both sides were talking about it. Everyone was most focused on how to get out of this quandary."

Kony insisted that the arrest warrants be lifted, but the mediation team knew that this was not legally possible, and they said this repeatedly to Kony and to other LRA representatives. Kony then asked for a deferral from the UN Security Council, as provided for in the Rome Statute, but the mediators explained that this would only be guaranteed for one year. But it was evident that Kony had many different and sometimes contradictory sources of information, and it was never clear who was whispering into his ear or what he chose to believe.

Regular public statements and seeming threats from the ICC Prosecutor, Luis Moreno Ocampo, were seen as making matters worse. Participants in the talks thought that a more sober presentation by the ICC and its supporters would have helped immeasurably, reducing the constant sense of threat that Kony was clearly reacting to.[14] The messages from the Prosecutor suggested that no alternative to arrest and extradition to the ICC would be possible for those who were indicted. It didn't help those trying to win Kony's trust in the idea that national alternatives were possible, which of course is both allowed and encouraged in the ICC Rome Statute.

The subject of accountability went beyond the issue of the ICC and beyond the narrow focus of the culpability of the LRA leadership. The mediation team hosted a workshop for the government and LRA negotiators to learn about other countries' experiences with victim reparations, truth commissions, memorials, and human rights screening for rebels and the army.[15] A chair of the workshop recalled the dynamics between the two parties, both of whom had harbored reservations about attending. "By lunchtime they were passing notes back and forth, suggesting the kinds of justice arrangements they wanted in an agreement."[16] These broader ideas captured their imagination in a way that other agenda items had not.

How Ugandans Viewed the ICC

The issue of justice was of great concern also to victim communities in northern Uganda. Unfortunately, the ICC lost considerable support there, where it should have found solid backing.

Victim communities were initially jubilant when they heard that the ICC was targeting Kony. Most knew little about the ICC, and many heard of its existence for the first time when it released the arrest warrants. They soon learned that the ICC had no means to arrest Kony and the others, and that to do so would rely on the same military forces that had been chasing him for more than two decades. This turned excitement into disappointment and worry. If the peace talks had some chance of succeeding, would the threat of prosecution not make it harder to agree a settlement and risk sending Kony further into the bush? The logic of the ICC engagement was lost on most northern Ugandans.

Population surveys from this time suggest that the public's views could be contradictory. The great majority agreed that those guilty of serious crimes should be punished, but many also supported an amnesty, forgiveness, and the notion that peace should be prioritized. Overall, there was a strong desire to end the war. While 44% said that peace was a top priority, only 3% prioritized justice.[17] An analysis of these results concluded:

> One explanation may be that while many people support accountability, they do not wish to jeopardize the current peace talks. In addition, other specific questions on accountability suggest that respondents differentiate between levels of responsibility for crimes. For example, respondents are more forgiving of the lower-ranking LRA than the LRA leaders.[18]

This position was logical, since the great majority of the lower-ranking combatants (and some who later became commanders) were recruited into the LRA through force. Many were abducted from their village as children, forced to commit terrible atrocities, and prevented from leaving the LRA on the threat of death. Their communities wanted them home.

Those whom I interviewed in northern Uganda in 2010, including community and religious leaders and civil society representatives, put forward an eloquent and nuanced view of the ICC. They expressed frustration with the timing and manner of its engagement, but insisted that they did not oppose the ICC in general. They said it was not a question of whether to have justice, but when and how. Most put a higher priority on ending the war. In effect, they worried that the ICC's engagement was badly timed and out of sync with their most urgent priorities.

Sheikh Karim, based in northern Uganda and long involved in peace efforts, described the dynamics during the very early period of ICC involvement:

> We met with the prosecutor in The Hague in early 2005, before the warrants came out. We put our position to him: we are not against the ICC. Our appeal was the timing: it was wrongly timed. We were already pushing at that time for a cessation of hostilities and a safe haven for the LRA. Thus we insisted: an ICC intervention at this moment is not well timed. If only people will give peace a chance, justice will come in. Once Kony is out of the bush, justice will be much easier. Throughout the talks, Kony's fear would be the ICC. The ICC would become the obstacle to a final end to the conflict . . . The prosecutor understood, and he agreed to give us some time. But our frustration was that he moved so quickly. We were trying for peaceful dialogue, and we knew that an arrest warrant would not help.

It later became clear that the Prosecutor requested the arrest warrants for the LRA leadership just six weeks after this meeting with the northern Ugandan community leaders.[19]

In addition, there was frustration that the ICC only targeted the LRA for prosecution, seeming to ignore the government's serious abuses. The press conference with the Ugandan president gave the impression that the ICC was too close to the government; many saw the ICC in "partnership" with the government, an impression that never changed over the next several years as the relationship with the community further soured. "The ICC did not investigate northern Uganda in its totality. Right from beginning, it was biased," Bishop Ochola told me, echoing many others.

When the ICC first engaged in Uganda, James Otto, head of the Ugandan nongovernmental organization Human Rights Focus, helped organize a dozen NGOs to act as an independent support group to the ICC process. "But when the ICC was seen as overtly taking sides, all twelve organizations withdrew," he recounted. Others described how this perception was confirmed when they saw that ICC investigators were guided by military intelligence officials during their visits to the north. When asked, the ICC clarified that it relied on Ugandan security officials for protection. Further, the ICC's Uganda cases were primarily based on case files supplied by the government. The ICC insisted that there was not enough evidence to prosecute government or military officials. It's also true that many of the army's worst abuses took place before July 2002, when the ICC jurisdiction begins. Nevertheless, a strong suspicion remained that the ICC hesitated to prosecute officials because it wanted to protect its cooperative relationship with the government. ICC insiders acknowledge that, whether intentional or not, this factor can indeed influence a prosecutor's calculations.

Misunderstandings worsened due to the lack of information available to local communities. The ICC began public outreach in the country a full two years after it opened investigations—a year after arrest warrants were announced—and visiting investigators generally tried to keep a low profile and avoid public attention.[20] Public attitudes thus formed in a vacuum and many misunderstandings took root, which were difficult to overcome.[21]

A local activist, Rosalba Oywa, head of the People's Voice for Peace, supported many victims of the LRA. She was initially very happy to hear about the warrants, assuming as others did that Kony would soon be arrested. But her direct experience with the ICC was more difficult.

> The ICC came with a high level of arrogance. They seemed to be saying: 'all your ways—cultural, traditional, etc.—don't have any value.' They're coming with their own culture. But two cultures should complement each other. You shouldn't come with a superior culture. And besides, what would we gain from five people being punished? . . . They were very secretive and did little outreach. They did a lot of things that were wrong, so people just didn't accept them. Ultimately we said, this is not

the time for this. To hell with your justice, if you don't respect our traditional justice.

This sense of offense at the ICC's perceived attitude of superiority highlighted underlying differences in conceptions of justice and who should define it. Prominent human rights advocates insisted that "justice" should be understood broadly and should not be reduced to criminal prosecution. Human rights advocate James Otto said, "Jail sentences and death penalties were brought by colonialists. If I wrong you, and I apologize, how can someone *else* come and say no, you can't allow him to apologize?" He acknowledged that things had changed over time and there was room for both traditional mechanisms and the ICC, but he argued that this required an impartial approach that the ICC was missing.[22]

Other local activists echoed this frustration. They felt that ICC investigators had failed to appreciate local dynamics, community interests, and the efforts by local authorities over many years to end the conflict.

Ugandan human rights lawyer Barney Afako, who became a key advisor to the mediation team, was pointed in his early criticism of those hailing the ICC prosecutions. "The fundamental question to be answered is whether the intervention of international justice is prolonging the conflict or hastening its solution," he told reporters. "Justice needs to be justified in terms of lives," he said, asking how many more Acholi would need to be slaughtered before the ICC was able to try the LRA leaders. "The [international] criminal justice system is isolated from the moral consequences of its intervention."[23]

An international participant in the Juba talks discussed these issues with many Ugandans and came away persuaded that the question of justice must be understood in context. " 'No justice' for the LRA leadership would probably mean: put them in a farmhouse somewhere and keep them quiet and out of trouble. Is it possible that a peace deal without accountability might in fact be more sustainable?"

Thus, there was an increasing perception in northern Uganda that the ICC was an irritant and an obstacle to peace. This view became widespread. A foreigner living in Gulu recounted the dynamic that prevailed at the time: "If you asked any small child at the time, why is there no peace in northern Uganda? He would say, 'The ICC!' "

International Perspectives

Foreigners who had been based in Uganda for many years were surprised at the often-incorrect assumptions made by the ICC and by its partners in foreign governments and NGOs. Some of the strongest international supporters of the ICC, such as ICC member states, had representatives in Uganda who followed local dynamics closely. These in-country representatives struggled to make sense of the ICC's manner of engagement: how it took decisions; how it related to local communities; its apparent lack of knowledge of the national context; and its limited representation in country. Many describe being surprised and frustrated by the Court's actions and its lack of political smarts. After the warrants were released, "Moreno Ocampo would simply say, 'it's up to member states to arrest Kony,' but this showed no understanding at all," said one foreign diplomat.

Those who followed the ICC's Ugandan engagement at a distance, from European capitals, for example, seemed to make assumptions about local dynamics that their Uganda-based colleagues found unrealistic. One political officer of a European embassy in Kampala described the views of an ICC Task Force at his headquarters in Europe. "They really believed that, as soon as he was indicted, Kony would come out of the bush because he would then be isolated and others would leave him." He and others based in Kampala thought this highly unlikely. A political officer at another European embassy remembers that a colleague in his Foreign Ministry proposed putting pressure on the LRA and increasing the likelihood of arrest by imposing a travel ban on its leaders—individuals who crossed international borders on foot and had lived in the bush for over two decades. He remembers thinking at the time that this showed a fundamental lack of understanding.

Some European states provided funds to buy food for the LRA when they moved into their designated camp. This met a basic security need, so that the LRA camp could be visited safely and the LRA would not raid local villages for supplies (although some raids were reported). One participant in the talks recalled being stupefied when the ICC Prosecutor lobbied states (unsuccessfully) to terminate these food provisions and suggested that states that provided humanitarian aid to the LRA might somehow incriminate themselves before the ICC. Asked later to comment, Moreno Ocampo agreed that food aid should be allowed to parties in peace talks, under appropriate conditions.[24]

The Proposed Agreement on Justice

After the workshop on transitional justice in early 2007, described above, agreement on many aspects of the justice agenda was reached relatively quickly. The first justice accord was concluded in late June 2007. A more detailed annex was initialed eight months later, in February 2008.

The International Center for Transitional Justice (ICTJ) summarized the approach, which was largely defined by the fact of the ICC warrants:

> While the ICC Prosecutor made clear that he could not withdraw the arrest warrants, parties to the negotiations began to discuss putting in place a national procedure to deal with the LRA. This would allow Uganda to potentially challenge the admissibility of the ICC case against LRA leaders in the future, thereby seeking to exert control over the fate of the LRA. The parties at Juba took the view that national criminal proceedings, rather than any alternatives such as traditional justice, were most likely to meet the complementarity threshold.[25]

The only option for avoiding the ICC warrants in the long term, while fully respecting the legal requirements of the ICC system, was to establish a national mechanism that could fulfill the "complementarity" requirements of the Rome Statute, combined with a short-term deferral by the UN Security Council to allow the national system to be established. Ugandan lawyer Barney Afako, who served as legal advisor to the mediation team, drafted an option along these lines.

The agreement stated that the parties were committed to preventing impunity through the use of the "formal courts and tribunals" of Uganda. A special division of the High Court of Uganda would be established to try "any individual who is alleged to have committed serious crimes or human rights violations in the course of the conflict."[26] The agreement explicitly notes that state actors accused of crimes would be processed through normal criminal justice procedures, not through these special mechanisms.

An important measure of flexibility was provided both in the kinds of sentences that were foreseen and in the explicit recognition of local, traditional justice practices. The new war crimes division would develop a "regime of alternative penalties and sanctions," to be incorporated through legislation, to address crimes by non-state actors. Just as the parties to the peace agreement in Colombia were to conclude eight years later, the Ugandans found a solution to the criminal justice quandary in the discretion that is allowed in sentencing. The agreement stated:

> Alternative penalties and sanctions shall, as relevant: reflect the gravity of the crimes or violations; promote reconciliation between individuals and within communities; promote the rehabilitation of offenders; take into account an individual's admissions or other cooperation with proceedings; and, require perpetrators to make reparations to victims.[27]

At the same time,

> Traditional justice shall form a central part of the alternative justice and reconciliation framework . . . The government shall, in consultation with relevant interlocutors, examine the practices of traditional justice mechanisms in affected areas, with a view to identifying the most appropriate roles for such mechanisms.[28]

An unnamed body was to be established to undertake an inquiry into the conflict and the violations committed. While not calling it a truth commission, the agreement set out the tasks that are typical of such an official truth body: analyze the history of the conflict, inquire into rights violations, hold public hearings, promote reconciliation, and publish a report with recommendations.

Individual and collective reparations would be provided for victims, the agreement said, but details of such reparations were left open for later consideration by the government. It also hinted at the idea of linking reparations to the penalties of perpetrators, as Colombia later did: "Reparations, which may be ordered to be paid to a victim as part of penalties and sanctions in accountability proceedings, may be paid out of resources identified for that purpose."[29]

The agreement specifically noted that "Uganda has institutions and mechanisms, customs and usages as provided for and recognized under national laws, capable of addressing the crimes and human rights violations committed during the conflict," thus suggesting that an international court was unnecessary. The government would "undertake any necessary representations or legal proceedings nationally or internationally," it said, and "address conscientiously the question of the ICC arrest warrants."[30]

The agreement did not address how these various mechanisms would work together, nor whether some cases would be addressed through traditional justice approaches and others through the new war crimes division of the High Court. The LRA continued to raise these questions up to the final days of the talks, worried that the text left open too many questions.

Apparently, some elements of the overall package were not included in the written text, but rather in an informal pact quietly reached on the side. This pertained in particular to what was planned for Joseph Kony's future. A report by the London-based Conciliation Resources reported that:

> A 'gentleman's agreement' was reached that the Ugandan government would bring a challenge to the Security Council to suspend the ICC indictment, opening the way to establishment of a Special Court that could try and sentence Kony . . . Kony would be imprisoned in the north, though the conditions of this imprisonment would be sufficiently flexible to meet the international requirement for Kony's freedom and movement to be significantly curtailed while sparing him the humiliation of formal incarceration in a prison.[31]

Kony was informed that he would have to accept public declarations that would differ from this informal agreement, and that he would have to trust the good will of President Museveni.[32] But, as outlined below, Kony remained very worried about the ICC's reach as well as his own security, and never fully trusted these promises; he continued to insist that the arrest warrants should first be withdrawn before he would agree to disarm.

Relationship to the Existing Amnesty Law in Uganda

This conversation on justice within the Juba peace process took place in a context in which ex-combatants from the LRA and other illegal armed groups had for many years been granted blanket amnesty with no questions asked. This amnesty law was still in place while the peace talks with the LRA were under way. Many former LRA fighters and commanders had benefited from it and lived freely in northern Uganda.

The amnesty was instituted, Ugandans explain, for practical reasons, and there was little public opposition to it. Administered by a state-appointed Amnesty Commission, it was established in 2000 to facilitate the reintegration of ex-combatants from the country's various armed conflicts since 1986. "Currently, whatever the crime, in Uganda, he would be absolved," the chair of the Amnesty Commission, Justice Peter Onega, told me in 2010. The process was simple. An individual was only required to surrender a weapon, denounce the rebellion, and complete a simple application form. "After that, he is deemed to be granted amnesty and receives an amnesty certificate," Onega explained. The whole process could take a day. If an individual was clearly traumatized, the Commission would try to provide counselling for a few days, working in conjunction with outside partners, before releasing him with the amnesty certificate. The Commission provided amnestied individuals with a small reintegration package: seeds and tools for planting, a plate, utensils, a mattress and blanket, and the equivalent of about one hundred U.S. dollars in cash.

The application form asked individuals to identify the armed group they were leaving and whether they joined willingly or were recruited by force, as well as what kinds of weapons they used. Justice Onega explained,

> We don't ask about their involvement in killings, abductions, or looting. This is something that was seriously debated in Parliament: should the amnesty be blanket, or conditional? The amnesty is now structured to make it easy for people to come back. The first version of the law prohibited amnesty for serious crimes like murder, and the government was being blamed by the Acholis for the fact that their children were not coming back.

By 2010, the Amnesty Commission had granted amnesty to over 26,000 applicants, of whom nearly half were from the LRA. Commission Chair Onega estimated that the majority of these people had probably committed serious crimes.

There was an intention to change the law if a final peace agreement was signed with the LRA, to introduce a more thorough review of applicants and ensure that those accused of serious crimes would enter a separate process; this may have included prosecution before the new special division of the High Court.

Mr. Onega was in touch with LRA commanders by telephone before and during the Juba talks.

> I had long discussions with them, and I was very honest with them. They understood: no blanket amnesty. Kony was not resisting the idea of coming out. They didn't expect to get off; instead, they were insisting on the idea of being tried domestically.

But Onega concluded that Kony never understood the options set out in the agreement and still feared he would be sent to The Hague: "The ICC was a major factor in the failure of the talks, even if this was based on a misunderstanding by Kony."

Distrust and Collapse of the Talks

As the Juba talks continued, preliminary agreements were initialed by the LRA representatives at the table. But Kony slowly lost trust in the process and never gained sufficient trust in the text. Both of these aspects played an important role in his refusal to sign the final agreement and ultimately the collapse of the peace process.

Even when the text of the agreement was finalized, some of Kony's fundamental questions seemed to remain unanswered. The mediation team felt that the elements were in place that could resolve the inherent challenges around justice and accountability, but this solution was apparently not explicit or secure enough for Kony to put his faith in.

Kony spoke in detail about these concerns with members of the mediation team and others who visited, throughout the two years of talks. He emphasized four points:

He spoke most frequently, at greatest length, about his concerns in relation to the ICC. He wanted to know in explicit terms what would happen to the outstanding arrest warrants and what forms of judicial sanction might be imposed. As the agreement was finalized and awaiting his signature, he again flagged concerns. One person who visited him late in the process quoted him as saying: "I'm very confused about the ICC. My name is there. But also, in Uganda the Special Division of the High Court is waiting for me. And also in the agreement there is *Motu Oput*," the traditional Ugandan ceremony to address crimes. So, he asked, why are there all three of these mechanisms?[33]

Second, Kony asked for assurances that he and other top commanders would be safe if they returned to Uganda. "I won't just be an ordinary person," he would say. "We may need protection. Where will I settle? What will the arrangements be?"

Third, he was concerned about his and his family's welfare. "How will I begin my life, once I drop my gun? I have a family: how will they be taken care of?"

Finally, he asked whether LRA leaders could participate in government. "I agree that I won't be part of the government, as I've been indicted. But there are others here who could," he said, pointing to members of his leadership team. "If there is peace, why can we not sit together?"

These questions on criminal accountability, personal security, and the LRA's political role were not addressed with sufficient clarity in the agreement that Kony was asked to sign. But some of those closest to the talks saw other factors that were just as important, and perhaps more important, in the ultimate breakdown of the negotiations.

A key weakness in the process was a fundamental lack of trust, in particular between the LRA leadership and the delegates representing them at the peace table. The LRA delegation was largely composed of people who had never fought with the LRA, and most only met Kony upon joining the negotiation team. For a brief period, two active LRA fighters joined the delegation, but Kony worried about their security if the talks failed and withdrew them. Kony and the other LRA leaders subject to ICC warrants were unwilling to leave their protected base and certainly unwilling to attend the talks themselves, where they assumed they would be at risk of arrest.

The trust between Kony and his delegation in Juba worsened as direct consultation became less frequent, and the sense of ownership and understanding of the text by the LRA leadership decreased. The chair of the LRA delegation during the first eighteen months, Martin Ojul, visited the LRA base a number of times and spent days going over details of the discussions and proposed agreements, with Kony and others. But as suspicions increased, Ojul suddenly resigned, fearing that Kony was planning to have him killed.[34] The new delegation chair consulted less frequently with the LRA leadership, mostly by telephone. Kony apparently held little trust in the process by the time the final proposals were made.

The talks were said to be riddled with backhanded deal making. Rumors circulated that the LRA delegation in Juba was compromised and that some LRA representatives were even under pay of the Ugandan government. This was unproven, but fed into Kony's distrust.[35]

Vincent Otti, the deputy to Kony and the second most prominent leader in the LRA, was more supportive of the peace talks and had regular contact with internationals, although he was also under an ICC arrest warrant. In a peak of anger in late 2007, Kony suddenly ordered Otti killed, reportedly on suspicion that Otti was plotting against Kony and negotiating with the government for a secret defection deal. Many saw Otti's death as the beginning of the end of the peace process. Kony became increasingly disengaged from the peace process.

Many in the Ugandan government and in the international community don't believe the ICC was the major impediment to an agreement. They concluded instead that Kony may have never intended to reach a peace deal, and that he was only using the talks to gain strength and rearm. From this perspective, the warrants and the other issues were only an excuse not to sign.

It's impossible to know Kony's intentions, and he was certainly known to be cunning and calculating. But his conduct and communications over a number of years suggested that he was genuinely interested in coming out of the bush, and he had good reason to want to do so.

In the end, none of these issues was the reason why the peace process came to a final, irreversible end in late 2008. When Kony repeatedly failed to turn up for scheduled signing ceremonies, the government lost patience. Ugandan community leaders were pushing the government to keep the channel of negotiations open and to try to address Kony's concerns. Instead, the

Ugandan military launched a major attack on the LRA base where Kony and others had been settled for over two years, just over the border in Congo. But the LRA learned of the attack in advance and most were able to escape. They scattered deep into Congo's forests. There has not been regular or reliable communication with the LRA since.

Conclusion

In 2016, eight years after the Juba talks were brought to a definitive end, northern Uganda was mostly at peace. The LRA never returned to Uganda, but it was still very active, operating in small bands and attacking civilian populations in the Democratic Republic of Congo, the Central African Republic, Sudan, and South Sudan. During this period, it continued to forcibly abduct over 600 civilians each year, primarily women and children, from a broad swath of territory spread over these four countries.[36]

The Ugandan government allowed the national amnesty law to lapse in 2012, on the grounds that the war in Uganda was over. This sparked protest from the very communities most affected by the war, and led to an organized effort to lobby for the reinstatement of the amnesty. While it was true that the LRA was no longer fighting in Uganda, many Ugandans remained within its forces. Their families and communities saw amnesty as a critical component to encourage defections and to hold open the possibility that their loved ones would return. Uganda had a "moral obligation towards the many innocent children who were enlisted . . . against their will, through abduction," declared twenty-two Ugandan and international organizations in a joint statement.[37] They also insisted that amnesty was necessary to promote peace and reconciliation. They celebrated when the government reinstated the amnesty the following year.

With the return of peace to northern Uganda, the ICC now had more support from conflict-affected communities, compared to the "stiff opposition" it had met ten years earlier from religious leaders, traditional leaders, civil society organizations, and other peace activists worried that it would be a destabilizing factor in the peace effort.[38] Ironically, the government of Uganda had become a vocal critic of the ICC, not only for its engagement in Uganda but throughout the continent.

ICC Chief Prosecutor Fatou Bensouda visited northern Uganda in early 2016. As she concluded her trip, she made a statement encouraging LRA fighters to defect and to return home, thus implicitly giving her support to the Ugandan amnesty, including its coverage of serious crimes. Kony had been using the threat of the ICC in order to deter his fighters from escaping. The Prosecutor thus stressed that she had no intention to prosecute more LRA crimes: "We have seen encouraging trends: many LRA fighters are returning home and reintegrating into their communities," she said. "I urge those still in the bush to also seize any opportunity to stop fighting and return home, where you have a chance to rebuild your lives."[39]

In 2015, the ICC obtained custody of one of the five people that it had indicted in 2005. It was an uncomfortable match, because this accused perpetrator, Dominic Ongwen, was also a victim: he had been forcibly abducted by the LRA at age ten. He fought with the LRA for twenty-three years and became a senior commander. Fearing for his life after Kony killed other LRA commanders, he fled the LRA and turned himself in. He was then transferred to the ICC in The Hague. Some in Uganda, including for example Bishop Ochola, felt that he was being "punished twice" and that the trial was a form of injustice, since he was first a victim.[40]

The only remaining person under ICC arrest warrant who was still alive was Joseph Kony himself. Despite an international force tracking Kony, with African Union and U.S. military support, it seemed he was as far from arrest as he was when the ICC entered thirteen years earlier.

We are left with uncomfortable questions about the timing, nature, and public posture of the ICC Prosecutor at the height of sensitive peace talks, which in this case was the last good hope for peacefully disarming a fearsome rebel group. A better appreciation for the concerns of victim communities, such as was reflected in the ICC Prosecutor's statement in 2016, might have improved how it was seen at the height of that once-promising peace process. A more modest public posture might also have granted more space for the talks to mature and for the key parties to gain confidence in alternative criminal justice solutions.

Notes

1 This case study is based in part on interviews in Kampala and Gulu, Uganda, and in Juba, Southern Sudan, undertaken by the author in October and November 2010.
2 The World Health Organization estimated that over one thousand persons were dying every month in these camps due to the poor conditions.
3 Phuong Pham, Patrick Vinck, Marieke Wierda, Eric Stover and Adrian di Giovanni, *Forgotten Voices: A Population-Based Survey on Attitudes about Peace and Justice in Northern Uganda* (Berkeley: International Center for Transitional Justice and the Human Rights Center, University of California, July 2005); Phuong Pham, Patrick Vinck, Eric Stover, Andrew Moss, Marieke Wierda and Richard Bailey, *When the Wars Ends: A Population-Based Survey on Attitudes About Peace, Justice, and Social Reconstruction in Northern Uganda* (Berkeley: International Center for Transitional Justice; the Human Rights Center, University of California; and the Payson Center for International Development, Tulane University, Dec 2007).
4 Interview by author with former LRA commanders who had helped to facilitate Bigombe's contacts with the LRA when they were still in the bush, Gulu, Nov 2010.
5 Bigombe's last attempt to meet with Kony failed after President Museveni did not authorize such a meeting. (Betty Bigombe, interview by author, Kampala, Nov 2010.)
6 Barney Afako, "Not a Crime to Talk: Legal Aspects of Dialogue With the Lords Resistance Army," unpublished paper, 25 June 2006, 1 (on file with author).

7 Ibid., 8–9.
8 For example, Kony had a serious infection of the mouth that deformed his face, making him almost unrecognizable, as described by one person who met him.
9 Interview, Gulu, Nov 2010.
10 Mark Kersten, *Justice in Conflict: The Effects of the International Criminal Court's Interventions on Ending Wars and Building Peace* (Oxford: Oxford University Press, 2016), 114.
11 Michael Otim and Marieke Wierda, "Justice at Juba: International Obligations and Local Demands in Northern Uganda," in Nicholas Waddell and Phil Clark, eds., *Courting Conflict? Justice, Peace and the ICC in Africa* (London: Royal African Society, March 2008), 23.
12 "UN Official Urges Ugandan Parties to Put Human Rights at the Centre of Talks," 11 May 2007, www.un.org.
13 Warner ten Kate and Sarah M. H. Nouwen, "The Globalisation of Justice: Amplifying and Silencing Voices at the ICC," in Jeff Handmaker and Karin Arts, eds., *Mobilising International Law for 'Global Justice* (Cambridge: Cambridge University Press, 2018).
14 See, for example, Peter Clottey, "Uganda's LRA Rebels Displeased With ICC Chief Prosecutor," Voice of America, 15 Oct 2007, in which an LRA negotiator complains at length about Moreno Ocampo's public statements, saying that "the chief prosecutor's recent statement could seriously destabilize the peace negotiations."
15 This workshop was co-sponsored by the International Center for Transitional Justice.
16 Interview by author.
17 "The main priorities for respondents (who could give more than one response) were health care (45%), peace (44%), children's education (31%), and livelihood concerns (including food, 43%; agricultural land, 37%; money and finances, 35%). These priorities had not changed substantially since 2005, although the emphasis on health care was new. Only 3% of respondents mentioned justice as their top priority." Pham, Stover, Moss, Wierda and Bailey, *When the Wars Ends*, 3.
18 Ibid., 5.
19 "Statement by the Chief Prosecutor on the Uganda Arrest Warrants," ICC Office of the Prosecutor, 14 Oct 2005, noting that the OTP's application for the arrest warrants was submitted on May 6, 2005; "Statements by ICC Chief Prosecutor and the visiting Delegation of Acholi leaders from Northern Uganda," ICC Office of the Prosecutor, The Hague, 18 March 2005.
20 An often-recounted story was that a local political leader, Norbert Mau, invited visiting ICC investigators onto his radio program to explain the Court. They declined. In response, out of frustration, Mr. Mau announced their vehicle license plate numbers on the radio, urging listeners to find them and speak with them directly.
21 For example, many people told me that they thought the ICC was prosecuting only one side of the conflict because it had been invited in by the government and worked on its behalf. This seemed to be a widely held misunderstanding, including among community leaders. Interviews by author, Gulu and environs, Nov 2010.
22 James Otto, telephone interview, Nov 2010.
23 Katy Glassborow, "Peace Versus Justice in Uganda," Institute for War and Peace Reporting, 15 Feb 2010, iwpr.net/global-voices/peace-versus-justice-uganda.
24 Interview, Luis Moreno Ocampo, The Hague, Nov 2011.
25 Michael Otim and Marieke Wierda, "Uganda: Impact of the Rome Statute and the International Criminal Court," International Center for Transitional Justice, May 2010, 3.

26 "Agreement on Accountability and Reconciliation," 29 June 2007, para. 4.1.

27 Ibid., para. 6.4.

28 "Annexure to the Agreement on Accountability and Reconciliation," 19 Feb 2008, para. 19–20.

29 "Agreement on Accountability and Reconciliation," 29 June 2007, para. 9.3.

30 Ibid., para. 5.1, 14.5, and 14.6.

31 Dylan Hendrickson and Kennedy Tumutegyereize, "Dealing With Complexity in Peace Negotiations: Reflections on the Lord's Resistance Army and the Juba Talks," Conciliation Resources, Jan 2012, 24, citing interview with Barney Afako, the lead legal advisor to the chief mediator.

32 Ibid.

33 As described by Michael Otim, an advisor to the mediation team, who met Kony a number of times during the talks. Interview by author, Nov 2010.

34 Martin Ojul, interview by author, Nov 2010.

35 See the detailed discussion of this, including that many delegates were interested in prolonging the talks for personal financial gain, in Kersten, *Justice in Conflict*, 97–98.

36 Some of those forcibly abducted were released after a short period, after they were used to transport goods, for example. "LRA Crisis Tracker: The State of the LRA in 2016," Invisible Children and The Resolve, March 2016, www.theresolve.org.

37 "Communiqué of traditional and religious leaders, civil society, and other organizations concerning the decision of the Minister of Internal Affairs of Uganda to declare, on 23 May, 2012, the lapse of the amnesty provisions of the Amnesty Act of Uganda," 12 June 2012, Kampala.

38 Lino Owor Ogora, "A Reversal of Roles: How the Government and Victims in Northern Uganda Have Switched Their Positions on the ICC," *International Justice Monitor*, 4 Nov 2016, www.ijmonitor.org.

39 "Message from the Prosecutor of the International Criminal Court, Fatou Bensouda, calling for defection by LRA fighters," statement from the Office of the Prosecutor of the ICC, 1 Apr 2016, www.icc-cpi.int.

40 "Ongwen Trial Provokes Strong Opinions in Uganda," *Justice Hub* (blog), 15 Jan 2017, www.justicehub.org.

13 Libya

The great hopes of the Libyan revolution have faded in the years since the extraordinary events of 2011. Things haven't developed well. By mid-2017, there were three competing governments, operating in different parts of the country, in addition to many competing armed militias under no central command. It remained a tragic, complex, and uncertain situation, in which violence abounds.[1]

This chapter is not about the challenges of present-day Libya, which has so radically changed over a few short years. Rather, it looks at the dynamics around the 2011 revolution and the two or three years immediately following. Specifically, it is focused on the issues that are central to this book, in particular the impact of the International Criminal Court in the immediate context of ongoing conflict. This analysis is based on interviews that I undertook in Libya and elsewhere from 2011 to 2013.

The Libyan Revolution

Libyans took to the streets in February 2011 to challenge the Muammar Gaddafi government after more than forty years of dictatorship, in the context of the "Arab Spring" sweeping across the region. These demonstrations met a violent response, and the country soon descended into civil war.

The international community played a defining—and still contested—role in events. Just ten days after the revolution began, the UN Security Council referred the situation to the ICC. Three weeks later, it passed another resolution that authorized "all necessary measures" to protect civilians in Libya. This led to a sustained NATO air campaign against government military installations and ground forces.

The ICC Prosecutor moved quickly, and by late June the ICC Pre-Trial Chamber confirmed arrest warrants for President Gaddafi, his son Saif al-Islam Gaddafi, and his intelligence chief Abdullah al-Senussi. President Gaddafi was on the run. In the final act of the war, on October 20, the opposition captured Gaddafi fleeing in a vehicle convoy; he was fairly quickly shot and killed. Thus, after eight months of war and with thousands dead on both sides, the opposition declared the liberation of the country. Saif Gaddafi and al-Senussi were arrested soon thereafter.

The former regime's many crimes were prominent on the political agenda after Gaddafi's fall. The transitional government grappled with massive challenges, including a compromised judiciary and physical damage to many courthouses and prisons. Militias associated with the new government held thousands from the former army or regime in unofficial detention centers, where there were increasing reports of torture. Libyans demanded restitution of the many properties that had been appropriated by Gaddafi and his cohorts. Local conflicts rose up from long-suppressed grievances. A transitional justice law was passed quite early, including a loose mandate for a fact-finding commission, but this was never implemented. Another controversial law was put in place to exclude all persons from public positions who had even the slightest link to the former regime.

The ICC was perceived as playing an outsized role during this period, although it was focused on only two of the many thousands of people in detention, and on a narrow set of crimes. This chapter aims to understand the impact of the ICC engagement in Libya, from the Security Council referral so early in the conflict to the arrest warrants at the height of the war. Did the Court's engagement, as many worried at the time, prolong the conflict by narrowing Gaddafi's options? Or did it reduce support for Gaddafi and strengthen the opposition? Did the careful watch of the ICC Prosecutor affect the behavior of combatants and deter atrocities? To address these questions, we must look at events, decisions, and assumptions in New York, The Hague, and Libya, as well as important efforts by the African Union in Addis Ababa.

The View From New York: Security Council Referral to the ICC

There were two remarkable things about the Security Council referral of the Libyan case to the ICC. First, it happened extremely quickly, even before organizations in support of the ICC had suggested such a move. Second, the referral was unanimous, with ICC-skeptical states neither vetoing nor abstaining, but in fact positively voting in favor. The resolution also imposed an arms embargo, a travel ban, and the freezing of assets of senior members of the Gaddafi regime.[2]

The early referral to the ICC startled human rights advocates in New York who closely followed the Security Council; they were not expecting and had not proposed an ICC referral at that time. The day before, the UN Human Rights Council in Geneva had created an International Commission of Inquiry on Libya; typically, the Security Council might express support for such an inquiry and urge cooperation by all UN member states, and consider additional measures later, usually after the commission of inquiry would report. This was what many expected.

The resolution passed during a forty-five-minute meeting of the Security Council on the evening of Saturday, February 26. The Council was deeply influenced by a letter from the Libyan ambassador to the UN, who supported the referral of his own country to the ICC. It was a short letter, stating simply:

> With reference to the Draft Resolution on Libya before the Security Council, I have the honour to confirm that the Libyan Delegation to the United Nations supports the measures proposed in the draft resolution to hold to account those responsible for the armed attacks against the Libyan Civilians, including through the International Criminal Court.[3]

Equally, the Council was influenced by statements by the Arab League, the African Union, and the Secretary-General of the Organization of the Islamic Conference. In official comments after the vote, many Council members made reference to the views of these regional bodies and to the views of Security Council members from the region. The Indian ambassador, for example, noted that as a non-ICC state party, India

> would have preferred a calibrated and gradual approach. However, we note that several members of the Council, including our colleagues from Africa and the Middle East, believe that referral to the Court would have the effect of an immediate cessation of violence and the restoration of calm and stability.

He also referred to the letter from the Libyan ambassador, which he said "strengthened this view."[4]

The representative from China called for the resolution of the crisis through dialogue, but "taking into consideration the special situation in Libya at this time and the concerns and views of the Arab and African countries," it had voted in favor.[5]

Some observers also recall a general view at the time—in these very early days of the conflict—that Gaddafi was losing the war. The opposition seemed to quickly take control of a large swath of the country, with Gaddafi pulling back his forces. In addition, the regional context, with the successful, rapid revolutions in Tunisia and Egypt, created an impression of the inevitability that Gaddafi would fall. But this was misleading. It was only a few days before Gaddafi's forces hit back with vengeance. Its march forward against the revolutionary forces was only stopped with the NATO military intervention that began in late March.

How Did the ICC Affect the Conflict?

Once referred, the next surprise was how quickly the ICC Prosecutor moved from investigation to arrest warrants. What had taken several years in other cases, such as Sudan, was accomplished in three months in the case of Libya.

The result was that the announcement of warrants was made at the height of the war, in late June 2011.

To understanding how the ICC intervention might have affected the conflict and any prospects for peace, it is useful to ask four questions. First, was there an impact on the possibility of a negotiated solution? Second, how did the indictments affect the perceived legitimacy of Gaddafi? Third, did the arrest warrants have an impact on the choices available to the government, and on its decisions and actions? Finally, did the engagement and oversight of the ICC affect the opposition fighters, perhaps deterring potential abuse? Each of these will be addressed below.

Assessing the Impact on the Possibility of Negotiations

Was there any real possibility of an end to the conflict in Libya in any way other than through a military solution? The received wisdom, in retrospect, is that the idea of a negotiated resolution was far-fetched and never had enough traction to become a serious possibility. At the time, however, this was not so evident, including for some of those at the heart of the Libyan opposition.

The key member states behind the NATO military campaign (the U.S., the UK, and France) were not enthusiastic about a negotiated solution and made little effort to support such an option. Indeed, analyst Bridget Conley later wrote that as early as March 2011,

> [T]he P3 (France, Britain and the United States) had already made their decision that military action would continue until regime change had been achieved. The UN was of the opinion that there was no opportunity for negotiations until the killing of civilians had ceased. The AU's position was that there was always time for negotiation, and that an attempted military solution would have high costs for Libya and unknowable repercussions for the region.[6]

The UN appointed a special envoy on the matter, Abdel-Elah al-Khatib, but he made little headway, hitting intransigence from both the government and the opposition. The African Union is described as having the most robust plan for a ceasefire, negotiations, and an "inclusive, consensual interim government, leading to democratic elections," as reported by Alex de Waal, based on a study of Africa's role in the Libyan conflict.[7] De Waal concludes that the AU initiative was effectively squelched by actions and statements of the P3 NATO states. He suggests that there was potential for a negotiated solution:

> The AU plan for a negotiated transition to a post-Gaddafi order in Libya had no guarantee of success. Libya's political and military dynamics made it a difficult proposition. However, a coordinated approach by the P3 and the AU would undoubtedly have stood a good chance of achieving a peaceful outcome, especially if pursued consistently from the outset of the

conflict. The AU could have persuaded Gaddafi to step aside, with P3-led military pressure forcing his hand.[8]

Indeed, the AU roadmap for a resolution of the conflict "failed primarily due to opposition from the P3," Conley wrote.[9]

Members or advisors of the main opposition body at the time, the National Transitional Council (NTC), echo the sentiment that there was never a serious attempt by the international community, and especially NATO states, to negotiate a resolution. Some (although a minority) within the NTC leadership thought a compromise solution would have been better, especially after Tripoli fell, in order to avoid the costs in deaths and destruction that came from a full military victory.

In interviews with persons in or close to the NTC, I was told of serious initiatives by the UK and by France to find a resolution to the war and in particular to Gaddafi's fate, in addition to the efforts of the AU. But the NTC held little trust in some of the ideas, such as a proposal from a Gaddafi envoy that he turn over power to his son and be allowed to settle in the south.

The International Crisis Group released a report in June 2011 that called for a ceasefire and negotiations, suggesting that the NTC would have to guarantee space for Gaddafi's supporters in a transitional government. The Crisis Group puts some blame on both the NTC leadership and its Western backers involved in the NATO military campaign for refusing negotiation initiatives, setting preconditions too high, and failing to come forward with their own proposals.[10]

How did the ICC arrest warrants play into these dynamics? There was strong and widespread support from the Libyan opposition for the referral to the ICC by the UN Security Council. But as time went on, the ICC was "definitely seen as an impediment to getting Gaddafi to possibly leave," as one NTC executive committee member put it.

At one point, when the NTC leadership thought there was movement on possible negotiations, they asked ICC Prosecutor Luis Moreno Ocampo to delay his announcement that he was requesting arrest warrants, so that they could push for a negotiated solution. The prosecutor complied with this request. Once the warrants were released, as they had feared, the opposition sensed that Gaddafi dug in his heels and decided to fight to the end.

Ahmed Gebreel, a senior political advisor to the NTC executive committee, lamented that an opportunity was lost to use the ICC, backed by the NATO military strikes, as a political tool to reach a compromise solution. "Divorcing peace from justice was unrealistic, given the situation on the ground. If you could have had a balanced approach and avoided tens of thousands killed, wouldn't you?"[11] While the NTC starting position was that Gaddafi must leave power, they also made clear that if Gaddafi left the country they would not pursue him. They were also prepared to ask for an Article 16 deferral from the UN Security Council, to halt ICC prosecutions for at least one year.

A compromise solution would have required serious engagement by several parties, in particular the U.S. (which Gaddafi saw as the key actor) and by the UN Security Council (to obtain the ICC deferral), Gebreel noted. There was just not much focus on this possibility either from the key Security Council members and NATO states or from within the NTC, where some resisted compromise. I spoke with Gebreel just six months after the end of the 2011 conflict, and stabilizing the country was already looking very difficult. Gebreel felt sure that a negotiated resolution to the war would have resulted in a Libya that was more inclusive and democratic, had more functioning institutions, and was less hampered by militia groups that remained outside central control after the war.

"It was the *warrant* that complicated everything, not the referral," Gebreel noted. "Once the arrest warrant was out, Gaddafi understood he had two options: either arrest and trial, or death. He chose the latter."

The AU also saw the ICC arrest warrants as hindering any peace option. Shortly after the warrants were confirmed by the ICC Pre-Trial Chamber, the AU declared that its members would not implement the warrants and that Gaddafi could freely travel in Africa.[12] This statement was apparently a product of considerable debate at the AU summit in late June 2011, but it was not clear how such an AU political decision could overrule the legal obligations of the then thirty-one African state parties to the ICC, who were required to cooperate with the Court and comply with the warrants.

At the international level, many commentators worried that such an early hail for justice would make a negotiated resolution more difficult, both in Libya and elsewhere. By April 2011, analysts were suggesting that other leaders throughout the Arab world, each confronting their own popular protests, were concluding that it was better to fight than quit. Whether the potential threat of prosecution was from international or national courts, it was increasingly clear that amnesty for their past deeds was not likely. This was certainly not only a question of ICC action: after all it was an Egyptian court that put the former President of Egypt Hosni Mubarak on trial after he ceded power— perhaps the most prominent attempt to hold a leader criminally accountable that emerged in the Arab Spring.

Delegitimizing Gaddafi

For most Libyans, the arrest warrants were a signal that the international community now considered Gaddafi a war criminal. Libyans describe how the announcement of the warrants had the immediate effect of delegitimizing him. Streets erupted in celebration in opposition-held areas. As the former chairman of the NTC Executive Committee, Mahmoud Jibril, told me, it was

> a very important moment. It was like a validating argument that said, 'these people have committed crimes against humanity, just like the opposition

has been saying.' Many saw the warrant for Gaddafi as effectively labeling him an international war criminal, thus providing clear moral support for the opposition.[13]

Many Libyans saw this as a turning point in the conflict, as the beginning of the collapse of the regime. Libyans who supported the government took a step back, and many who were on the fence began to pull away from the regime.

Members of the NTC had understood very early how important such a move would be, and it tasked the Legal Committee of the NTC to compile reports and evidence to be provided to the ICC Prosecutor, with the hope that this might lead to high-level indictments. The chair of this Legal Committee, Dr. Salwa El Daghili, described the long hours spent by the Committee to compile and send information to the Prosecutor, through a painfully slow internet connection. ICC representatives visited Benghazi twice, and El Daghili traveled to The Hague to meet with ICC Prosecutor Moreno Ocampo.

"Thank goodness," Dr. El Daghili said, when I met with her in Tripoli in 2012, "our efforts were a success: this resulted in three warrants. The warrants were our ultimate goal, in order to delegitimize Gaddafi. We wanted to make him an international criminal—this represented legitimacy for us. Gaddafi became wanted internationally."

But almost in the same breath, she also insisted that she had felt strongly at the time, and continued to believe, that the trials for those indicted by the ICC must take place in Libyan courts. "It has to be *our* process," she said. This was universally agreed at the time among her colleagues, and she made this view clear to the ICC when they met, she said. Indeed, she and her colleagues on the legal committee "were surprised when the ICC called for trials in an international court. We always discussed having trials at the national level, and always said this clearly to the ICC."

Why would the NTC push for international indictments if they had no interest that the ICC follow through? There are several reasons. Clearly, as noted, the indictments from an international court represented first and foremost a political strike against the regime and thus in support of the opposition. Second, if Gaddafi had fled Libya, he could be arrested overseas under an ICC warrant, and thus the engagement of the ICC was seen in part as an insurance policy. And third, although this may be forgotten with time, it wasn't at all clear during much of the conflict that the opposition would defeat the government and gain control of the whole country. If Libya had split into two states, the NTC would not have had access to put the Gaddafi leadership on trial, and thus again the international warrants would be critical.

The profound impact of the warrants on the legitimacy of the regime's leadership led some to conclude that, rather than lengthening the war, the Security Council referral and the arrest warrants shortened the war, by "taking the carpet out from under the regime," as a group of former opposition commanders told me. They felt that other countries significantly reduced contact with the government as a result.[14]

What Impact on the Regime's Actions and Choices?

The reaction to the arrest warrants by many international commentators was more one of increasing worry. Gaddafi's legitimacy was no doubt damaged, and his options had also considerably narrowed. As an editor of *The Guardian* wrote when the warrants were confirmed, "The ICC has added its weight to attempts to corner Gaddafi. But cornered, he is rendered all the more dangerous."[15]

The escape route had been narrowed: if he decided to flee the country, he would have to go to a non-ICC state party to avoid arrest. But Gaddafi would know that even in those countries, his security from arrest would not be sure.

Opinions from outside Libya were plentiful. But is there any way to know what Gaddafi was thinking, and how and whether the ICC's engagement affected his calculations? Very few people were close enough to Gaddafi to have discussed these matters with him.

One of the men who was close to Gaddafi, former Security Chief Mansour Dhao Ibrahim, was with him until his last hours. Dhao was in the convoy with Gaddafi that was attacked while it was departing from Sirte, resulting in Gaddafi being captured and killed. Dhao was struck by shrapnel and fell unconscious, presumed dead; it was probably for this reason that he lived, while many others were killed. I interviewed Dhao in a detention center in Misrata three months after the fall of the regime.

Dhao explained how Gaddafi intentionally used the ICC to rally more support to his side, decrying this form of international intervention into Libyan affairs. In Dhao's view, this initially increased the popular support for his regime and thus had the effect of prolonging the conflict.

But Dhao also described Gaddafi's frustration with the lack of apparent solutions during his last months. He was under military siege by the rebels on the one hand, but well aware that the ICC arrest warrant awaited him on the other. He couldn't see any options for escape. "He expected his friends in the international community to help guide him, to suggest what should be done," Dhao told me.

> He had this idea in mind until the last minute—that Berlusconi, Blair, or Erdogan, for example, would contact him to help. Especially Berlusconi: Gaddafi was very disappointed with him. He didn't understand why no one reached out to propose a solution.

When pressed, it became clear that Dhao had no appreciation—and neither had Gaddafi—that these international figures may well have been constrained to take any action to assist Gaddafi, in part due to the ICC warrants. Silvio Berlusconi, then the prime minister of Italy, represented an ICC state party, and was thus legally obliged to fully cooperate with the Court. Former British Prime Minister Tony Blair may also have felt constrained, although he was then a private individual. Turkish Prime Minister Recep Tayyip Erdogan (who received the Gaddafi International Prize for Human Rights three months before the Libyan revolution) represented a non-ICC state party, but may still have felt constrained by the UN Security Council's Chapter VII referral of the case.[16] The delegitimizing effect of the ICC warrants probably also played a role: even for those not legally constrained, there may have been limited interest in helping an indicted war criminal whose power was beginning to collapse.

Meanwhile, there is no evidence that the ICC engagement in Libya affected the fighting tactics of the regime's forces. They committed serious abuses throughout the conflict. The nature of these forces may have contributed to their lack of attention to the ICC referral and indictments: Gaddafi had a weak army, but strong independent brigades operating under Gaddafi's sons and trusted relatives, as well as informal forces and mercenaries.

There is no suggestion that Gaddafi, the army command, or the more informal forces fighting on behalf of the regime made any attempt to change their practices as a result of the threat of international prosecution.

Did the ICC Deter Abuses by Opposition Fighters?

Available evidence suggests that the worst and the greatest number of abuses during this period were by the regime's forces, including both the regular army and irregular forces that supported the regime. This included abuses in combat, torture and other abuse of detainees, and the treatment of civilians outside of conflict (such as violence against unarmed protestors).

There were, however, serious abuses by the opposition forces as well. Towards the end of the conflict, Human Rights Watch and others began to report on practices by the armed opposition that clearly constituted grave violations of the rules of war.[17] In particular, militia-controlled detention centers tortured detainees, including people detained solely for their association with the Gaddafi regime. A number of people died under torture.

The extent of opposition war crimes during the 2011 conflict is not clear. Former commanders and fighters, in an interview in Misrata, insisted that any abuses that took place were crimes of individuals, and did not take place by policy or with the knowledge or authorization of commanders.[18] They cited examples where they took steps explicitly to comply with international laws of war, such as halting the march on Sirte (a city allied with the regime) for a number of days in order to allow civilians to leave.

Did the engagement of the ICC affect the opposition fighters' actions? Did its watchful eye shape their policies and deter them from atrocities? There are mixed answers to these questions, but in sum the answer is, largely, no. Most opposition fighters didn't understand that the ICC applied to them.

Some within the opposition leadership were aware that the ICC jurisdiction would cover actions by either side of the conflict. "We discussed this from a very early stage, before the real battles began," NTC advisor Gebreel told me.

> We said, 'Be careful: the Security Council referral covers the whole country, not just Gaddafi. If you commit crimes, you might be accused of war

crimes.' But we didn't have a clear command structure. People were coming from the streets and just taking up arms. They didn't understand. And we had no means to reach them: there was almost no communication between the fighters and the NTC Executive Committee.[19]

This was echoed by others in the leadership. Former NTC Chairman Mahmoud Jibril reiterated the communications difficulties. "Fighters didn't know the rules of engagement or the law. And they were full of anger. It was a question of discipline." The respect for their commanders was the critical element that shaped their actions, he said. It is clear that any ICC deterrence effect will be much more limited in situations with irregular, decentralized, semi-autonomous security forces, as was true of the opposition forces.[20]

At the level of the front-line fighters, there was little to no understanding that the ICC might pertain to them. One former field commander told me that he was aware of the ICC applicability to his forces, and it was one of many factors that pushed him to comply with the rules of war.[21] But many others I spoke with made clear that they had understood the ICC to be an international court that was targeting the Gaddafi regime. After the three arrest warrants were released, no one thought there was any possibility of additional ICC indictments.

In the view of Libyans, the ICC made no attempt to suggest otherwise. An NTC Executive Committee member noted that the NTC was in touch with the Prosecutor's office from the beginning. I asked whether the Prosecutor made clear that NTC fighters could also be at risk of criminal investigations. "No, he really didn't. He didn't come across as very impartial; it was clear from the beginning that he was going after Gaddafi."

Mahmoud Jibril remembers, "We received two or three emails from NATO saying that we should respect human rights, and maybe making reference to the ICC. But not from the ICC itself; they never said this, nor suggested that we were also a target."

The International Committee of the Red Cross (ICRC) also held trainings very early on, trying to quickly provide basic information on the rules of war. There was apparently no mention in these trainings of the ICC factor.[22] The chair of the NTC legal committee told me,

> There was no sense that the ICC was a threat of prosecution for NTC fighters. I never heard this directly said in trainings on IHL [international humanitarian law]. I believe the UN may have said it once, but really it was never put on the table in any serious way. For revolutionaries, it was *never* in their mind that they might be condemned by a court outside of Libya. Fighters were oblivious of this. The ICC was only about the three who were indicted.

The Misratan former fighters explained, "We respected the rules of war for religious reasons, and common sense. And because we believed in our just cause." Religious leaders and civil society organizations gave lectures to the fighters, urging them not to commit crimes. "They were always telling us: 'Gaddafi was wrong to us, but we will succeed by not doing wrong to them.'"

A former field commander in Misrata briefly outlined the rules of war that had been emphasized, and in particular stressed by religious leaders:

> Prisoners would be treated humanely; civilians would not be targeted; ambulances would be given due respect, and ambulances could not be used to carry weapons; injured soldiers from Gaddafi's forces would be taken to hospital. All of these rules, we tried to respect them.[23]

Some former opposition fighters blame the ICC for not taking action against a broader number of regime commanders and for acting too slowly. They are convinced it would have had a deterrent effect. "The problem was that the ICC didn't go beyond the three initially indicted, to reach commanders on the ground, where there were many crimes. The delay in warrants meant that the regime's commanders didn't stop these abuses."

During the conflict, the NTC repeatedly stated its commitment to hold people responsible for alleged abuses on either side of the war. The international community accepted these intentions as genuine, which reduced any pressure for ICC to take action against the opposition. But the judicial system suffered serious deficiencies, many thousands of conflict detainees remained unprocessed, and there was no action against those from the revolutionary forces who were carrying out rampant torture or other abuses.[24]

While the former combatants recount their good intentions and play down any abuses, several key events colored the image of the revolution. The conflict between the city of Misrata and neighboring Tawergha was prominent among them. The revolutionary forces in Misrata fought for months to hold out against a sustained attack from the Gaddafi government. It was a brutal campaign, with huge losses and major destruction to the city. Tawerghans had fought enthusiastically in support of the government. When Misrata finally repelled the regime's forces in May 2011, the opposition forces turned their revenge on Tawergha. The retaliation was complete: they forcibly expelled the entire Tawerghan population of 40,000, who scattered to refugee camps and to other cities. Militias continued to target Tawerghans in the following years with reported abductions, torture, and killings.[25]

Misrata's image suffered further a few months after the war ended when an international group providing medical services in detention centers publicly accused the jailers of torture. The organization worried they were being asked to patch up torture victims only so that the detainees could be interrogated, and tortured, further. With such a rare public denouncement, the organization, Médecins Sans Frontières (MSF), quit their work in the Misrata detention centers.[26]

Three months later, the ICC Prosecutor visited Libya and traveled to Misrata. He visited the impressive war museum that honored the many thousands killed in the battle for Misrata. The prosecutor left a note in the visitors' book, which was displayed prominently at the entrance to the museum. The prosecutor wrote:

> I am honored to visit this museum. It is showing the courage and determination of Misrata people. They freed the city, the country, and are an example for the world. The Office of the Prosecutor of the International Criminal Court will present a case exploring the responsibility of those who ordered all these crimes.[27]

> The Prosecutor, with great admiration for Misrata
> Luis Moreno Ocampo
> 2012.4.20

The Prosecutor would surely have known about the allegations against the Misratan forces, both in Tawergha and in the prisons. Indeed, a few weeks later the Prosecutor made a presentation to the UN Security Council in which he outlined the Tawergha events and the reports of torture of detainees, indicating that these could constitute international crimes.[28] His public posture in Libya, however, helped explain why Misratans, and Libyans as a whole, never believed the ICC intended to focus on more than one side.

For any possible deterrent effect from an international court, the first step must be that those who might commit crimes are aware that the court has jurisdiction and is watching. It would seem natural for an international prosecutor to make this clear—as the ICC Prosecutor has done very forthrightly in other contexts, such as Côte d'Ivoire and Colombia. This did not take place in Libya.

Justice and the ICC After the Conflict

Serious abuses continued in Libya after the revolution, especially widespread torture. Human Rights Watch reported on the abuses, but saw no action from national authorities to investigate or stop these practices. In early 2012, Human Rights Watch released a statement warning that the ICC still held jurisdiction, hoping this might help deter abuses. This was apparently heard: while abuses didn't stop, the militias began to hide or cover up evidence in a way they hadn't before. International organizations found investigations more difficult, and local officials were reticent to grant access or share information; they were concerned these investigations might be linked to the ICC.

Speaking to the UN Security Council in May 2013, the new ICC Prosecutor, Fatou Bensouda, hinted that she might open additional cases against Gaddafi regime officials and said that the ICC was also concerned about alleged crimes by the former rebels, specifically mentioning the Tawergha events.[29] In 2016, the Prosecutor announced that Libya would be a priority in her investigations for 2017, referring back to cases from 2011 as well as more recent events. In describing their plans, the Prosecutor's office emphasized their hope and expectation that new arrest warrants would deter further crimes.

Meanwhile, in 2012 and 2013, the Libyan government challenged the ICC's jurisdiction over the two outstanding indictees, insisting that Libya could try them domestically. The ICC pre-trial chamber assessed Libya's ability and willingness to provide a fair trial: it decided that Libya could try former intelligence chief al-Senussi nationally, but that Saif Gaddafi should be transferred to the ICC. But Saif Gaddafi remained in the hands of a militia, and the government said it had to no power to transfer him. One consequence of these ICC admissibility proceedings was that Libya reformed some elements of its judicial system, in part to meet the requirements of the ICC.

Libya's insistence in trying the indictees in country, under national laws, was not only for reasons of national pride. There were important substantive reasons. The ICC jurisdiction only covered crimes committed after late February 2011. Al-Senussi, for example, was implicated in a massacre of over 1,200 prisoners at the Abu Salim Prison in 1996, one of the worst atrocities of the Gaddafi era. Libyans wanted justice for these and other pre-2011 crimes. Sentencing also differed: Libya could consider the death penalty, whereas the ICC could not.

Conclusion

The UN-backed military intervention in Libya has left lasting scars on the international community's understanding of the role it can or should play in attempting to halt threatened atrocities and to shape national political realities in such unpredictable and volatile contexts. The choice by the UN Security Council to refer the situation to the ICC so very early in the conflict is difficult to separate from this broader context of intervention. The ICC, of course, perceived itself as independent from the political and military forces holding sway in Libya, but in the end it was seen as an important factor shaping these very political realities.

In retrospect, it's easy to see that publicly announced arrest warrants will have a political effect—targeting such high-level persons who were literally fighting for their life—and it's hard to imagine the Prosecutor at that time keeping these warrants under wraps. If the Prosecutor hoped to deter further abuses, this also fell flat. It is true that deterrence is difficult if forces are not under central command and control, as many forces in Libya were not. But the ICC Prosecutor's exclusive focus on crimes of the Gaddafi regime did not help. The message from the Prosecutor should be clear and unambiguous that all sides fall under the Court's jurisdiction and are being watched. In Libya, this was not widely understood.

Notes

1 This case study is based in part on interviews undertaken by the author in Tripoli and Misrata, Libya, from 2011 to 2013.
2 UN Security Council Resolution 1970, 26 Feb 2011.
3 Letter to the President of the UN Security Council, 26 Feb 2011, from Abdurrahman M. Shalgham, Permanent Representative of Libya to the United Nations.

4 Statement of Hardeep Singh Puri, Permanent Representative of India to the United Nations, UN Security Council session of 26 Feb 2011, UN Doc. S/PV.6491.

5 Statement of Li Baodong, Permanent Representative of China to the United Nations, UN Doc. S/PV.6491.

6 Bridget Conley, "Libya in the African Context: A History Waiting to Be Written," *African Arguments* (blog), 10 Jan 2013, africanarguments.org, summarizing a meeting of Libya experts hosted by the World Peace Foundation.

7 Alex de Waal, "African Roles in the Libyan Conflict of 2011," *International Affairs* 89:2 (2013): 375.

8 Ibid., 379.

9 Conley, "Libya in the African Context."

10 "Popular Protest in North Africa and the Middle East (V): Making Sense of Libya," International Crisis Group, 6 June 2011, 28–29.

11 Ahmed Gebreel, interview by author, London, 25 Apr 2012.

12 The decision by the AU was attributed to "deep concerns" with the "manner in which the International Criminal Court (ICC) Prosecutor handles the situation in Libya" and worries that the Gaddafi warrant would complicate efforts to negotiate a political solution in Libya. "Decision on the implementation of the Assembly decisions on the International Criminal Court," para. 6, (17th AU Summit, 30 June—1 July 2011, Malabo, Equatorial Guinea), AU Doc.EX.CL/670(XIX). For analysis, see Antoinette Louw, "Perspectives on Africa's response to the ICC's arrest warrants in the Libya situation," Situation Report, Institute for Security Studies, 22 July 2011.

13 Mahmoud Jibril, interview by author, Tripoli, 16 Apr 2013.

14 Meeting with a group of seven former commanders and fighters in the opposition forces, Misrata, 17 Apr 2013.

15 Simon Tisdall, "This Arrest Warrant Could Make Gaddafi More Dangerous," Opinion Piece, *The Guardian*, 27 June 2011, guardian.co.uk.

16 The Security Council resolution referring the case to the ICC specifically states: ". . . while recognizing that States not party to the Rome Statute have no obligation under the Statute, urges all States and concerned regional and other international organizations to cooperate fully with the Court and the Prosecutor." Operative para. 5, UNSC Resolution 1970 (2011).

17 "Libya: New Proof of Mass Killings and Gaddafi Death Site," Human Rights Watch, 17 Oct 2012, www.hrw.org.

18 Interviews by author, Misrata, 17 Apr 2013.

19 Gebreel, interview.

20 Jibril, interview.

21 Interview by author, Misrata, 26 Jan 2012.

22 Interviews by author, Apr 2013, with Red Crescent Society staff, Misrata; former staff of ICRC who were present in the trainings in Benghazi in March 2011; former chair of legal committee of the NTC.

23 Interview by author, Misrata, Jan 2012.

24 Interviews by author, Apr 2013. For a thorough assessment of the judicial system in Libya as of 2013, see "Trial by Error: Justice in Post-Qadhafi Libya," International Crisis Group, 17 Apr 2013.

25 "Trial by Error," International Crisis Group, 7.

26 "MSF Quits Prisons in Libya City Over 'Torture'," *Reuters*, 26 Jan 2012, www.reuters.com.

27 As displayed on the wall of the Misrata Martyr's Museum, Apr 2013.

28 "Third Report of the Prosecutor of the International Criminal Court to the UN Security Council Pursuant to UNSCR 1970 (2011)," 16 May 2012, www.icc-cpi.int.

29 "Security Council: Libyan Trials Could Be 'Nuremberg Moment,' ICC Prosecutor Says," UN News Centre, 8 May 2013, www.un.org.

14 Colombia

The announcement in late 2015 that the Colombian government had reached an agreement on justice issues with the country's largest guerrilla group was received with jubilation in Colombia and abroad. An overall peace deal with the Revolutionary Armed Forces of Colombia, or FARC, now seemed within reach. While there were other difficult issues outstanding, such as the mechanics of ceasefire and demobilization, in the public mind the question of justice was always the most difficult, and no one was sure the parties would find a way out. The crimes were too great, and the culpability reached too high—and both national and international courts were watching closely and unlikely to allow an agreement that did not hold high-level perpetrators to account.[1]

To announce the justice agreement, Colombian President Juan Manuel Santos made his first trip to the site of the talks that had been under way for three years, in Havana, Cuba. With his first public handshake with the leader of the FARC, they agreed not only to a broad system for justice, reparations, and truth, but also to an intended deadline for a conclusion of the talks within six months. Now, finally, this seemed possible.

The prominence of accountability and victims' rights in the Colombia peace process was due in part to the large numbers of victims, but also to a strong legal culture in the country. A vibrant civil society has demanded the highest standards and helped shape policy through challenges in national courts and in the Inter-American human rights commission and court. Colombian judges had repeatedly confirmed strict obligations of the state, sometimes even surpassing the requirements of international law. From 2003, when Colombia ratified the Rome Statute, the ICC Prosecutor had also actively monitored the country, threatening to open prosecutions if national efforts fell short.

Even before the talks began, it was widely assumed that grappling with the many crimes of the war would be the central and possibly insurmountable challenge. The FARC was accused of many atrocities in its fifty-year war, and so were the state's armed forces and the brutal paramilitary forces that supported the state. It was clear that granting impunity would be unacceptable to broad constituencies within Colombian society.

Fifty Years of War and Attempts at Peace

The judicial opinions, legalistic culture, and even stated policies of government in favor of human rights stood in stark contrast to the levels of human rights violations and war crimes that continued over decades of war, including targeted assassinations, kidnappings, disappearances, and massacres. Even as the FARC peace talks were under way, rights activists received regular death threats, and labor, land, and human rights activists were targeted and killed. While government forces were not always directly responsible, there were too few efforts to halt the abuses, and many were linked to the paramilitary forces that operated at one-step remove from the government. In a country of forty-eight million, over five million people were direct victims, mostly of forced displacement. Some 220,000 have died in the conflict since 1958, most of them civilians.[2]

As the country's largest armed opposition group, the FARC was at its strongest in the 1990s and up until 2002, when at certain times it controlled 40% of the country and had an armed force of close to 20,000. By 2012, when the most recent peace process began, the group and its range of control was much reduced as a result of a strong military counter-offensive by the government, with heavy financial and technical support from the U.S., but it was still estimated to have over 9,000 troops. Other armed groups, such as the National Liberation Army (ELN), were smaller, but also an important presence. Frequent clashes between the army and guerrillas still caused some 1,500 deaths each year when the 2012 talks began.

The Colombian army began a particularly egregious practice in the mid-2000s of capturing and killing random young men—several thousand in total—and passing them off as guerrilla fighters; this resulted in financial and other benefits for the soldiers whose kill count was high. These came to be known as "false positive" cases, and hundreds of mostly low-level soldiers were eventually prosecuted and imprisoned for these crimes.

There have been many peace negotiations in Colombia with many armed groups, going back decades.[3] In almost every case, the talks began with a promise of an amnesty, and there were many such amnesties granted since the 1950s for conflict-related offenses. As early as the 1980s, these amnesty agreements usually stated that serious human rights violations would not be covered, and this kept some convicted combatants in jail even after a peace agreement was signed, but in every case the leaders of these armed groups were amnestied without investigation or prosecution. Some former guerrilla leaders later held important political roles, including mayor of Bogota and member of Congress.

But it did not always go well for leftist guerrillas who demobilized and joined civilian life. Most notoriously, members of the Patriotic Union, a political party founded by the FARC after a 1985 ceasefire agreement, were systematically tracked down and assassinated by right-wing paramilitary forces. It is estimated that an extraordinary three to five thousand Patriotic Union members were killed over a several-year period, including eight Congressmen and two presidential candidates. This well-known history served as a dark shadow over later peace processes.

From the early 1990s, Colombia saw an increase in paramilitary groups that were aligned with the government, often had the support of local business leaders or landed elite, and, as it became clear later, received direct support and cover from members of Congress and other senior officials. They targeted and killed trade unionists, journalists, human rights activists, and anyone they believed was associated with a guerrilla group.

The decision by President Uribe to demobilize the paramilitaries, beginning in 2002, coincided with the moment when the International Criminal Court came into force, and Colombia was among the first states to submit to its jurisdiction.[4] The ICC would play more of a role in setting the parameters for peace agreements going forward than the government may have expected. Many policies, laws, and national court decisions were pushed to take this international framework into account, and both the arrangement with the paramilitary forces and the agreement with the FARC were shaped in part by the fact of the ICC. Colombia has consistently pledged its support to complying with requirements of both the ICC and the Inter-American human rights system, in particular the Inter-American Court of Human Rights. But more immediate constraints emerged from Colombia's own laws and the jurisprudence of its courts. The ICC and the Inter-American Court would watch how the national system handled these issues before deciding their response.

The below will first track the legally fraught efforts to hold the paramilitaries to account, and then turn to the negotiations and agreement with the FARC.

A Justice System for Paramilitary Forces

The creation of a special system of justice for the paramilitaries, referred to as the "Justice and Peace" process, received intense scrutiny from human rights advocates and from Colombian courts over a number of years. This complex regime set out new ground, intending to process thousands of demobilized paramilitary members through a new court structure and legal framework. It was years in development, but its implementation was slow and ineffective, and it ultimately lost support even from those who initially pushed for such a system. This legal and political precedent set important background to the FARC talks that followed.

President Uribe began negotiations with the paramilitary forces in 2002. Of course, these paramilitaries were considered allies of the government, so these talks were not peace negotiations in any traditional sense. Uribe readily promised that these paramilitary forces would walk free without fear of prosecution once they demobilized. The paramilitary leadership welcomed this, and they and their members began to turn in their weapons and demobilize (although some did not fully demobilize and continued to operate illegal networks). However, over the next two years, this impunity agreement was challenged and overturned, due to strong public opposition and multiple court decisions.[5] The basic assumptions on which the demobilization had taken place had suddenly changed.

President Uribe then proposed a scheme by which perpetrators could confess to crimes in exchange for a considerably reduced sentence. Congress passed this as the Justice and Peace Law, which created "justice and peace" hearings, magistrates, courtrooms, and sentences. This was also challenged in the Constitutional Court by victims and human rights advocates. Thus began a long process by which the Court interrogated the very core of the proposed arrangement that limited justice for the sake of (it was hoped) peace, or at least demobilization of one major actor in the violence. These high court decisions significantly strengthened the Justice and Peace Law in favor of justice, but also put a greater burden on implementation.

In a major decision in 2006, for example, the Constitutional Court ruled that parts of the Justice and Peace Law were unconstitutional. The decision accepted that the imperative of peace justified a reduction of penalties—a maximum of eight years in prison—but that this had to be balanced with victims' rights. Thus, the Court said, confessions by perpetrators had to be true and complete, with all of their crimes included. Second, the perpetrator's duty to provide reparations to victims required that he surrender all assets, not only those illegally obtained. The decision as a whole was explicitly framed as providing an equilibrium between justice and peace, based on core principles of transitional justice.

The Justice and Peace regime intended to process thousands of paramilitary members. The procedure ultimately worked as follows:

- The president's office provided a list of over 4,000 persons who should be included in the Justice and Peace process. These were each accused of serious crimes such as killings, torture, disappearances, and massacres. Once referred to the Justice and Peace process, they were known as *postulados* in Spanish. However, only about one thousand reported for the process, and there was apparently little effort to track those who were missing.

- These *postulados* were required to provide full information about their crimes, in sessions known as *versiones libres*, or freely stated accounts, where they were not restricted by time nor guided by a prosecutor or magistrate. Some *versiones libres* lasted for weeks, and the system was criticized for allowing *postulados* to carry on extensively, sometimes off-topic, sometimes trying to justify their acts. Victims could listen from a separate room and occasionally submit a question, but they had little role in this stage of the process. These hearings were otherwise closed to the public and press.

- A multiple-step process followed, including public hearings to review the charges by the prosecutor, some opportunity for victims or their representatives to challenge their account or ask for further details, and questions from the magistrates overseeing the process. A final reparations hearing required each *postulado* to list their assets, and compensation was awarded to victims. This reparations procedure was also criticized, in that many were said to hide their assets to avoid paying reparations.

- If the *postulado* was determined to be telling the truth and provided all the information requested, he would be given a sentence of five to eight years. If they did not fully cooperate with the process, including providing a full and truthful account, they could be removed from the process and tried in a normal court, where sentences for these crimes ranged from forty to sixty years.

But the process moved very slowly. After seven years of Justice and Peace hearings, only ten cases had been concluded, raising serious concerns. By 2015, 115 had been sentenced. But the initial confessions from people entering the process had already identified an extraordinary 70,000 individual crimes. It became clear that this alternative but heavily judicialized approach would have a very hard time processing the thousands of individuals and tens of thousands of crimes outstanding within any reasonable period of time.

The magistrates explained that their first cases intentionally included an in-depth and lengthy inquiry into each paramilitary block, resulting in major judgments of up to 800 pages, with the idea that later cases could be attached to these and would therefore move more quickly.[6] They pressed the prosecutor's office to bring cases against commanders first, so that the magistrates could explore questions beyond the narrow specificity of individual crimes. The first judgments indeed provided extensive detail on the inside workings of each paramilitary block: where they obtained weapons, the source of financing, command structure, and types of human rights violations. But while the decisions were public, they received little public or media attention. Then, as time passed, former paramilitary members began to be released before their cases had even been heard, having served the maximum eight years in prison.

The Justice and Peace hearings were managed by magistrates and took place in a courtroom, but they were very different from normal criminal court hearings. The questions from the magistrates, from the prosecutor, and occasionally from victims' representatives pertained less to the guilt of the individual and more to the reasons why such severe abuses took place, where the remains of the victims could be found, how they learned certain torture practices, and even why they decided to kill certain victims over others.

I attended a Justice and Peace hearing in May 2012 during the "confirmation of charges" phase. The eight *postulados* were transported to the court in a secure prison vehicle and in handcuffs, with heavy police accompaniment. There was no question that these were prisoners. While responses to the many specific questions were not always readily provided—and the lower level perpetrators in particular often couldn't or didn't provide any contextual information about why things happened as they did—the exchanges still proved very interesting. Box 14.1 provides a sample.

Box 14.1   Justice and Peace Hearing—May 2012

Excerpts of questions to members of a group of eight former paramilitaries ("postulados") accused of torture, killings, and a massacre in Arauca, Colombia:

Magistrate: Do you remember where this man was assassinated?
Postulado: No, I wasn't there.
Magistrate: Do you know why he was killed?
Postulado: No, I don't know why. I was told the next day that he was killed.
Magistrate: Did you always assassinate people who were detained and accused of being a Guerrilla?
Postulado: Yes, generally we would.

The Magistrate tried to explore the origin of use of torture by this paramilitary group, and particularly why they used a certain form of electrical shock—which entailed putting a tube of toothpaste in the victim's mouth so that electricity applied elsewhere on the body would be intensified:

Magistrate: The cruelty—why such cruelty? This is representative of many other cases.
Postulado: In the moment, you didn't have control of yourself . . .
Magistrate: Was it taught to you during your training?
Postulado: I was in the army before. This never occurred to me at that time. . . . That humans could do this to another person, this level of cruelty. . . .
Magistrate: When did it occur to you? You were prepared to do it. It's not something that occurred to you at that moment. Where did it come from?
Postulado: The use of electric shock, for example: it was what we had on hand. A tube of toothpaste for example—all the materials were there. Using a gun would make too much noise. So other things had to be used to not cause panic in the population.
Magistrate: You needed *preparation* to do these things, such as knowing to use toothpaste to make the electricity more intense. You say this was decided "in the moment," but that can't be. Was there a commander who ordered this?
Postulado: These were difficult moments. . . .

The Magistrate then turned to the commander of the group:

Magistrate: What do you know about these acts, and particularly the massacre?

Postulado:	Arauca is one of the most isolated areas covered by our Block. So we would send the most experienced people, with military experience. They were trained in the military.
Magistrate:	What orders did you give? Was it just "do what you want"?
Postulado:	The order was to combat the guerrilla.
Magistrate:	Did anyone comment, either from the civilian population, or from your members, about the cruelty that was being used and the other abuses? Or if the results achieved were acceptable, then that was sufficient?
Postulado:	I generally didn't have this kind of information.

In early hearings of the process, paramilitary commanders named many civilians as close collaborators, including Congressmen and businessmen. This fed into the quickly developing "parapolitics" scandal that revealed the close relationship between the paramilitaries and many politicians. Over 130 members of Congress were prosecuted, and by 2015 over 60 had been convicted and jailed. Thousands of other officials around the country were suspected of direct links to the paramilitaries, according to the national prosecutor's office. The Justice and Peace Law did not apply to politicians complicit in these crimes, as they were not paramilitary members but rather provided political or financial backing and helped cover up crimes.

In 2008, as the hearings were underway, and cutting off key testimony, President Uribe authorized the immediate extradition to the U.S. of over a dozen paramilitary commanders, on drug trafficking charges. Colombian rights groups accused Uribe of intentionally cutting the testimony short to protect those who might be named. Over the next years, some of these commanders, now serving long sentences in U.S. prisons, were able to testify in Justice and Peace hearings through a video link. Some observers thought they were revealing more from afar because their security was at less risk, and perhaps also in anger over their extradition.[7]

Meanwhile, the Colombian courts also set out clear limitations on immunities for the other paramilitary members—the over 20,000 who had demobilized without specific accusations against them, and were therefore not part of the Justice and Peace process. The state intended to allow their demobilization without a judicial process. But this was also challenged at the Constitutional Court and overturned. Although they were not accused of war crimes, their paramilitary membership and activities were by definition criminal, and the courts threw out two attempts to provide them with de facto amnesty. Because the paramilitaries were allied with the government, these crimes could not be considered treason or any other form of "political crime" for which unconditional amnesty might be possible, the Court said.

Ultimately, these 20,000 paramilitary members were required to make individual "truth" statements to a state-funded Center for Historical Memory, in which they documented their own actions and all they knew about how the paramilitary structures worked.[8] This process effectively clarified their legal status.

By the time this third attempt at legislation to handle these paramilitary members was finally approved by the Constitutional Court by a narrow 5–4 decision, in 2011, the very limited flexibility that the courts would allow on justice and impunity had become very clear. The initial impunity agreement between the paramilitaries and President Uribe, nine year earlier, seemed very long ago indeed. The national courts had clearly established that blanket impunity was not a policy option for any Colombian peace process.

This background set out a tough challenge for those beginning to think about a new peace process with the FARC.

Peace Talks With the FARC

Early in his administration, President Santos envisioned the possibility of a peace process with the FARC and understood that justice for past crimes would be one of its most difficult issues. In November 2010, a full two years before negotiations formally began, he met with legal advisors in his office and asked that they prepare options for dealing with the issue of justice in relation to the ICC, in the event that peace talks took place. He wanted to protect both the space for talks and ultimately any final agreement. This meant providing legal security to the parties and predictability, and thus keeping justice at home.

The legal experts reported back that there were just four possibilities, as recounted by a senior government official. First, the ICC Prosecutor's office might make use of the Rome Statute's "interests of justice" clause to decide not to open cases in Colombia while peace talks were under way. Second, the UN Security Council could pass a resolution deferring any ICC action on Colombia, under Article 16. Third, Colombia could choose to leave the ICC, although this would have no retroactive effect and thus effectively wouldn't respond to the issue at hand. And fourth, Colombia could make it clear that it was able and willing to prosecute serious crimes, and in this way keep the ICC out.

President Santos considered their report and made up his mind. "We'll comply. That is our route. Option four," he said. And this indeed framed the tenor of all of Colombia's actions going forward: an insistence that there was no need for the ICC to enter, and that any agreement with the FARC would fully comply with its legal obligations, including those under the Rome Statute.

But Santos also concluded that it would be impossible to meet the requirements of Colombian law at that time. He thus proposed a constitutional amendment that would allow some flexibility. A contentious debate in Congress reflected the strong opposition to any hint of reduced accountability for the FARC. The "Legal Framework for Peace" was finally approved: this said that in a transitional, peace-accord context, all cases of serious crime would not have to be prosecuted, but rather that prosecutors could focus on those "most responsible," and that reduced or alternative sentences would be possible for those convicted. Those found responsible for crimes against humanity or genocide would be barred from elected office. All provisions were applicable to "armed groups at the margin of the law" as well as to agents of the state.

Some Colombian human rights groups challenged this Framework for Peace in the Constitutional Court, arguing that the state was obliged to prosecute all serious crimes. The Inter-American Commission on Human Rights published a lengthy analysis arguing that a "selective" approach to prosecutions was unacceptable.[9] Human Rights Watch, from New York, was especially critical, saying that the Framework for Peace "paves the way for widespread impunity for atrocities by guerrillas, paramilitaries, and the military."[10] However, other Colombian human rights organizations argued in favor of the Framework for Peace and the overall idea that there was no legal obligation for all of the war's many crimes to be prosecuted in court, and that such a requirement would be unrealistic and unhelpful.

The issue under examination by the Constitutional Court was thus the specific question of whether all or only a select number of accused must be prosecuted. Just weeks before the Court's decision, in August 2013, the Prosecutor of the ICC also intervened into the case, through letters to the president of the Constitutional Court that were labeled confidential but soon leaked to the press. The ICC Prosecutor's comments were primarily focused on a different matter that had not been up for discussion in the challenge before the Court: whether those responsible for crimes against humanity could receive suspended sentences. Some in Colombia thought that prosecuting and convicting perpetrators, and then promptly suspending their sentence, might be an effective resolution to the demand for justice and specifically the requirement for criminal prosecutions. The ICC Prosecutor argued in her letters that suspended sentences were unacceptable, but as many later pointed out, the issue of sentencing had never been analyzed by the judges of the ICC, and international law was not clear on the matter.

President Santos pushed against this level of intervention by the ICC. He insisted in his public statements that preventing future victims was as important as providing justice for past victims. In an address to the UN General Assembly, weeks after the ICC Prosecutor's letters leaked to the public, he insisted that the international community must respect Colombia's sovereignty and allow the country to find its own path to peace, while again promising that any agreement would respect human rights obligations.[11]

It seemed that these letters from the ICC Prosecutor did affect the Constitutional Court ruling, however. Although the Court's public statements and more detailed full decision were slightly contradictory, it generally indicated that suspended sentences were not acceptable for international crimes. But it otherwise confirmed much of the premise of the Framework for Peace.

The Legal Framework for Peace thus remained essentially intact, but it only provided a framework, opening the door for legislation that would set out details. Meanwhile, as the formal talks began, the FARC insisted that it was not in favor of the Framework, since it had been unilaterally proposed by the government and passed by Congress in a manner that gave them no voice in the matter. Thus, in many respects, the conversation in Havana on issues of justice started from a blank slate, even though the legal parameters had changed in important ways.

Norway and Cuba served as the "guarantor states" for the FARC talks, attending the negotiations, providing the meeting location and logistics, and facilitating visits from experts especially to meet with the FARC, who generally could not travel. Chile and Venezuela served as observer states.[12] In time, the U.S. appointed an envoy to the process, which was important given the outsized role of the U.S. in Colombia; other states and institutions such as the UN also increased their engagement over time. The agenda that was agreed between the parties comprised six points. One of these was called "Victims"; compared to the other agenda items, it was spare in detail. Its complete text said, "Compensating victims is at the center of the agreement. In this sense, the parties will treat 1) human rights of the victims and 2) truth." In addition, some other agenda items made reference to combatting impunity and addressing the phenomenon of paramilitaries. But it was understood that the victims agenda was where a host of justice issues would be addressed, including criminal accountability, a possible truth commission, and reparations. The parties didn't turn to this subject until they had concluded preliminary agreements on three prior agenda items: agricultural development, the problem of illicit drugs, and political participation.

The parties set out more details of their intentions only a few weeks after turning to the victims agenda item, eighteen months into the talks. The issue of impunity and justice in the FARC talks had become the most contentious issue in the presidential elections of June 2014. A week before the elections, with the possibility that the peace process might end if President Santos was not reelected, the parties announced a ten-point agreement of principles that they said would guide their discussions on the issue. This promised a robust commitment to a broad array of transitional justice fundamentals, from recognition of victims to clarification of the truth. Under a paragraph titled "recognition of responsibility," the parties specifically promised not to "exchange impunities."[13] Victims and rights advocates were pleased with the declaration, as indeed they should have been; there is no other example of such a robust and specific commitment to justice in the course of a peace negotiation, and in particular before parties have discussed the specifics of the issue. The only criticism on human rights grounds came from Amnesty International, who warned that the joint statement "failed to guarantee" full criminal justice for all perpetrators.[14]

Difficult Issues

The negotiations that followed were in-depth and slow going, requiring another eighteen months before a final, lengthy, detailed agreement on justice would be signed. The parties grappled with a host of complex issues.

As indicated in the statement of ten principles, the parties envisioned a multifaceted agreement on justice that would meet international standards and prioritize victims. Agreements on a truth commission and on victim reparations were expected to be relatively uncomplicated, but even there issues arose. Would the parties accept a truly independent investigation into this painful history? Could the truth commission identify those it found to be responsible for past crimes? Each of these issues was difficult in part because they were directly linked to questions of individual accountability, political legacy, and legitimacy.

The biggest challenge was always seen to be the question of criminal accountability. This was not a theoretical question, nor would the parties allow it to remain undefined for resolution in the future: most of the FARC leadership had already been convicted in absentia and had long prison sentences awaiting them. They couldn't conclude the peace negotiations without a clear understanding of what would happen not only to these existing sentences but also to any other charges that might be brought.

The FARC repeatedly insisted, from the start of the process, that they would not serve "even one day" in prison. They also said that whatever justice they might face must equally be applied to the government side, including the most senior military and political leaders, whom they considered their counterparts.

The parties were well aware of pressures that came from multiple sources, putting any agreement at risk if it was deemed to fall short on these issues. The pressures were in equal parts legal and political. The legal demands were inescapable: there was no question the Colombian Constitutional Court would review the terms of the justice deal, and the ICC had made clear that it would watch closely. Victim advocates might bring a challenge to the Inter-American Court as well. But despite these pressures, the specific legal requirements were actually not completely clear. There were differences in expert opinion on questions of minimal standards regarding who, how, what, how much, and what kind of justice was needed: how many people, at what level, and through what institutional means, must cases be investigated and/or prosecuted? Did these crimes require a prison sentence, and if so, for how many years? As explored in Chapter 8, the law was not clear on these questions.

Separate from these legal pressures, the parties knew that the accord could equally fail if the Colombian public found it too lenient and were simply unwilling to accept its terms of justice. President Santos had promised a referendum or popular consultation on the final accord. There was a strong and vocal political current that opposed any compromise with the FARC; led by former President Uribe, who still held considerable public support, many on the right opposed even the idea of negotiations with a "terrorist" group. Whatever final resolution was found, it would have to pass a tough test of public opinion.

The public focus on the FARC's crimes seemed to downplay the serious abuses that were committed also by the Colombian military and the paramilitaries. The military's opposition to any compromise for the FARC changed over time as they began to see advantages of a transitional justice arrangement for their own interests. The hundreds of low-level soldiers and the very few senior officers who were serving decades-long sentences could see a route out. The increasing threat of prosecution of other high-level military or political leaders, especially as the ICC increased its pressure, pushed the military to consider an overall compromise on justice.

The idea that state agents and the FARC might receive equivalent benefits was controversial; most human rights advocates opposed this approach. The state held a special responsibility to protect and uphold the law. They were not an illegal armed group that needed to be disarmed and reintegrated into society. The abuses of the state were thus of a different quality, advocates insisted, and they resisted the idea that a peace deal should give them equal treatment to the armed opposition. But, as others noted, it was not tenable to think that a peace deal would allow FARC leaders to walk away with significant reductions in punishment, while generals served out forty-year prison sentences for similar crimes.

The ICC Prosecutor's office made clear, in a detailed assessment report and in regular visits to the country, that it was most focused on the need for accountability for high-level military personnel in relation to the "false positive" cases. It was satisfied there had been sufficient justice for the FARC leadership through the in absentia trials, "subject to the appropriate execution of sentences of those convicted."[15] Needless to say, determining the "appropriateness" of sentences would not be such a simple matter, but the ICC Prosecutor made clear that a conviction alone was not enough. As the parties grappled with these questions, the ICC's Deputy Prosecutor, James Stewart, gave a speech in Bogota that set out a very interesting set of parameters that might be used to assess the legitimacy of alternative or reduced sentences. These included an assessment of the broader transitional justice context, such as a perpetrator's engagement in processes of acknowledgement and truth telling, or a possible ban on taking part in public affairs.[16]

It became clear early on that an agreement would need to be built on amnesty for "political" crimes, and also for those crimes considered "connected" to political crimes. This legal notion had a long history in Colombia and internationally, although the parameters of what would be covered were not at first clear.[17] Most difficult was defining what crimes could be considered "connected" crimes. Certainly, joining an armed group or illegally transporting weapons were political crimes, but what about those acts that provided financial support to the armed struggle but were of a different quality: most prominent was the FARC's well-known practice of kidnapping, as well as acts linked to the illegal drug trade.

Whatever criminal investigations or prosecutions might take place, it was clear that the FARC would never allow these to run through the national judicial system. They would not trust its impartiality, and in any case, as they pointed out, the judiciary was in the midst of a crisis and considered even by neutral observers to be weak and possibly corrupt at that moment. So a new tribunal and independent prosecutor would be required. At first, the FARC pressed for a new international ad hoc tribunal, but this suggested long delays in its creation and set up, a huge expense, and big questions about ensuring legitimacy and impartiality. There would also be a risk of international judges applying strict, maximalist standards in relation to penalties, out of context of the broader transitional justice system operating in Colombia, if the judges might not appreciate or accept the exceptionalism of a peace process.

Those debating and brainstorming on possible models and those advising both parties struggled with the difficulty of finding an approach that might work. To provide legal security, some proposed, there should be a set number of cases for prosecution agreed in advance. Or there should be a deadline after which no more prosecutions could take place. Some advocated a confession-based system that prioritized truth for the victims over punishment for the perpetrators. If international law required punishment of some kind, there was considerable debate over what kinds of alternative sentencing might be possible, such as community service or house arrest. There was also the thorny question of whether there would be restrictions, or perhaps explicit allowances, for former combatants to play a political role, maybe even while serving out sentences.

The challenges around nonprosecutorial justice measures, including truth and victim reparations, were different. The government had already created a significant reparations program, years earlier, that on paper was excellent, but its implementation was plagued by inefficiencies and complaints. The parties, and especially the FARC, hoped to improve this existing program, but the best way to do so was not obvious. Ultimately, the main point of contention was whether the FARC would put its resources into a general reparations fund, as the government insisted, or whether it would be allowed to control its own FARC-funded reparatory program.

There was early agreement on having a truth commission. In the interest of meeting best-practice standards, considerable attention was dedicated to how the members and commission chair would be selected, the commission's powers, and especially how the evidence uncovered by the truth commission would pertain to criminal justice. If one goal of the criminal justice mechanism were to provide early clarity on who was to be prosecuted, what would happen three years hence when the truth commission released its report and might implicate more people in serious crimes?

The final agreement tried to address all of these issues, as described further below. But the means of reaching the agreement and working through all of these complex and interlinked issues was not easy. Several of the processes and substructures that were put in place to help arrive at a solution were in themselves precedent setting.

Innovations in the Process

The Colombian negotiations benefited from an overlapping series of initiatives, developed organically over time, that gave shape to the agreement on justice. This included direct involvement of victims in the process, an intensive but informal parallel brainstorming group, a preliminary historical review commission, and a legal subcommission to draft the specific agreement for a special tribunal.

The parties' initial agreement on guiding principles, mentioned above, committed to placing victims at the center of the process. This was followed by a more detailed plan to invite victims to speak to the negotiating table in Havana: a total of sixty individual victims in five delegations were invited to present their own story of loss, recounting events that were often the direct result of actions of one of the parties sitting in front of them. In one case, a victim directly accused an army general who was on the government delegation of personal responsibility for a killing. These meetings were not public, but participants recount powerful exchanges that clearly affected how the parties addressed the issue at hand. These victims also gave public voice to a sentiment increasingly heard from those who suffered the war: in their public statements, most spoke forcefully in favor of finding peace and preventing further violence, and the need for truth and reparations, and did not emphasize a demand for criminal prosecution and punishment.

In addition, the parties created an online portal to collect submissions from victims and from the public at large; and the UN, the Catholic Church, and a policy center at the National University organized a series of regional victims fora, gathering thousands of direct victims to discuss policy proposals to put to the parties.[18] A total of 23,000 submissions on the victims agenda item were received through either the online portal or the victims fora. Both the FARC and the government dedicated time and resources to distill and give consideration to these proposals.[19]

Early in the process, Norway convened a group of seven Colombian and international experts to brainstorm on parameters and possible solutions to the justice dilemmas. The group included two legal advisors to the FARC, as well as persons in touch with the government delegation in the negotiations. The group met regularly over two years, operating in confidence; while it had no formal mandate from the parties, both the FARC and the government knew of and were in support of its work. I served as chair of this group.

This brainstorming experts group, known as the "New York Group," held a total of thirteen meetings of two days each, gathering in New York, Bogota, Panama, Madrid, and once in Havana to meet with the parties. By identifying and debating challenges and possible approaches to a resolution, the group provided a sounding board, a channel to feed new ideas into the formal negotiating table, and a means by which the FARC, through its legal advisors, could present and defend its positions to independent experts for reaction. The group included experts on the ICC and on Colombian law, thus serving as an informal check on whether proposals would likely meet Colombia's international obligations as well as pass muster with the Constitutional Court. But it also grappled with the many nonjudicial issues, such as the mandate and selection process for the truth commission, how to improve the existing reparations program, and how the various parts of the overall transitional justice system could work together. As a "guarantor state" in the peace negotiations, Norway took the initiative to create (and cover the costs for) this brainstorming group, and senior Norwegian representatives attended the group's meetings as observers. Cuba, as the second guarantor state, also attended a number of the meetings at a high level. This informal and off-the-record brainstorming, with a direct feedback loop back into Havana, was helpful in advancing and deepening the discussions that took place directly between the parties, according to those closest to the process.[20]

Meanwhile, very early in the negotiations, the FARC pushed for the parties to create a historical review commission even while the talks were still under way, which it hoped would change how the conflict and the FARC itself were perceived. An honest review of history, they believed, would show both the social justice roots of their struggle and the true record of violations by their opponents. The government eventually conceded, and they jointly appointed a Historical Commission on the Conflict and its Victims; each named six members and one co-coordinator, primarily academics, and gave them six months to report. The members each prepared separate reports, focusing on their specific area of expertise. They were not able, however, to agree to a joint consensus report, an outcome that some observers feared would only exacerbate the deep divisions in society. Ultimately, this exercise may have only highlighted the need for a deeper consideration of these complex historical and societal issues by a well-appointed truth commission that would have the time and resources necessary for the task.

The parties released a detailed agreement for a truth commission a full year after they had formally opened their deliberations on the victims agenda item. But issues of criminal accountability remained complex and contentious, and especially because the parties held fundamentally different views on a number of central questions. Both the parties and the Colombian public were increasingly worried about the slow progress in the talks. The parties thus decided to appoint a subcommission to work independently from the negotiating table to try to break through the impasse. This "legal subcommission" was comprised of three experts appointed by each side; it met intensively over five months to prepare a detailed proposal on criminal justice. When both parties agreed to the approach the subcommission proposed, a final agreement on the full justice package was finally announced.

A Final Agreement on Justice

The justice agreement that the parties finalized in December 2015 stood apart not only for its great detail and length, but also for its intentional construction of what it called a "system of comprehensive justice." The section on justice was 63 pages of the almost 300 pages of the full peace agreement. It included sections on a truth commission, victim reparations, a special entity to search for the disappeared, measures to prevent further abuses, and a special mechanism on criminal justice. The last of these, a plan for prosecutions and amnesty, took the greatest space and received the most focus and concern in the negotiations and also the most attention in the reaction from the public, press, and victim advocates. (Later, after the public referendum, some changes would be made, as set out further below, but the essential elements and overall structure of the justice arrangements remained.)

The "Special Jurisdiction for Peace," as the new criminal justice system would be called, is a complex, multi-layered special tribunal (and more) that would be created at the national level but operate independently from the existing judiciary. It includes a special prosecutor's office, pre-trial chambers to receive confessions and consider amnesties, and several chambers for prosecuting cases.

The system is built on a presumption of perpetrators confessing. The incentive for perpetrators is both to avoid a full trial and to benefit from significantly lighter sentences as compared to the forty to sixty years that was typical for these kinds of crimes.

Amnesty or pardon would be granted for political or related crimes, including "rebellion, sedition, assault, as well as the illegal bearing of weapons, combat deaths consistent with international humanitarian law, conspiracy to commit crimes for the purpose of rebellion, and other related offenses."[21] The accord also spelled out the crimes that would not be covered by an amnesty.[22]

Those who confess to crimes that cannot receive amnesty and who cooperate fully with the broader transitional justice system, such as providing information to the truth commission, will be sentenced to "effective restriction of liberty" for five to eight years, during which time they will undertake reparative or restorative work. The accord stated that this restriction of liberty "would not be understood as jail or prison," but the important question of how these reparatory sentences would be structured, and how such a complex program would be managed, was not initially detailed.

Those who fully confess to their crimes but late in the process, after prosecution has begun and up until sentencing, will receive a reduced sentence of five to eight years in prison. They must commit to work, study, or training while serving their sentence, for the purpose of "re-socialization," and as appropriate to take part in other activities to promote the non-repetition of crimes.[23] Finally, those who do not recognize their responsibility for crimes will be tried before the special tribunal and if convicted will receive a prison sentence of fifteen to twenty years in prison.

In addition to the FARC and state agents, this would be applicable to those who participated in crimes of the conflict in an indirect manner, such as providing financial support.

There were differences of understanding, when the agreement was announced, as to whether it required that all crimes and perpetrators must be individually processed through the system (with either a confession or full prosecution) or only those persons considered most responsible for the most serious crimes. The agreement included contradictory language on this, while the government's public statements suggested that only those "most responsible" would have to go through the system. Some human rights advocates insisted that a selective approach would not sustain a legal challenge.[24]

The system was complex and would be expensive. The structure required over forty judges. Initially, no one knew how many cases would go through the special tribunal; experts first suggested anywhere from a few thousand to 30,000 or more.[25] The general prosecutor then announced that, based on case information in his office, some 24,400 state officials and 12,500 civilians would have to be processed for war-related crimes, as well as between 6,200 and 20,000 FARC members.[26]

At least some of those who designed the new transitional justice system were convinced that cases could be processed quickly, with an expedient procedure of matching the confessions against the accusations and evidence submitted from the national prosecutor and information from human rights organizations. Others worried about the legal complexity and extraordinary workload that could burden the system, in addition to the considerable difficulties in constructing the necessary legal framework and putting it all into operation. Identifying acceptably impartial judges would be one considerable challenge, for example.

The agreement for a truth commission largely satisfied best-practice standards. The "Commission for the Clarification of Truth, Coexistence and Non-Repetition" was given a robust mandate to investigate events, practices, and the impact of the conflict, covering "the period of the conflict" (over fifty years) and to report in three years.

The most controversial element in the truth commission accord was the explicit prohibition of information "produced or received" by the truth commission being used in criminal prosecutions. Information and activities of the commission would have "no judicial character" and could not be transferred to nor requested by judicial authorities.[27] The intention of the parties was to allow perpetrators to freely engage with the truth commission without fear of consequence. Indeed, there was a stated requirement that those who benefited from reduced penalties through the Special Jurisdiction must cooperate fully with the truth commission and other transitional justice bodies.[28] Still, rights advocates criticized this restriction on sharing information, and it seemed likely to be reviewed by the courts.

The parties also agreed to a special commission to search for the missing and disappeared. It would try to locate the remains of the tens of thousands of persons who were forcibly disappeared or killed in combat without a trace. This body could share forensic or scientific information with the tribunal, but not other analysis or conclusions. It should have a close relationship with the truth commission, the agreement said, although the disappearances commission was expected to operate for many more years.

While the reaction to the justice agreement was overall quite positive, the loudest critics focused on the Special Jurisdiction, specifically its sentencing regime, saying that it did not meet international standards. This criticism came primarily from the Colombian political right, which had vociferously opposed the talks from the start. Human Rights Watch and to a lesser degree Amnesty International were also very critical, focusing their analysis and critique almost exclusively on the question of prosecutions and sentencing. Sentences that did not include prison were not "meaningful punishment," Human Rights Watch said, and the agreement's "tangle of ambiguities, omissions, and loopholes" added up to "an empty promise."[29] Human Rights Watch's immediate comment to the press in Colombia was that the agreement was a "piñata of impunity" and that the ICC Prosecutor would surely open prosecutions as a result.[30] Amnesty International was concerned that the penalties did "not appear to be proportionate to the severity of crimes."[31]

This couldn't have been more of a contrast with the views and statements from Colombian human rights organizations, the United Nations human rights office, and many other commentators worldwide, including even the ICC Prosecutor. National human rights advocates and victims were very positive about the agreement. The Colombian Commission of Jurists, for example, which has fiercely advocated for accountability for many years, received the agreement "with enthusiasm," calling it "unprecedented, necessary, and timely." The agreement set a path to "satisfy the rights of victims, end the cycle of impunity and silence the guns so that political violence is no longer an instrument of repression," it said.[32]

The ICC Prosecutor released a statement saying that while she would monitor implementation of the agreement, she "noted with optimism" that amnesty was excluded for war crimes and crimes against humanity, and that the agreement was a "significant step" towards ending the decades-long armed conflict. "Any genuine and practical initiative that achieves this laudable goal, while paying homage to justice as a critical pillar of sustainable peace, is of course welcomed," she said.[33]

More sober and in-depth analysis by, for example, the Washington Office on Latin America, an NGO, highlighted a number of specific areas that remained unclear or raised concern. These included the question of whether "false positives" (the army's killing of civilians) would be considered violations of international humanitarian law; whether the accord's definition of command responsibility was too weak, making it difficult to hold commanders to account; whether ex-guerrilla leaders would be allowed to campaign or even hold political office while serving sentences of restricted liberty; and how the special tribunal's judges would be chosen.[34]

A Referendum and Further Revisions to the Agreement

After the parties concluded other aspects of the overall peace agreement, such as cease-fire and demobilization plans, they finally celebrated the official signing of the accord with a large and joyous public ceremony in Cartagena, Colombia, in late September 2016. But the long-promised popular vote on the approval of the agreement only took place a week after the signing ceremony.

Despite polls predicting easy passage, Colombians were shocked to see the agreement rejected by the slim margin of 50.2% opposed versus 49.7% in favor. In a telling analysis of the voting patterns, it was found that the areas of the country most directly affected by the conflict voted overwhelmingly in favor of the accord, and those more removed from the violence were more likely to be opposed. The "no" campaign played strongly on worries of impunity for the FARC. At the international level, commentators questioned the role of Human Rights Watch in so vehemently attacking the accord; indeed HRW had released three different strongly worded statements in the week prior to the vote.[35] There were also other important factors pertaining to distinct aspects of the 300-page agreement beyond concerns in the justice chapter: these included the economic interests of large landowners (affected by land reforms) and opposition from the conservative Catholic Church to the accord's reference to gender rights.

President Santos immediately pledged to a process of consultation and further negotiations, and the FARC also reiterated its commitment to finding a deal. The government sat with the organizations and political parties that had supported the "no" vote, coming out with a list of over 500 proposed changes to the accord. Armed with this list, the government then spent two weeks negotiating intensively with the FARC. Forty-one days after the failed plebiscite, the parties announced a new agreement, which incorporated many of these points.

The greatest number of changes were made to the Special Jurisdiction, including in sentencing, but there were also important changes in regards to the legal status of the overall accord, the political rights and representation of the future FARC political party, and related areas.

The new accord on justice, now over seventy pages, included for example the following substantive changes:[36]

- The meaning of "effective restriction of liberty" was clarified: these non-penal sentences would be served in zones no larger than a small rural hamlet. This was much more limited than what the original accord might have allowed. On the other hand, the FARC refused to give in to pressure that these sentences should be served in prison.
- The Special Jurisdiction was first envisioned to include ten foreign judges, but this was changed so that all will be Colombian; instead, there will be ten foreign legal experts as observers.
- The legal definition of "command responsibility" was tightened to better reflect international standards and to prevent commanders from easily escaping responsibility for war crimes.
- The new accord stated that war crimes committed for "personal enrichment" could not benefit from the new transitional justice system; this effectively excluded the army's "false positive" cases.
- The revised accord also clarified whether drug trafficking by the FARC would be considered to be "connected" to a political crime, and thus receive amnesty. This will be decided on a case-by-case basis, depending on whether the proceeds of the drug trafficking went towards the war effort or for personal enrichment.
- The initial plan was for the entire accord to de facto become part of the Colombian constitution; this was limited so that only the parts pertaining to humanitarian law would be given constitutional status.
- While the special tribunal would remain largely independent from the national judiciary, it was agreed that specific rulings of the tribunal could be appealed to the Colombian Constitutional Court.
- After first resisting, the FARC finally agreed to provide a full inventory of its assets, and also that these would go towards victim reparations.
- The special tribunal would have ten years to operate, with a possible extension of five years further.

The FARC would still be granted ten automatic Congressional seats, for eight years, as originally envisioned. The new accord also maintained the explicit right to participate in politics while serving sentences under this system.[37]

To avoid the delay and cost of a second plebiscite, Colombia approved this final agreement through special procedures in Congress. The accord was finally complete, and the FARC began the process of demobilizing in the first weeks of 2017, bringing the 52-year war to an end.

Conclusion

More than any other peace process to date, Colombia's negotiations with armed groups have been heavily defined by conversations about law and the legal intricacies of the state's international and constitutional obligations. The resulting agreements have been reviewed in detail by national and international courts, sometimes compelling significant changes to the plans.

Knowing that these reviews would take place, and knowing also that prosecution and significant prison time was a certainty if another arrangement was not found, both parties in the FARC talks focused intensively on finding a workable and acceptable solution that would comply with legal requirements. The extraordinary complexity, detail, and length of the final justice agreement was perhaps a natural result.

But even such an intense focus, including by many eminently qualified and independent experts, cannot fully resolve the issue. There are too many factors that cannot be predicted or controlled: the agreement will require legislation in Congress, which might result in changes; the Constitutional Court may review important aspects; and there are elements that depend on interpretation by those responsible for implementation, most importantly the special prosecutor, the magistrates of the special tribunal, and the members of the various commissions.

There are also many questions in relation on how all the elements of the full "comprehensive system" of transitional justice will work together. Some aspects of the interrelationship between the new special tribunal and the other mechanisms are addressed in the agreement. But the little that is indicated leaves much open for negotiation between the bodies, or perhaps argued and resolved in court. Based on experience elsewhere, we can assume that many operational questions, such as how much information can be shared between them, will be strongly influenced by the personalities of those heading these institutions. It is nearly impossible to set out this level of specificity in advance, and it would be unwise to try to do so.

One of the greatest risks to the justice plans in Colombia is in the area of access and guarantees for those who suffered violence. The large numbers of direct victims in Colombia together with the country's very legalistic culture may spell trouble for those who envision an effective and efficient victim-centered process. The parties tried to include strong victim guarantees and repeatedly insisted that this was a priority, but it is easy to imagine the difficulties that could arise for both the truth commission and the search for the tens of thousands of missing, as well as in the judicial procedures of the new tribunal, where victims' procedural rights are not clear.

Some of these are the very problems that have plagued the Justice and Peace process for the paramilitary forces. Although that process also tried to accomplish a difficult feat through a creative legal approach, it pales in comparison to the extraordinarily ambitious, multi-pronged transitional justice system that Colombia has set out in its agreement with the FARC.

As the FARC talks were in their last stages, Colombia was preparing to launch a separate line of talks with the other significant guerrilla group that remained, the National Liberation Army, or ELN. Early signals suggested that the ELN was unlikely to simply agree to the justice components included in the FARC accord. If they push for a wholly different kind of justice approach, it could be an extremely difficult negotiation indeed.

Notes

1 Research for this chapter is based in part on interviews during several visits to Colombia between May 2012 and January 2016. The peace negotiations and specifically the issue of justice were the subject of intense attention from the media and analysts, with daily in-depth articles and commentary. For ease of access, this chapter errs on the side of English-language resources, where available. I was involved in the process as an advisor to Norway on transitional justice, and specifically as coordinator of the New York Group, described further below.

2 Centro Nacional de Memoria Histórica, *¡Basta Ya! Colombia: Memorias de Guerra y Dignidad* (Bogota: Centro Nacional de Memoria Histórica, 2013), centrodememoriahistorica.gov.co.

3 Most recently, attempted peace negotiations with the FARC from 1999 to 2002 were criticized for giving up too much to the FARC (such as granting a large "demilitarized zone" to fall under the full control of the FARC) and working with an agenda that was unrealistically ambitious. Conversations with the ELN in 2005–2006 were also inconclusive.

4 It postponed for seven years the application of jurisdiction in relation to war crimes, which became applicable in 2009.

5 A useful history of the negotiations around the Justice and Peace Law can be found in Maria Paula Saffon and Rodrigo Uprimny, "Uses and Abuses of Transitional Justice in Colombia," in Morten Bergsmo and Pablo Kalmanovitz, eds., *Law in Peace Negotiations*, 2nd ed. (Oslo: Torkel Opsahl, 2010), 354–400, www.fichl.org.

6 Interviews by author with magistrates in the Peace and Justice system, Bogota, 2012.

7 While extremely important to the process in Colombia, these video transmissions did not always work well at an operational level. The audio quality was sometimes poor, and the schedule of appearances was erratic. Prison officials in the U.S. were not always supportive of the participation of their detainees in this foreign process.

8 Known as Law 1424. A useful account of this process can be found in Silke Pheiffer, "Transitional Justice for Rank-and-File Combatants in Colombia: Insights From Law 1424," Norwegian Peacebuilding Resource Centre, Feb 2015, www.noref.no.

9 Inter-American Commission on Human Rights, *Truth, Justice and Reparation: Fourth Report on Human Rights Situation in Colombia*, 31 Dec 2013, www.cidh.org.

10 Human Rights Watch, *World Report: 2015* (New York: Human Rights Watch, 2015), 170.

11 President Juan Manuel Santos, "Statement before the UN General Assembly in its 68th Session," 24 Sept 2013.

12 For a more detailed summary of the negotiations, including the role of various international entities, see Renata Segura and Delphine Mechoulan, *Made in Havana: How Colombia and the FARC Decided to End the War* (New York: International Peace Institute, Feb 2017).

13 National Government of Colombia and the FARC, "Statement of Principles for the Discussion of Item 5 of the Agenda: Victims," Joint Communiqué Havana, 7 June 2014, www.mesadeconversaciones.com.co.

14 Amnesty International, "Historic Colombia-FARC Declaration Fails to Guarantee Victims' Right to Justice," Press Release, 9 June 2014.

15 In a 2012 preliminary report on Colombia, the ICC Office of the Prosecutor stated, "The information available indicates that eight current or former members of the FARC Secretariat, its highest leadership body, and four current members of ELN's Central Command, have been convicted in absentia. Subject to the appropriate execution of sentences of those convicted in absentia, the Office has no reason at this stage to doubt the genuineness of such proceedings." ICC, Office of the Prosecutor, *Situation in Colombia: Interim Report*, Nov 2012, 5, para. 12.

16 James Stewart, "Transitional Justice in Colombia and the Role of the International Criminal Court," 13 May 2015, www.icc-cpi.int.

17 See, for example, Fernando Travesí and Henry Rivera, "Political Crime, Amnesties, and Pardons: Scope and Challenges," International Center for Transitional Justice, March 2016.

18 See *Sistematización* and *Informe y Balance General: Foros Nacional y Regionales Sobre Víctimas* (Bogota: UN Colombia Office and Centro de Pensamiento y Seguimiento al Diálago de Paz, Universidad Nacional de Colombia, 2014).

19 The government contracted an independent NGO, Fundación Ideas para la Paz, to analyze and present summaries of these many thousands of submissions. The FARC prepared a document outlining key ideas from these inputs and from NGO reports or submissions, and they incorporated many of these ideas into their proposals.

20 See Hugo García Segura and Juan David Laverde Palma, "Los Arquitectos del Acuerdo," *El Espectador*, 27 Sept 2015, 2–5. See also Segura and Mechoulan, *Made in Havana*, 17.

21 *Acuerdo Final para la Terminación del Conflicto y la Construcción de una Paz Estable y Duradera*, 24 Nov 2016 (hereafter *Acuerdo Final*), 150, para. 38. To avoid confusion, the language from the final, revised 2016 version of the accord is cited here.

22 The final accord states: "There shall be no amnesty or pardon or equivalent benefits for crimes against humanity, genocide, serious war crimes—that is, any violation of international humanitarian law committed systematically—hostage-taking or other serious deprivation of liberty, torture, extrajudicial executions, enforced disappearance, violent carnal access and other forms of sexual violence, child abduction, forced displacement, as well as the recruitment of minors, all in accordance with the Statute of Rome," *Acuerdo Final*, 151, para. 40.

23 *Acuerdo Final*, 175.

24 Interview, Gustavo Gallon (Colombian Commission of Jurists, Jan 2016) who insisted that Colombian law required that all must go through a court-sanctioned process.

25 Interviews by author with several people involved in the initial design of the system.

26 After demobilization of the FARC in the first months of 2017, the number of FARC members expected to go through the special tribunal was reduced to 1,400. 24,400 state officials (some elected) and 12,500 private individuals remained. Adriaan Alsema, "Santos Decrees Amnesty for 3500 FARC rebels, 1400 guerrillas expected in court," *Colombia Reports*, 11 July 2017.

27 *Acuerdo Final*, "Extra-Judicial Mechanism," 134, section 5.1.1.1.1.

28 "To have access to special treatment . . . it is necessary to provide the full truth, provide reparations to the victims and ensure non-repetition. Provide the full truth means to relate, whenever such information is available, in an exhaustive and detailed manner, the conduct committed and the circumstances of how it was committed, as well as necessary and sufficient information to attribute responsibilities, in order to guarantee the satisfaction of the rights of the victims to reparation and non-repetition," *Acuerdo Final*, 146, para. 13.

29 Human Rights Watch, "Colombia: Agreeing to Impunity: Government, FARC Deal Sacrifices Victims' Right to Justice," 22 Dec 2015.

30 "Pacto de justicia en Colombia es una 'piñata de impunidad', denuncia HRW," *El Espectador*, 22 Dec 2015. See also Human Rights Watch, "Human Rights Watch Analysis of Colombia-FARC Agreement," 21 Dec 2015, www. hrw.org. A year later, Human Rights Watch had softened its position demanding that sentences must be served in prison. "Our view on this has evolved," acknowledged Richard Dicker, HRW director of international justice (interview by author, 10 May 2017). It was still concerned for "meaningful punishment," but generally accepted the model of modified restrictions on liberty. It remained concerned about the definition of command responsibility and opposed the idea that those serving a sentence could simultaneously play a political role. See "Letter to President Santos on the New Peace Agreement with the FARC," 22 Nov 2016, www.hrw.org.

31 Amnesty International, *Annual Report 2016* (London: Amnesty International, 2016).

32 Comisión Colombiana de Juristas, "Acuerdo sobre víctimas: Necesario y oportuno," press release, 21 Dec 2015.

33 ICC Office of the Prosecutor, "Statement of the Prosecutor on the Agreement on the Creation of a Special Jurisdiction for Peace in Colombia," 24 Sept 2015.

34 Washington Office on Latin America, "9 Unanswered Questions About Colombia's Victims and Justice Accord," 23 Dec 2015, colombiapeace.org. See also the detailed analysis by the Asociación de Oficiales Retirados de las Fuerzas Militares, "Las Diez Cosas que se Necesitan para que la Justicia Transicional no sea un Fiasco," 17 Dec 2015, www.acore.org.co.

35 See Greg Grandin, "Did Human Rights Watch Sabotage Colombia's Peace Agreement?" *The Nation*, 3 Oct 2016.

36 A good summary was produced by the Washington Office on Latin America: "Key Changes to the New Peace Accord," 15 Nov 2016, colombiapeace.org.

37 "The imposition of any sanction [under the Special Jurisdiction] will not disqualify persons from political participation nor limit the exercise of any right, active or passive, of political participation, for which the parties will agree the necessary constitutional reforms," *Acuerdo Final*, 150, para. 36.

Index